JUSTICE SOCIETY OF AMERICA

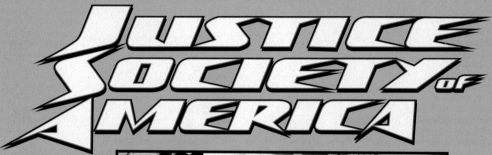

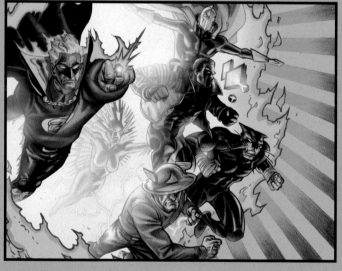

SUPERTOWN

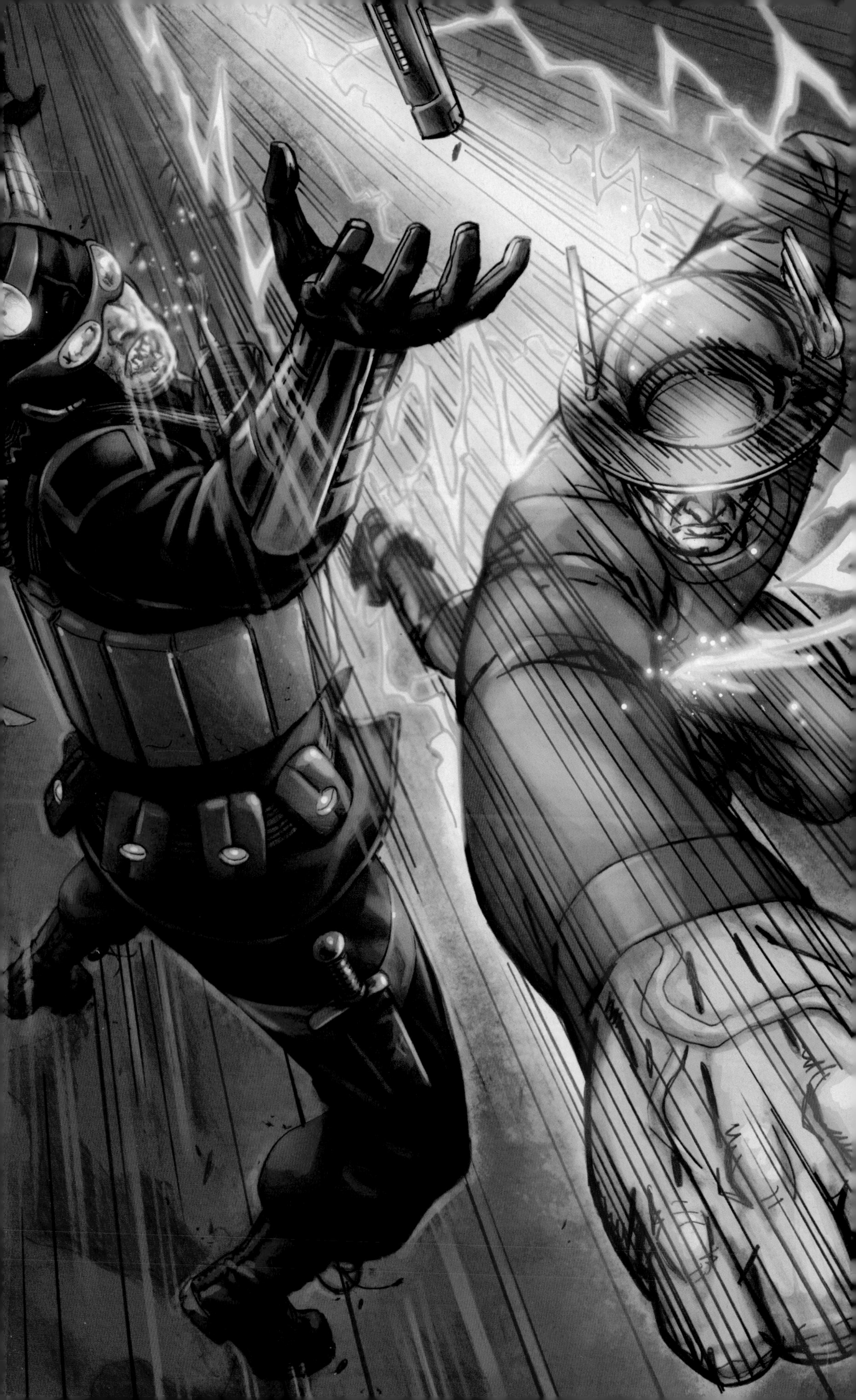

JUSTICE SOCIETY OF AMERICA

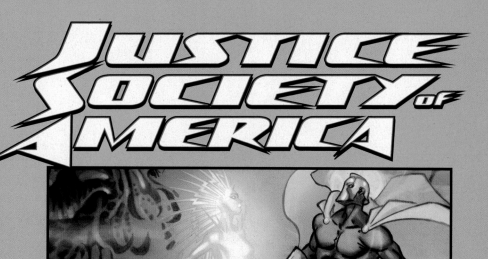

SUPERTOWN

MARC GUGGENHEIM
WRITER

SCOTT KOLINS
MIKE NORTON (PART THREE)
ARTISTS

MIKE ATIYEH
COLORIST

ROB LEIGH
LETTERER

SCOTT KOLINS WITH **MIKE ATIYEH**
COLLECTION COVER

SPECIAL THANKS TO **JAMES ROBINSON**

MIKE CARLIN
JOEY CAVALIERI
Editors – Original Series

RACHEL GLUCKSTERN
CHRIS CONROY
Associate Editors – Original Series

IAN SATTLER
Director Editorial, Special Projects and Archival Editions

ROBBIN BROSTERMAN
Design Director – Books

EDDIE BERGANZA
Executive Editor

BOB HARRAS
VP – Editor in Chief

DIANE NELSON
President

DAN DIDIO and JIM LEE
Co-Publishers

GEOFF JOHNS
Chief Creative Officer

JOHN ROOD
Executive VP – Sales, Marketing and Business Development

AMY GENKINS
Senior VP – Business and Legal Affairs

NAIRI GARDINER
Senior VP – Finance

JEFF BOISON
VP – Publishing Operations

MARK CHIARELLO
VP – Art Direction and Design

JOHN CUNNINGHAM
VP – Marketing

TERRI CUNNINGHAM
VP – Talent Relations and Services

ALISON GILL
Senior VP – Manufacturing and Operations

DAVID HYDE
VP – Publicity

HANK KANALZ
Senior VP – Digital

JAY KOGAN
VP – Business and Legal Affairs, Publishing

JACK MAHAN
VP – Business Affairs, Talent

NICK NAPOLITANO
VP – Manufacturing Administration

RON PERAZZA
VP – Online

SUE POHJA
VP – Book Sales

COURTNEY SIMMONS
Senior VP – Publicity

BOB WAYNE
Senior VP – Sales

JUSTICE SOCIETY OF AMERICA: SUPERTOWN

DC Comics, 1700 Broadway, New York, NY 10019
A Warner Bros. Entertainment Company
Printed by RR Donnelley, Salem, VA, USA. 8/26/11.
First Printing.
ISBN: 978-1-4012-3284-9

SUSTAINABLE
FORESTRY
INITIATIVE

Certified Chain of Custody
Promoting Sustainable
Forest Management

Fiber used in this product line meets the
sourcing requirements of the SFI program.
www.sfiprogram.org SGS-SFI/COC-US10/81072

SUPERTOWN Part One

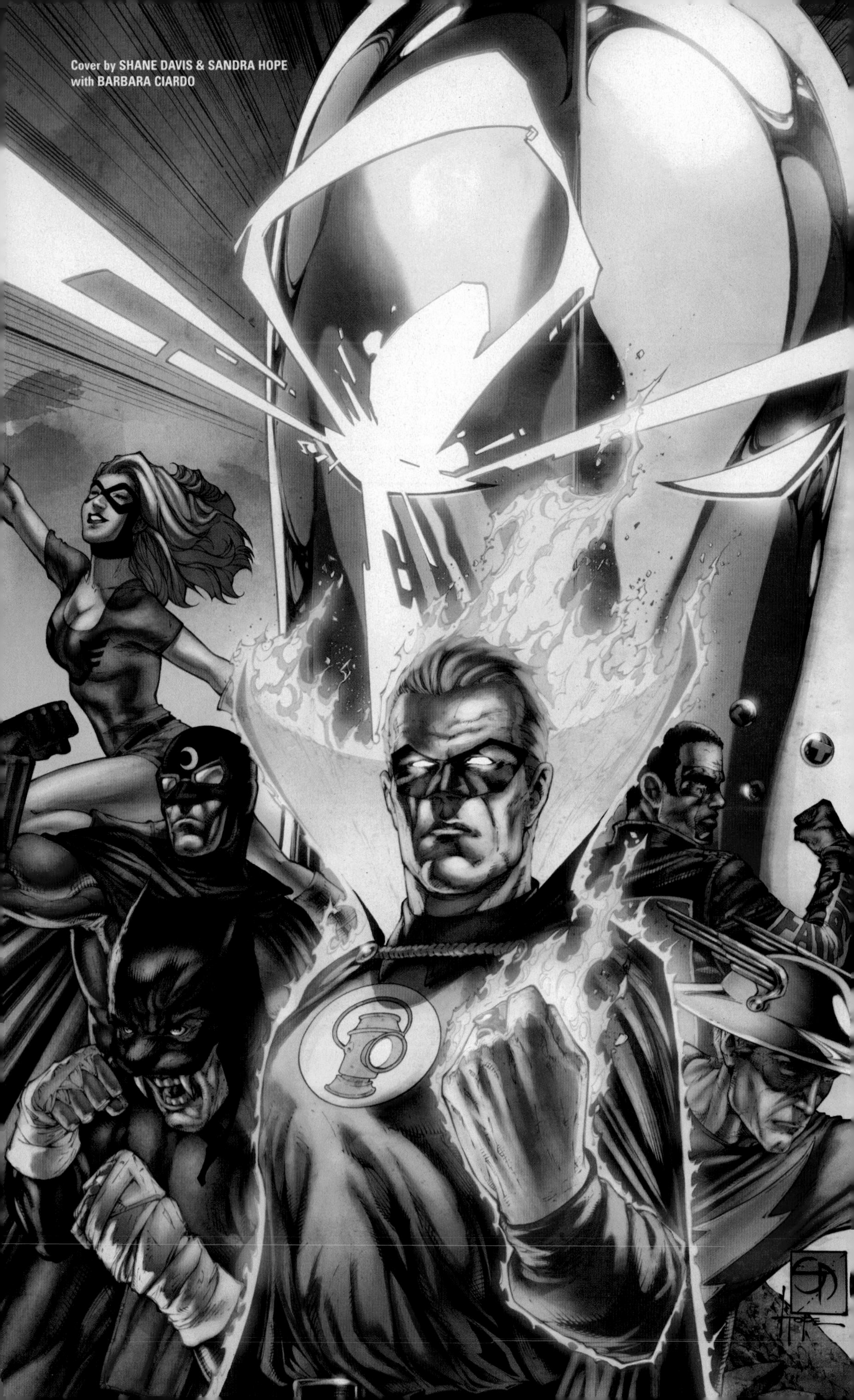
Cover by SHANE DAVIS & SANDRA HOPE
with BARBARA CIARDO

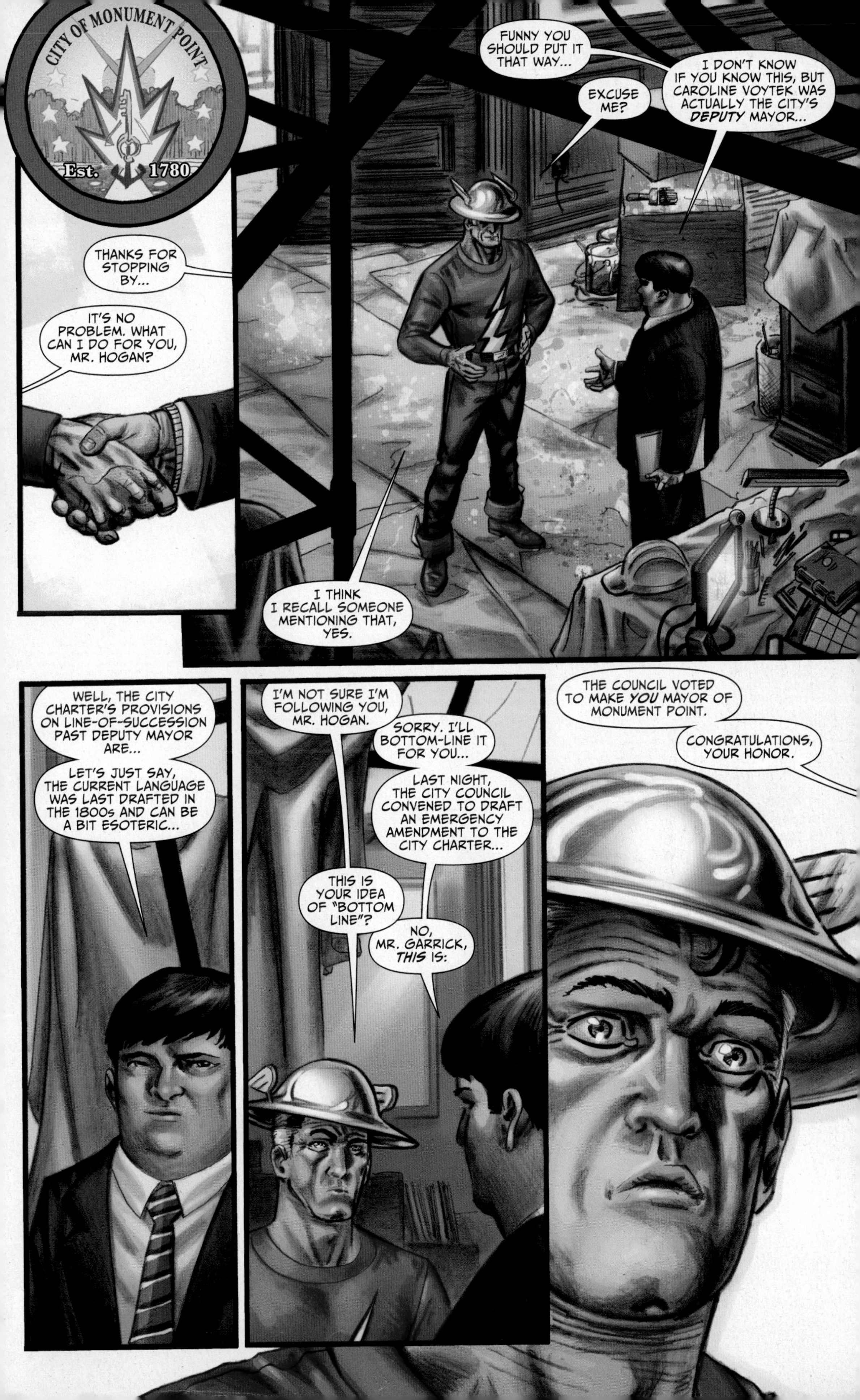
CITY OF MONUMENT POINT
Est. 1780
THANKS FOR STOPPING BY...
IT'S NO PROBLEM. WHAT CAN I DO FOR YOU, MR. HOGAN?
FUNNY YOU SHOULD PUT IT THAT WAY...
I DON'T KNOW IF YOU KNOW THIS, BUT CAROLINE VOYTEK WAS ACTUALLY THE CITY'S DEPUTY MAYOR...
EXCUSE ME?
I THINK I RECALL SOMEONE MENTIONING THAT, YES.
WELL, THE CITY CHARTER'S PROVISIONS ON LINE-OF-SUCCESSION PAST DEPUTY MAYOR ARE...
LET'S JUST SAY, THE CURRENT LANGUAGE WAS LAST DRAFTED IN THE 1800s AND CAN BE A BIT ESOTERIC...
I'M NOT SURE I'M FOLLOWING YOU, MR. HOGAN.
SORRY. I'LL BOTTOM-LINE IT FOR YOU...
LAST NIGHT, THE CITY COUNCIL CONVENED TO DRAFT AN EMERGENCY AMENDMENT TO THE CITY CHARTER...
THIS IS YOUR IDEA OF "BOTTOM LINE"?
NO, MR. GARRICK, THIS IS:
THE COUNCIL VOTED TO MAKE YOU MAYOR OF MONUMENT POINT.
CONGRATULATIONS, YOUR HONOR.

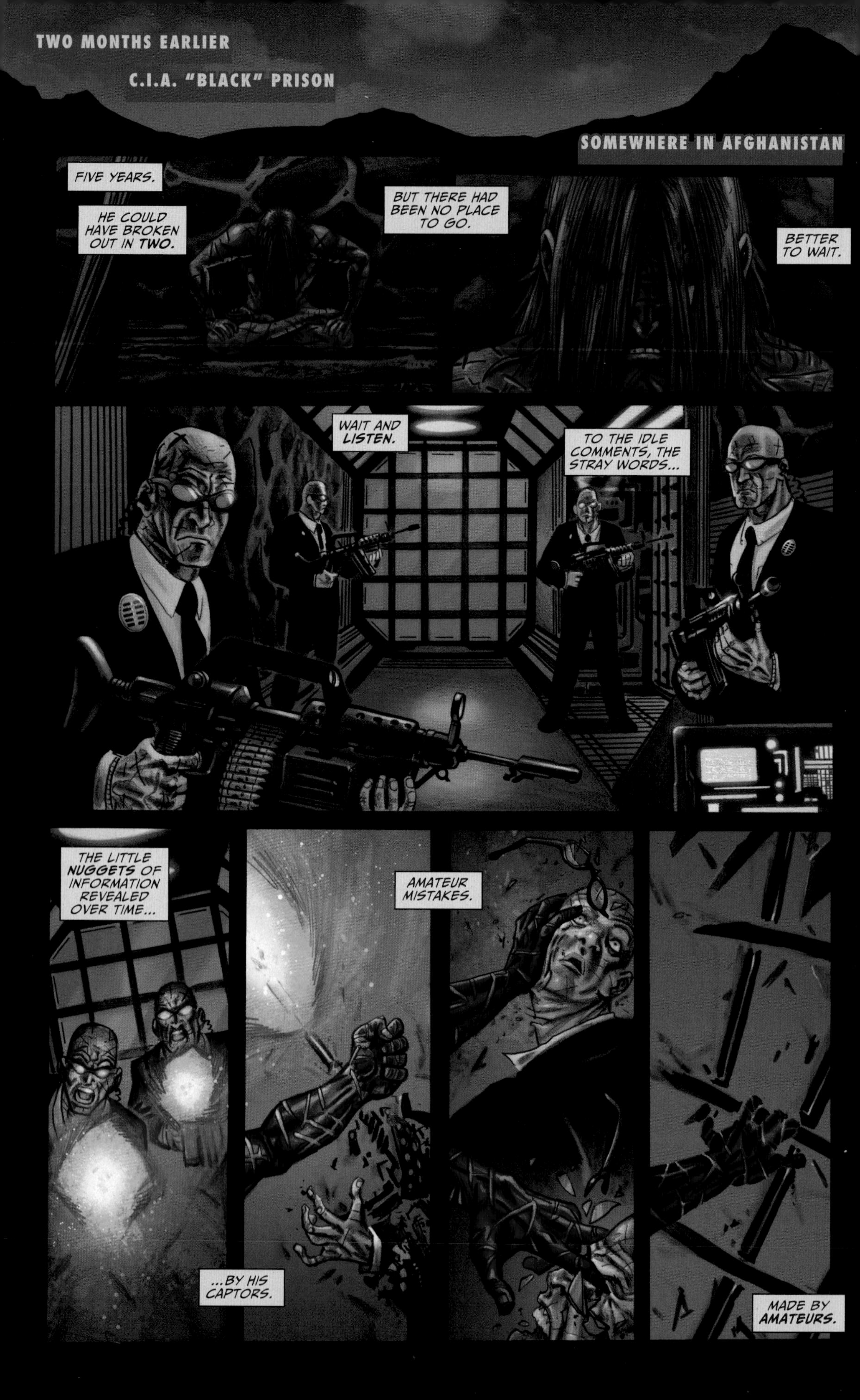
TWO MONTHS EARLIER
C.I.A. "BLACK" PRISON
SOMEWHERE IN AFGHANISTAN
FIVE YEARS.
HE COULD HAVE BROKEN OUT IN TWO.
BUT THERE HAD BEEN NO PLACE TO GO.
BETTER TO WAIT.
WAIT AND LISTEN.
TO THE IDLE COMMENTS, THE STRAY WORDS...
THE LITTLE NUGGETS OF INFORMATION REVEALED OVER TIME...
...BY HIS CAPTORS.
AMATEUR MISTAKES.
MADE BY AMATEURS.

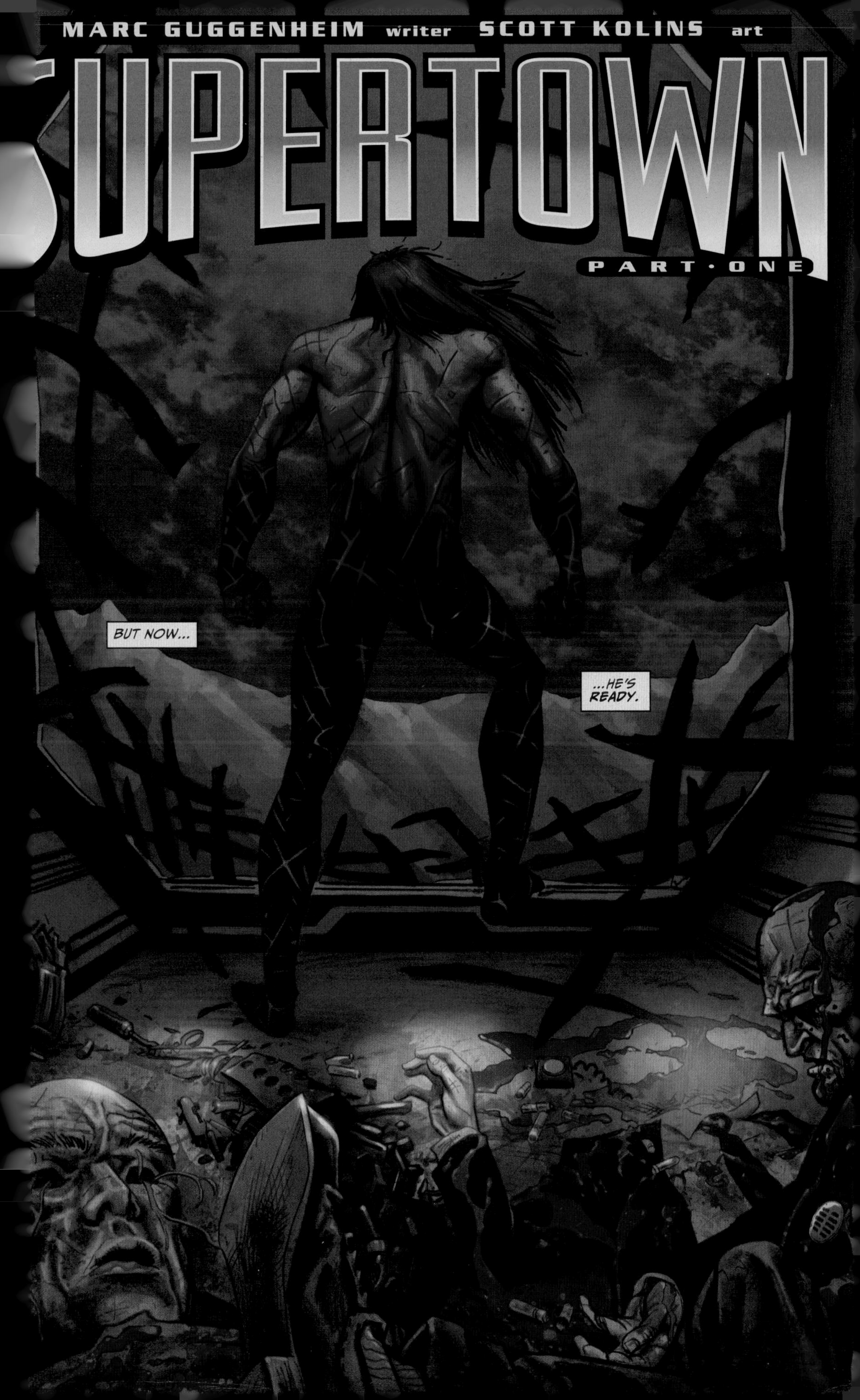
MARC GUGGENHEIM writer SCOTT KOLINS art
SUPERTOWN
PART·ONE
BUT NOW...
...HE'S READY.

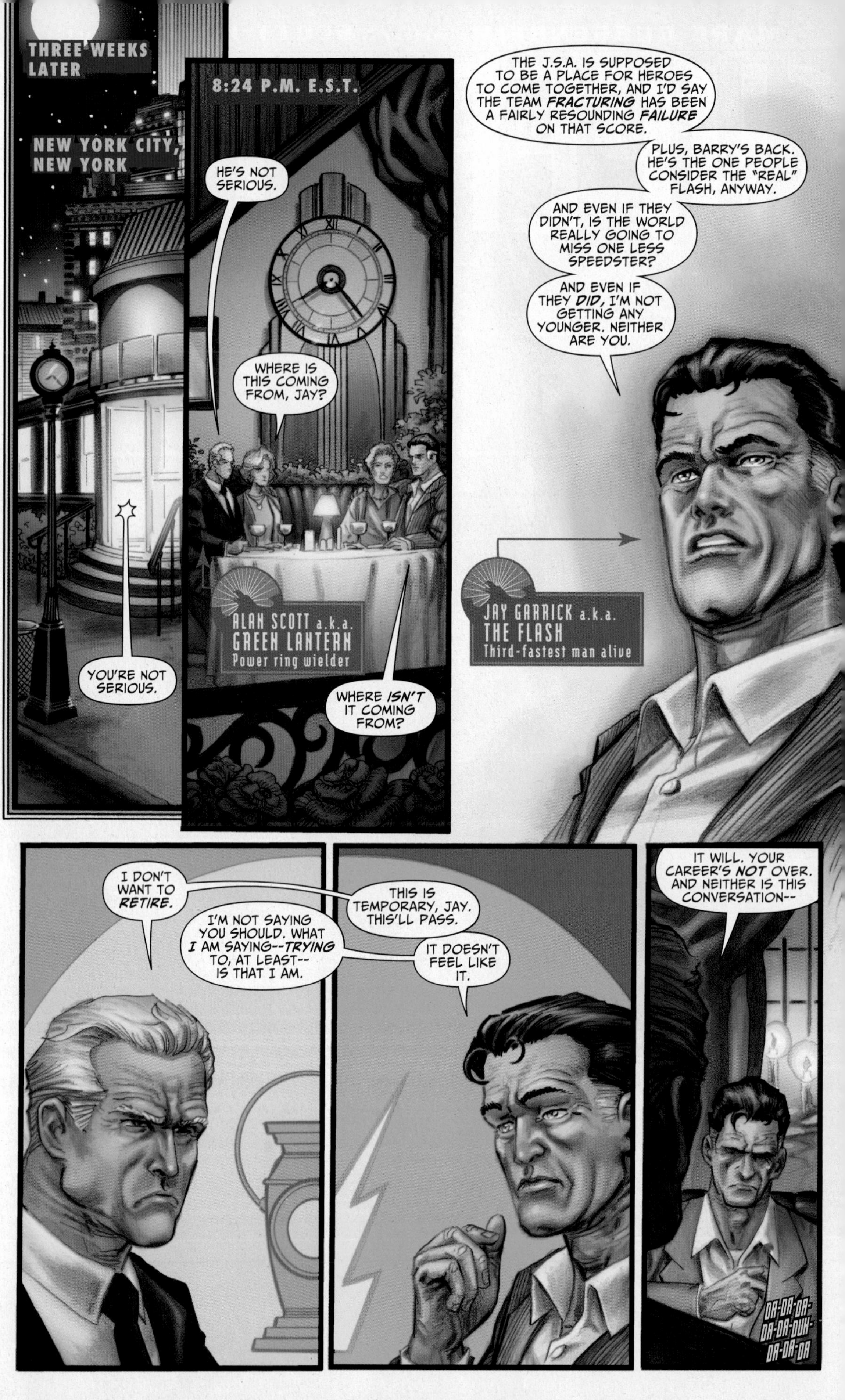
THREE WEEKS LATER
NEW YORK CITY, NEW YORK
YOU'RE NOT SERIOUS.
8:24 P.M. E.S.T.
HE'S NOT SERIOUS.
WHERE IS THIS COMING FROM, JAY?
ALAN SCOTT a.k.a. GREEN LANTERN Power ring wielder
WHERE ISN'T IT COMING FROM?
THE J.S.A. IS SUPPOSED TO BE A PLACE FOR HEROES TO COME TOGETHER, AND I'D SAY THE TEAM FRACTURING HAS BEEN A FAIRLY RESOUNDING FAILURE ON THAT SCORE.
PLUS, BARRY'S BACK. HE'S THE ONE PEOPLE CONSIDER THE "REAL" FLASH, ANYWAY.
AND EVEN IF THEY DIDN'T, IS THE WORLD REALLY GOING TO MISS ONE LESS SPEEDSTER?
AND EVEN IF THEY DID, I'M NOT GETTING ANY YOUNGER. NEITHER ARE YOU.
JAY GARRICK a.k.a. THE FLASH Third-fastest man alive
I DON'T WANT TO RETIRE.
THIS IS TEMPORARY, JAY. THIS'LL PASS.
I'M NOT SAYING YOU SHOULD. WHAT I AM SAYING--TRYING TO, AT LEAST--IS THAT I AM.
IT DOESN'T FEEL LIKE IT.
IT WILL. YOUR CAREER'S NOT OVER. AND NEITHER IS THIS CONVERSATION--
DA-DA-DA-DA-DA-DUH-DA-DA-DA

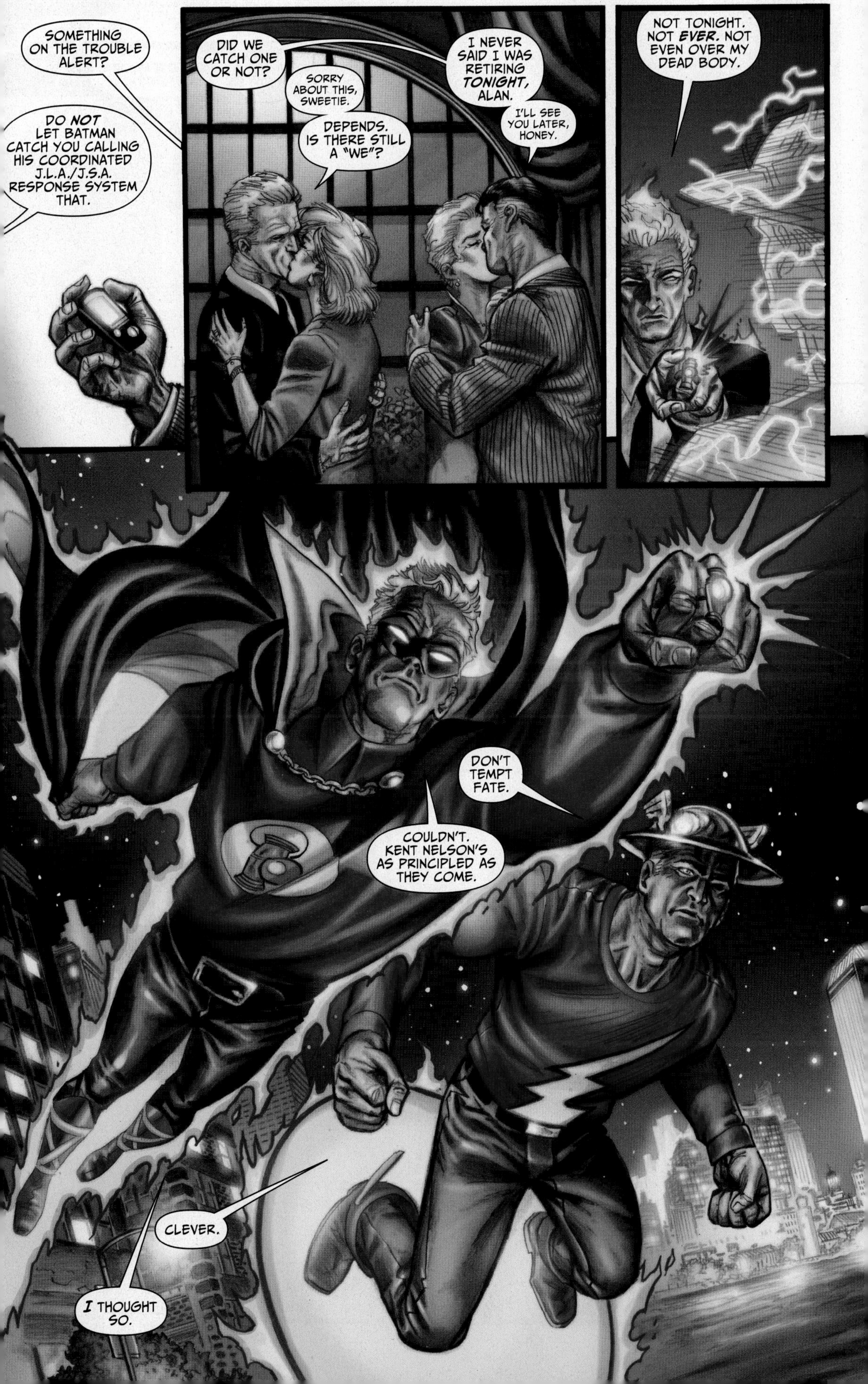
SOMETHING ON THE TROUBLE ALERT?
DO NOT LET BATMAN CATCH YOU CALLING HIS COORDINATED J.L.A./J.S.A. RESPONSE SYSTEM THAT.
DID WE CATCH ONE OR NOT?
SORRY ABOUT THIS, SWEETIE.
DEPENDS. IS THERE STILL A "WE"?
I NEVER SAID I WAS RETIRING TONIGHT, ALAN.
I'LL SEE YOU LATER, HONEY.
NOT TONIGHT. NOT EVER. NOT EVEN OVER MY DEAD BODY.
DON'T TEMPT FATE.
COULDN'T. KENT NELSON'S AS PRINCIPLED AS THEY COME.
CLEVER.
I THOUGHT SO.

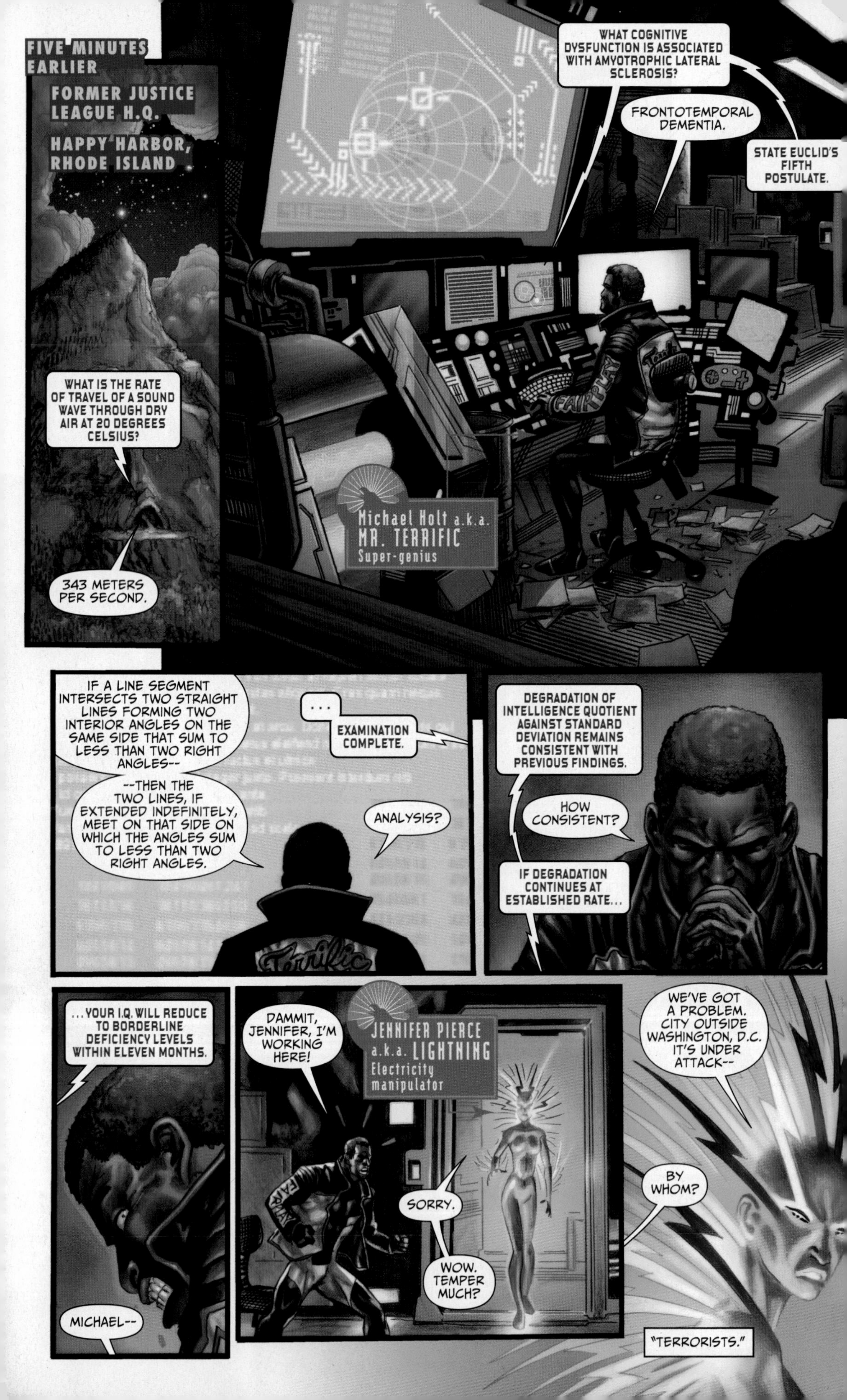
FIVE MINUTES EARLIER
FORMER JUSTICE LEAGUE H.Q.
HAPPY HARBOR, RHODE ISLAND
WHAT IS THE RATE OF TRAVEL OF A SOUND WAVE THROUGH DRY AIR AT 20 DEGREES CELSIUS?
343 METERS PER SECOND.
WHAT COGNITIVE DYSFUNCTION IS ASSOCIATED WITH AMYOTROPHIC LATERAL SCLEROSIS?
FRONTOTEMPORAL DEMENTIA.
STATE EUCLID'S FIFTH POSTULATE.
Michael Holt a.k.a. MR. TERRIFIC Super-genius
IF A LINE SEGMENT INTERSECTS TWO STRAIGHT LINES FORMING TWO INTERIOR ANGLES ON THE SAME SIDE THAT SUM TO LESS THAN TWO RIGHT ANGLES--
--THEN THE TWO LINES, IF EXTENDED INDEFINITELY, MEET ON THAT SIDE ON WHICH THE ANGLES SUM TO LESS THAN TWO RIGHT ANGLES.
...
EXAMINATION COMPLETE.
ANALYSIS?
DEGRADATION OF INTELLIGENCE QUOTIENT AGAINST STANDARD DEVIATION REMAINS CONSISTENT WITH PREVIOUS FINDINGS.
HOW CONSISTENT?
IF DEGRADATION CONTINUES AT ESTABLISHED RATE...
...YOUR I.Q. WILL REDUCE TO BORDERLINE DEFICIENCY LEVELS WITHIN ELEVEN MONTHS.
MICHAEL--
DAMMIT, JENNIFER, I'M WORKING HERE!
JENNIFER PIERCE a.k.a. LIGHTNING Electricity manipulator
SORRY.
WOW. TEMPER MUCH?
WE'VE GOT A PROBLEM. CITY OUTSIDE WASHINGTON, D.C. IT'S UNDER ATTACK--
BY WHOM?
"TERRORISTS."

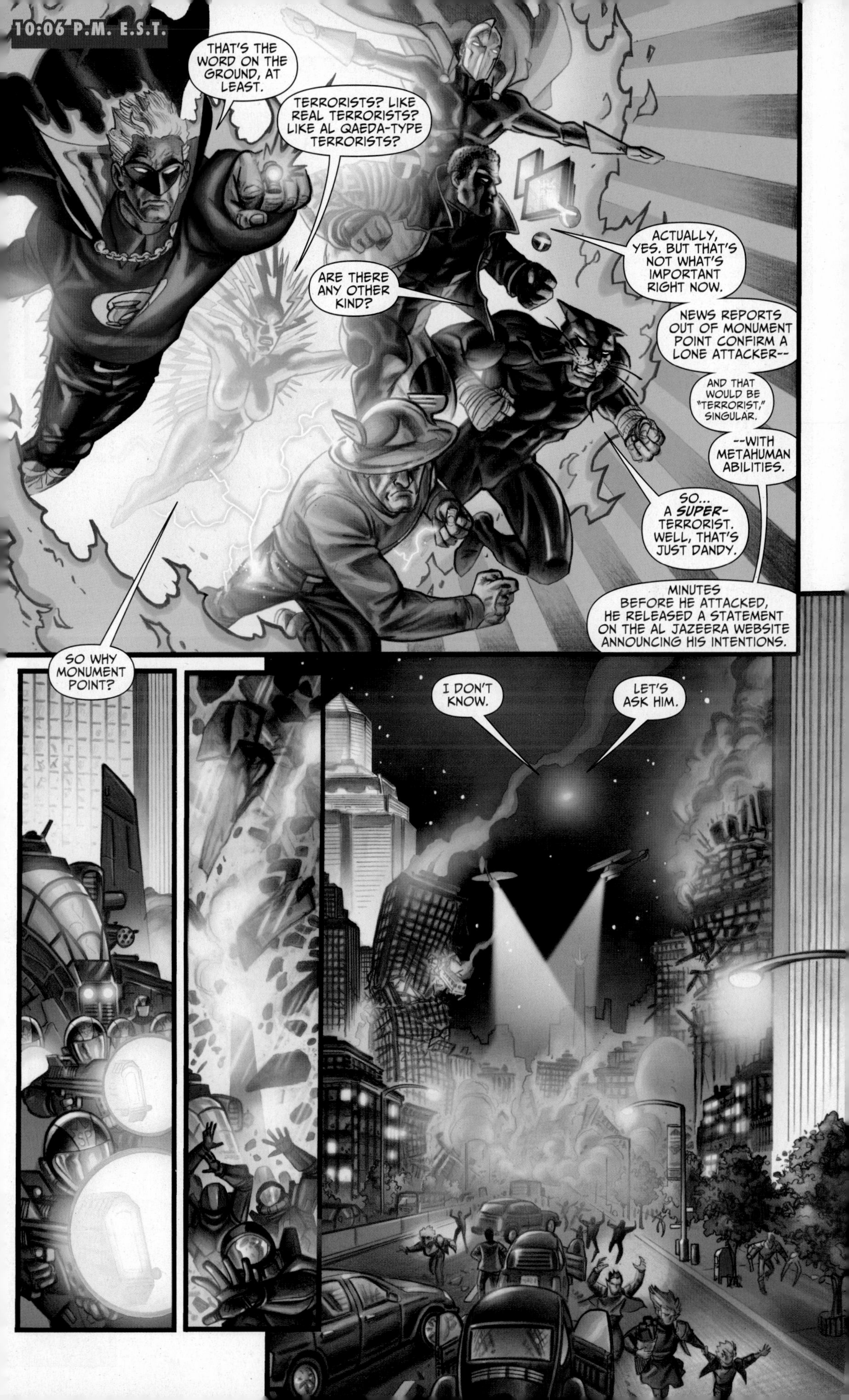

10:06 P.M. E.S.T.
THAT'S THE WORD ON THE GROUND, AT LEAST.
TERRORISTS? LIKE REAL TERRORISTS? LIKE AL QAEDA-TYPE TERRORISTS?
ACTUALLY, YES. BUT THAT'S NOT WHAT'S IMPORTANT RIGHT NOW.
ARE THERE ANY OTHER KIND?
NEWS REPORTS OUT OF MONUMENT POINT CONFIRM A LONE ATTACKER--
AND THAT WOULD BE "TERRORIST," SINGULAR.
--WITH METAHUMAN ABILITIES.
SO... A SUPER-TERRORIST. WELL, THAT'S JUST DANDY.
MINUTES BEFORE HE ATTACKED, HE RELEASED A STATEMENT ON THE AL JAZEERA WEBSITE ANNOUNCING HIS INTENTIONS.
SO WHY MONUMENT POINT?
I DON'T KNOW.
LET'S ASK HIM.

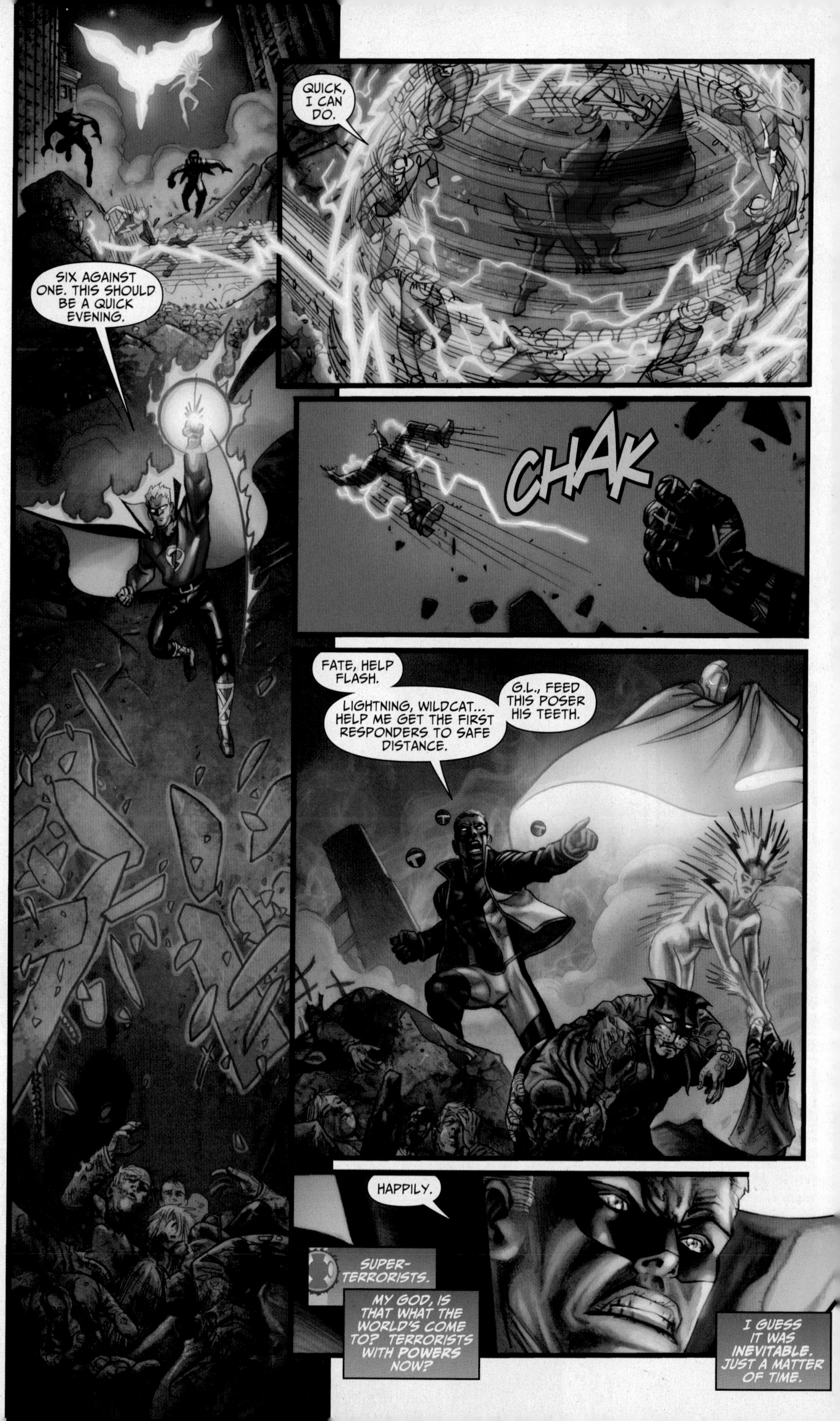
SIX AGAINST ONE. THIS SHOULD BE A QUICK EVENING.
QUICK, I CAN DO.
CHAK
FATE, HELP FLASH.
LIGHTNING, WILDCAT... HELP ME GET THE FIRST RESPONDERS TO SAFE DISTANCE.
G.L., FEED THIS POSER HIS TEETH.
HAPPILY.
SUPER-TERRORISTS.
MY GOD, IS THAT WHAT THE WORLD'S COME TO? TERRORISTS WITH POWERS NOW?
I GUESS IT WAS INEVITABLE. JUST A MATTER OF TIME.

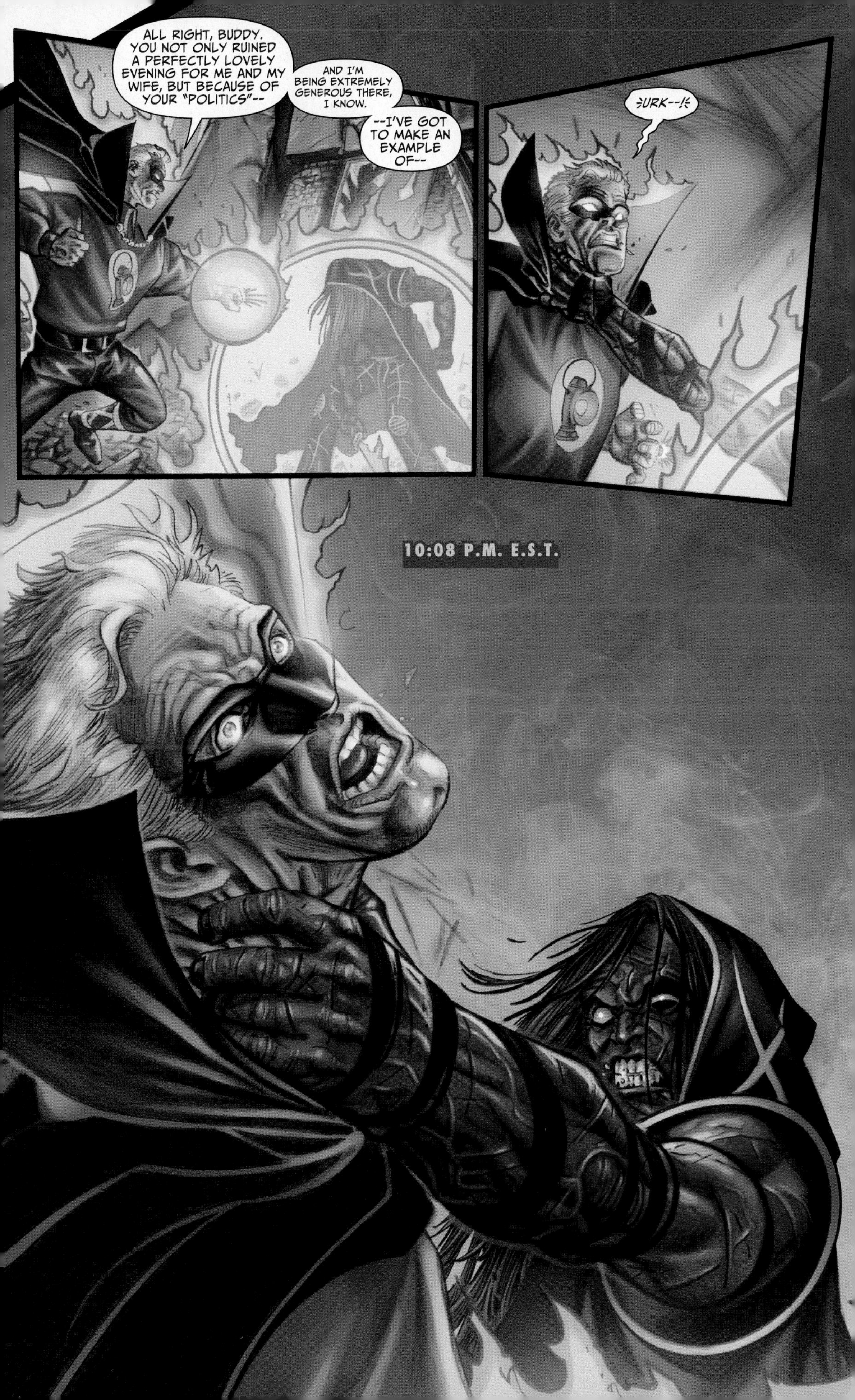

ALL RIGHT, BUDDY. YOU NOT ONLY RUINED A PERFECTLY LOVELY EVENING FOR ME AND MY WIFE, BUT BECAUSE OF YOUR "POLITICS"--
AND I'M BEING EXTREMELY GENEROUS THERE, I KNOW.
--I'VE GOT TO MAKE AN EXAMPLE OF--
URK--!
10:08 P.M. E.S.T.

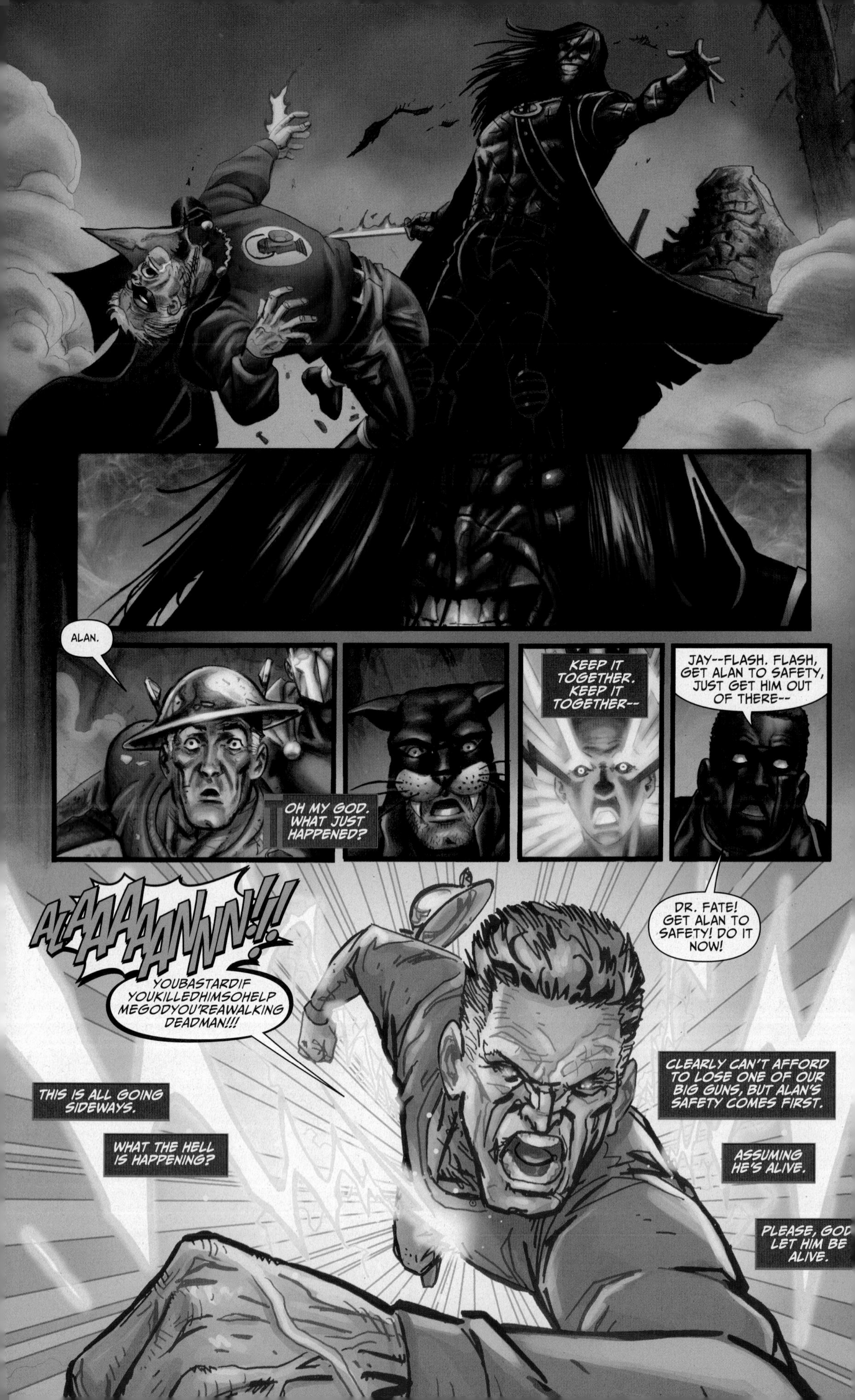
ALAN.
OH MY GOD. WHAT JUST HAPPENED?
KEEP IT TOGETHER. KEEP IT TOGETHER--
JAY--FLASH. FLASH, GET ALAN TO SAFETY, JUST GET HIM OUT OF THERE--
DR. FATE! GET ALAN TO SAFETY! DO IT NOW!
ALAAAAANNN!!!
YOUBASTARDIF YOUKILLEDHIMSOHELP MEGODYOU'REAWALKING DEADMAN!!!
THIS IS ALL GOING SIDEWAYS.
WHAT THE HELL IS HAPPENING?
CLEARLY CAN'T AFFORD TO LOSE ONE OF OUR BIG GUNS, BUT ALAN'S SAFETY COMES FIRST.
ASSUMING HE'S ALIVE.
PLEASE, GOD LET HIM BE ALIVE.

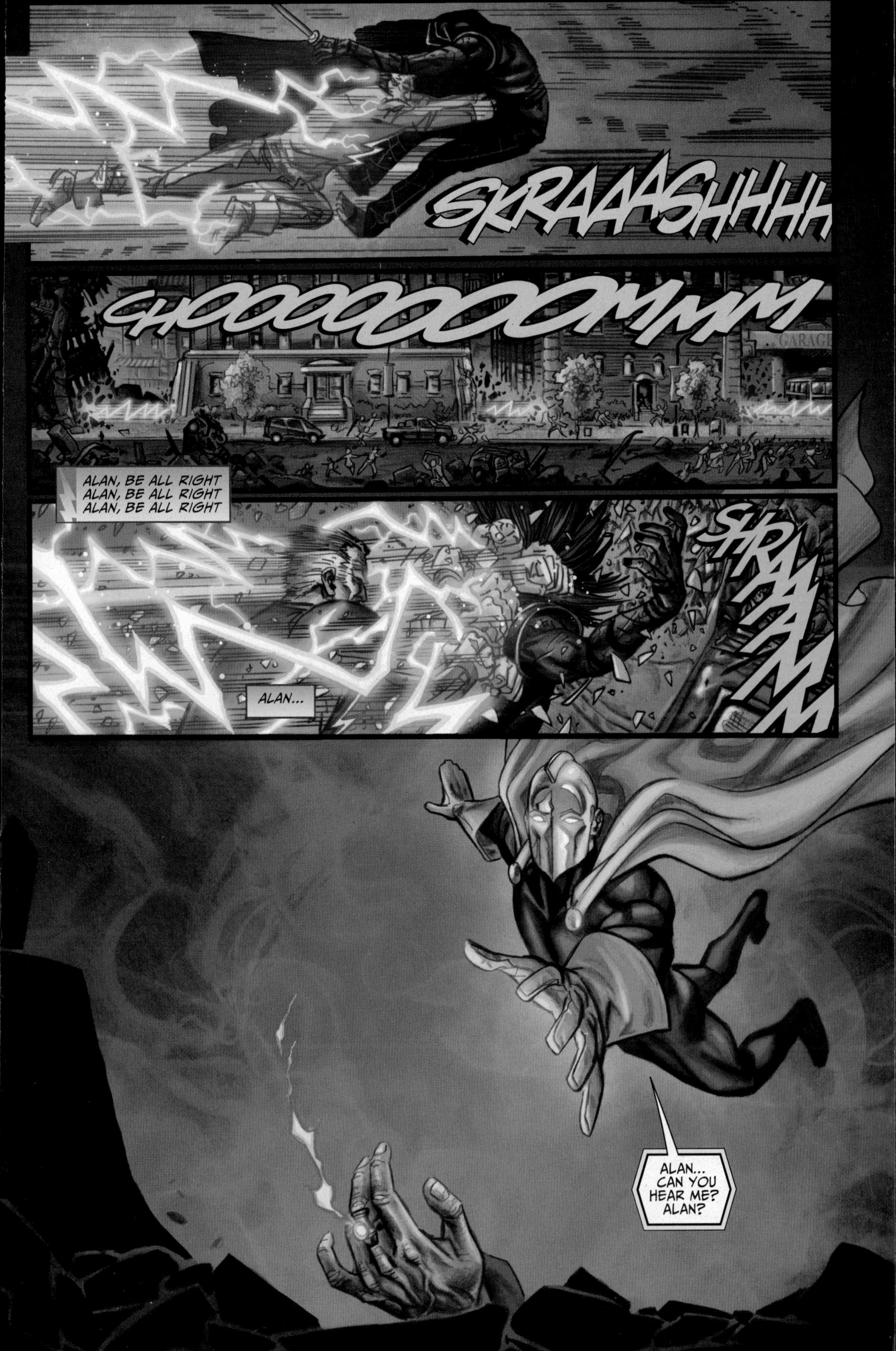
SKRAAASHHHH
CHOOOOOOOOMMM
GARAGE
ALAN, BE ALL RIGHT
ALAN, BE ALL RIGHT
ALAN, BE ALL RIGHT
SHRAAAM
ALAN...
ALAN... CAN YOU HEAR ME? ALAN?

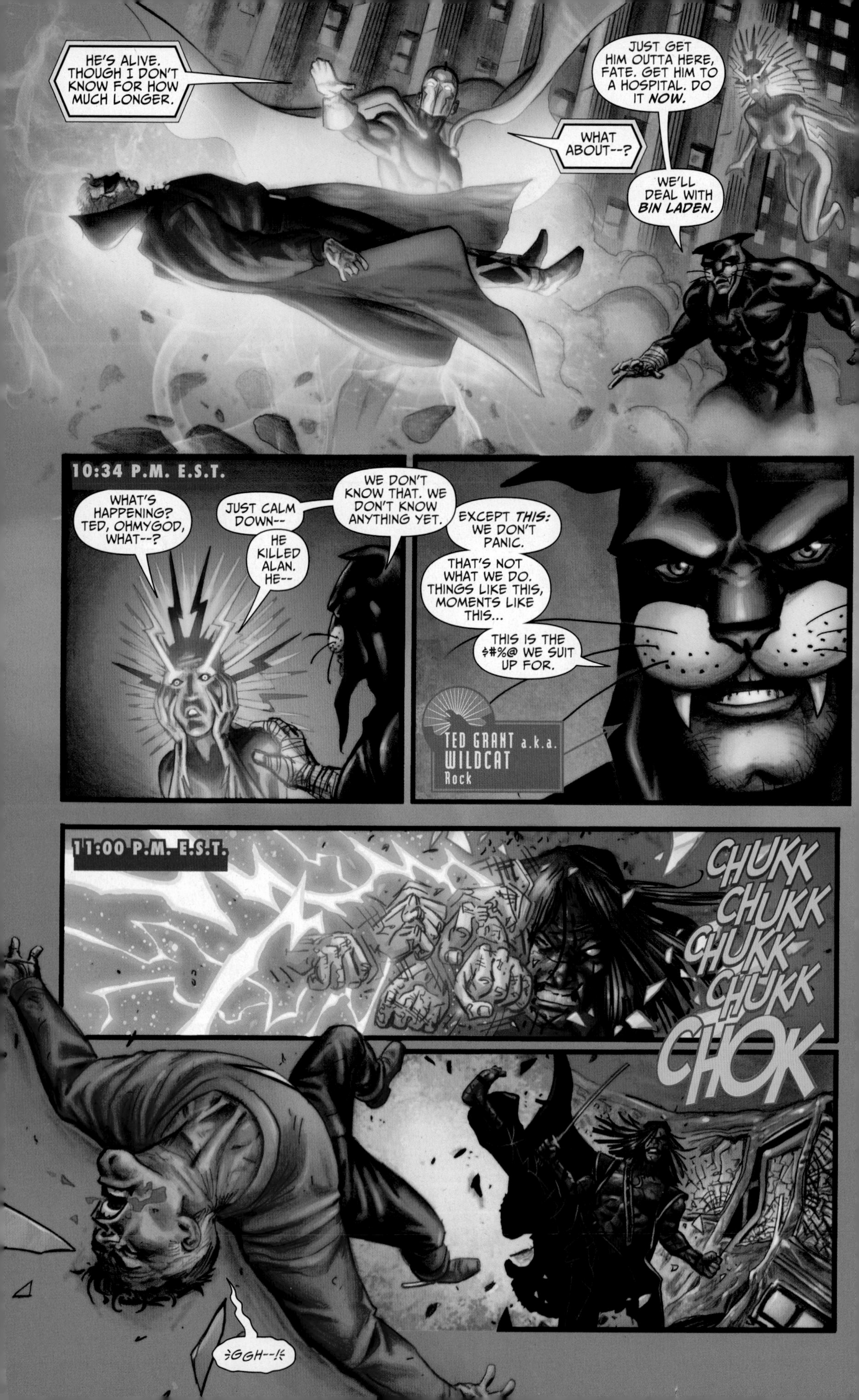
HE'S ALIVE. THOUGH I DON'T KNOW FOR HOW MUCH LONGER.
JUST GET HIM OUTTA HERE, FATE. GET HIM TO A HOSPITAL. DO IT NOW.
WHAT ABOUT--?
WE'LL DEAL WITH BIN LADEN.
10:34 P.M. E.S.T.
WHAT'S HAPPENING? TED, OHMYGOD, WHAT--?
JUST CALM DOWN--
WE DON'T KNOW THAT. WE DON'T KNOW ANYTHING YET.
HE KILLED ALAN. HE--
EXCEPT THIS: WE DON'T PANIC.
THAT'S NOT WHAT WE DO. THINGS LIKE THIS, MOMENTS LIKE THIS...
THIS IS THE $#%@ WE SUIT UP FOR.
TED GRANT a.k.a. WILDCAT
Rock
11:00 P.M. E.S.T.
CHUKK CHUKK CHUKK CHUKK
CHOK
GGH--!

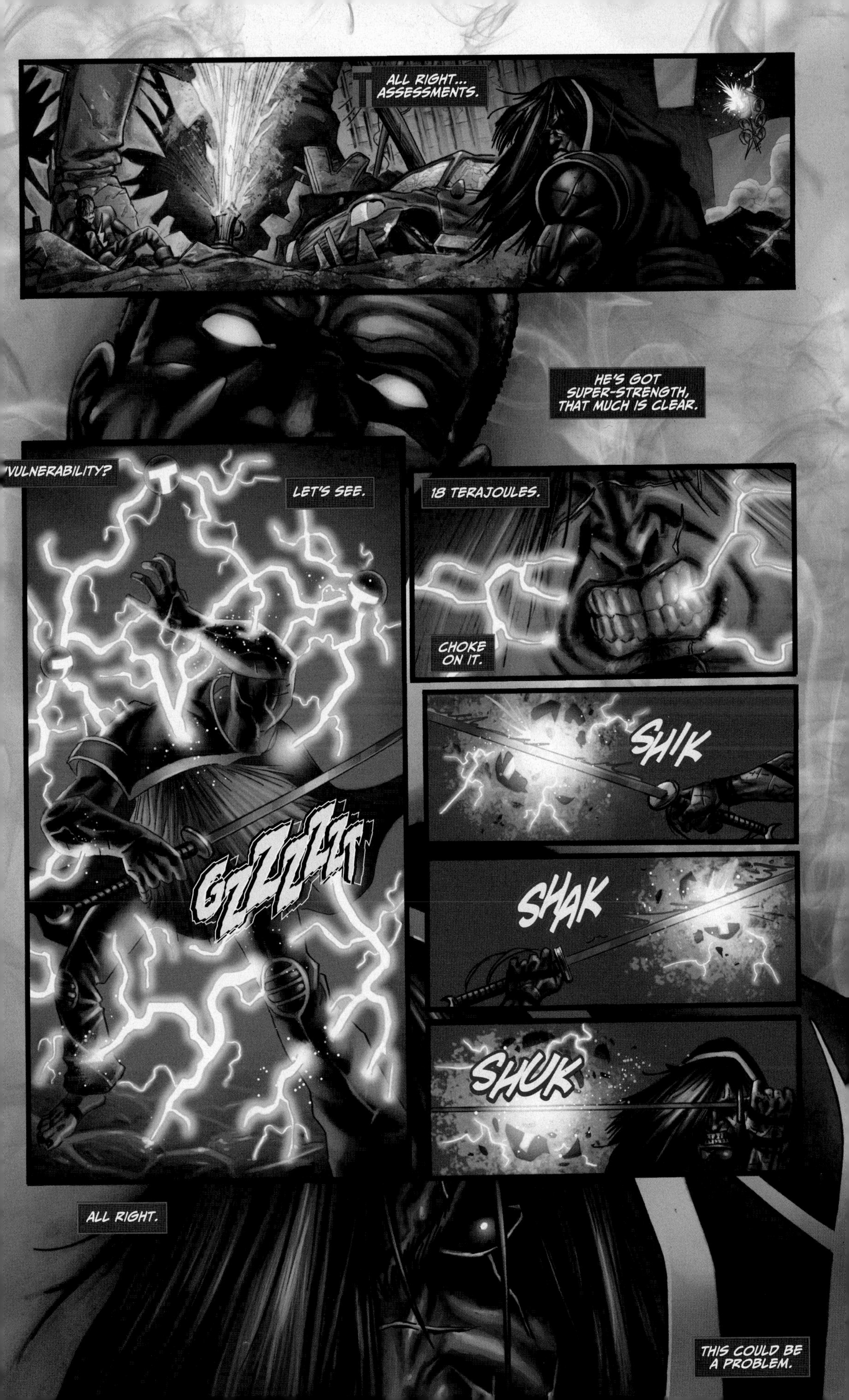
ALL RIGHT... ASSESSMENTS.
HE'S GOT SUPER-STRENGTH, THAT MUCH IS CLEAR.
VULNERABILITY?
LET'S SEE.
18 TERAJOULES.
CHOKE ON IT.
GZZZZZT
SHIK
SHAK
SHUK
ALL RIGHT.
THIS COULD BE A PROBLEM.

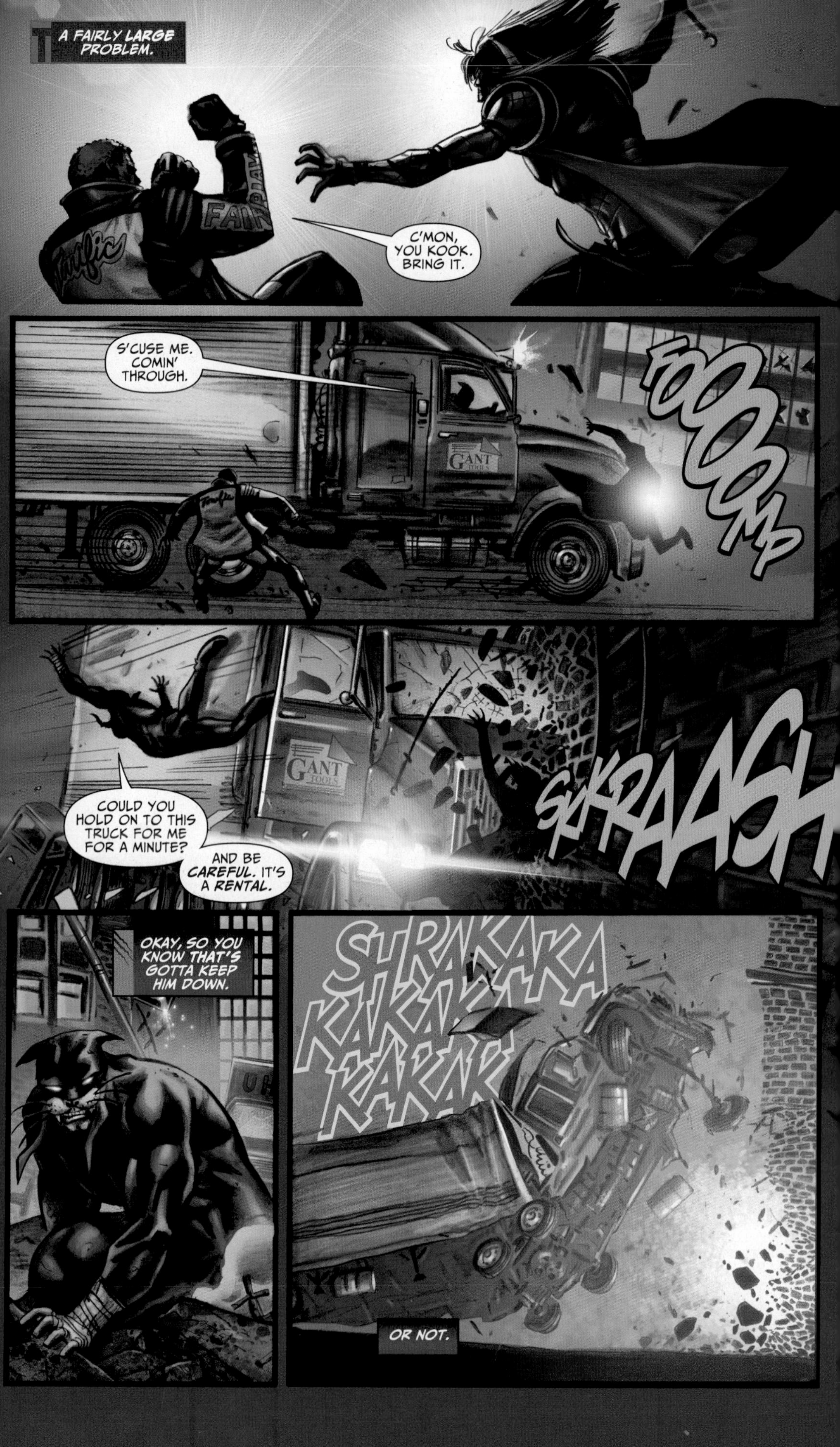
A FAIRLY LARGE PROBLEM.
C'MON, YOU KOOK. BRING IT.
S'CUSE ME. COMIN' THROUGH.
FOOOOOMP
COULD YOU HOLD ON TO THIS TRUCK FOR ME FOR A MINUTE?
AND BE CAREFUL. IT'S A RENTAL.
SKRAASH
OKAY, SO YOU KNOW THAT'S GOTTA KEEP HIM DOWN.
SHRAKAKA KAKAKAKA KAKAK
OR NOT.

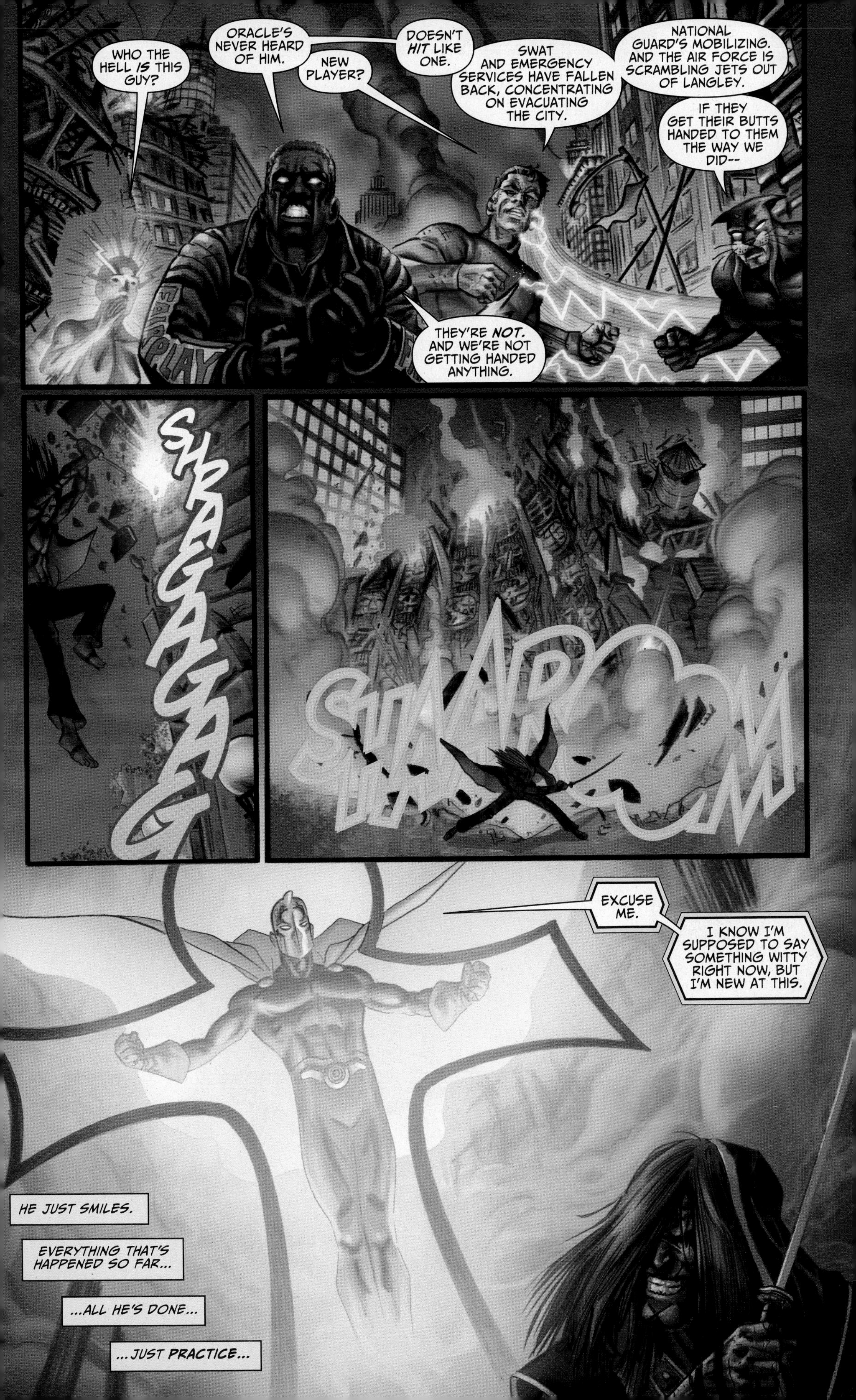
WHO THE HELL IS THIS GUY?
ORACLE'S NEVER HEARD OF HIM.
NEW PLAYER?
DOESN'T HIT LIKE ONE.
SWAT AND EMERGENCY SERVICES HAVE FALLEN BACK, CONCENTRATING ON EVACUATING THE CITY.
NATIONAL GUARD'S MOBILIZING. AND THE AIR FORCE IS SCRAMBLING JETS OUT OF LANGLEY.
IF THEY GET THEIR BUTTS HANDED TO THEM THE WAY WE DID--
THEY'RE NOT. AND WE'RE NOT GETTING HANDED ANYTHING.
SHRAGAGAGAG
SHAAROOM
EXCUSE ME.
I KNOW I'M SUPPOSED TO SAY SOMETHING WITTY RIGHT NOW, BUT I'M NEW AT THIS.
HE JUST SMILES.
EVERYTHING THAT'S HAPPENED SO FAR...
...ALL HE'S DONE...
...JUST PRACTICE...

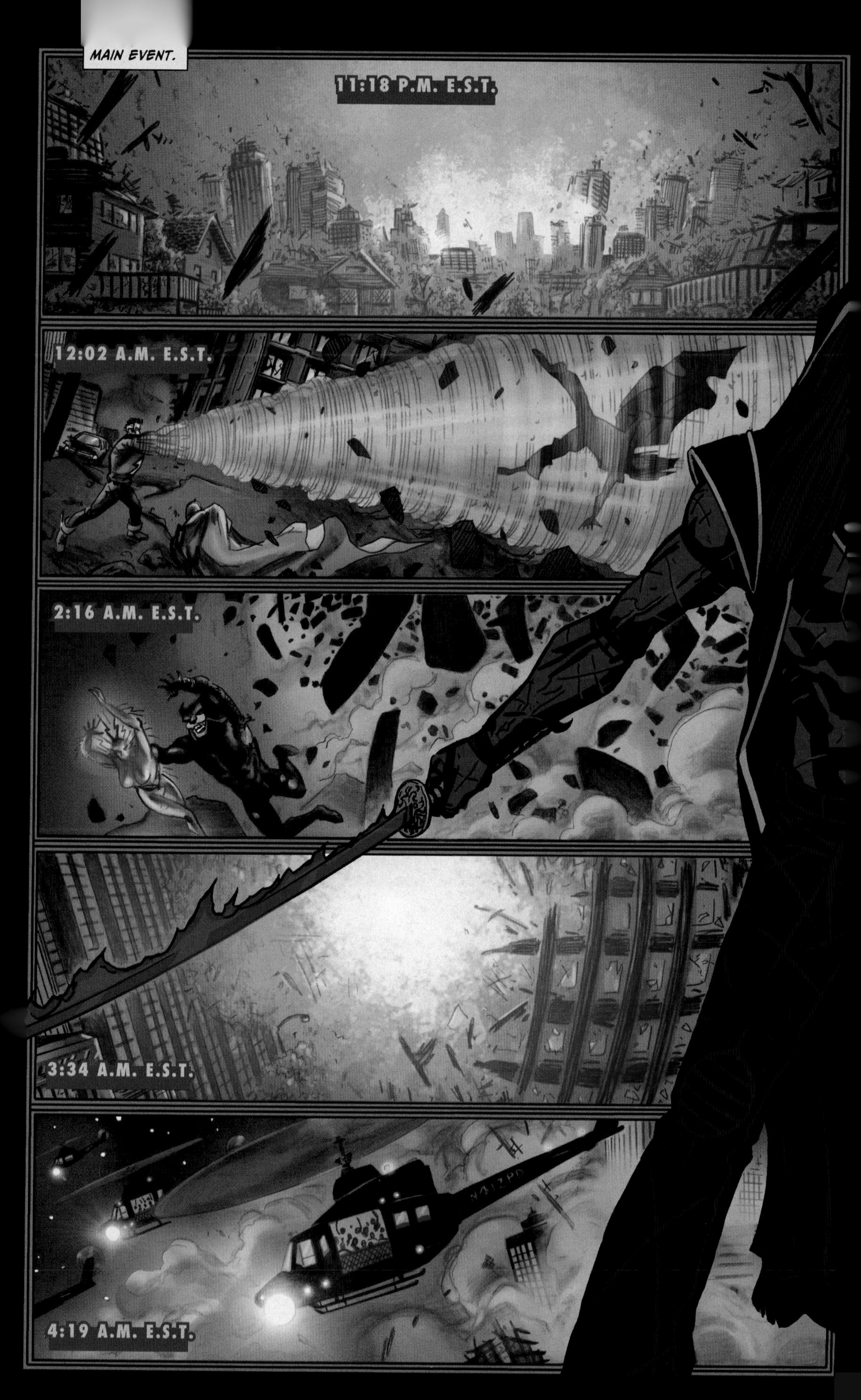
MAIN EVENT.
11:18 P.M. E.S.T.
12:02 A.M. E.S.T.
2:16 A.M. E.S.T.
3:34 A.M. E.S.T.
4:19 A.M. E.S.T.

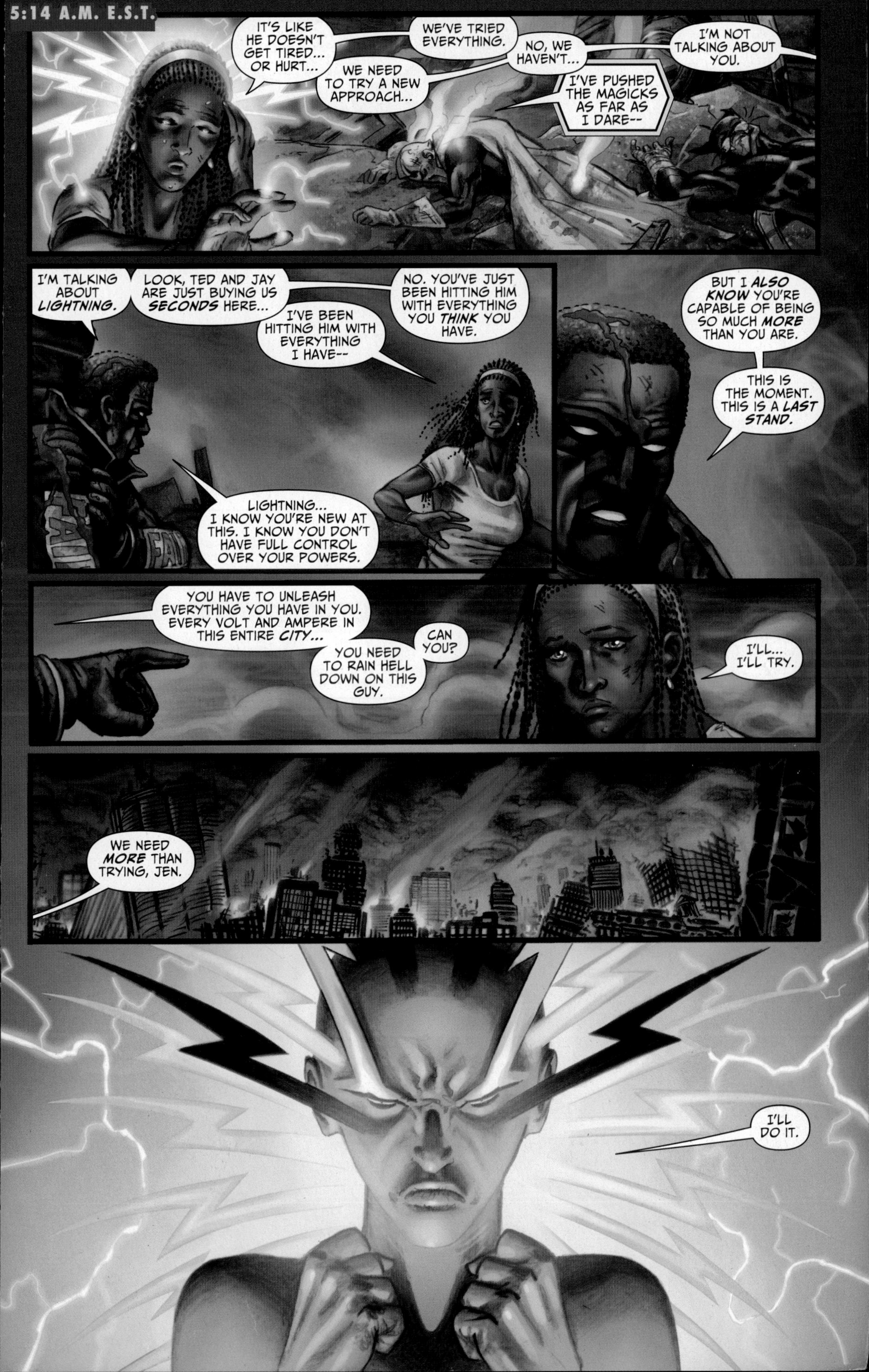
5:14 A.M. E.S.T.
IT'S LIKE HE DOESN'T GET TIRED... OR HURT...
WE'VE TRIED EVERYTHING.
WE NEED TO TRY A NEW APPROACH...
NO, WE HAVEN'T...
I'M NOT TALKING ABOUT YOU.
I'VE PUSHED THE MAGICKS AS FAR AS I DARE--
I'M TALKING ABOUT LIGHTNING.
LOOK, TED AND JAY ARE JUST BUYING US SECONDS HERE...
I'VE BEEN HITTING HIM WITH EVERYTHING I HAVE--
NO. YOU'VE JUST BEEN HITTING HIM WITH EVERYTHING YOU THINK YOU HAVE.
LIGHTNING... I KNOW YOU'RE NEW AT THIS. I KNOW YOU DON'T HAVE FULL CONTROL OVER YOUR POWERS.
BUT I ALSO KNOW YOU'RE CAPABLE OF BEING SO MUCH MORE THAN YOU ARE.
THIS IS THE MOMENT. THIS IS A LAST STAND.
YOU HAVE TO UNLEASH EVERYTHING YOU HAVE IN YOU. EVERY VOLT AND AMPERE IN THIS ENTIRE CITY...
YOU NEED TO RAIN HELL DOWN ON THIS GUY.
CAN YOU?
I'LL... I'LL TRY.
WE NEED MORE THAN TRYING, JEN.
I'LL DO IT.

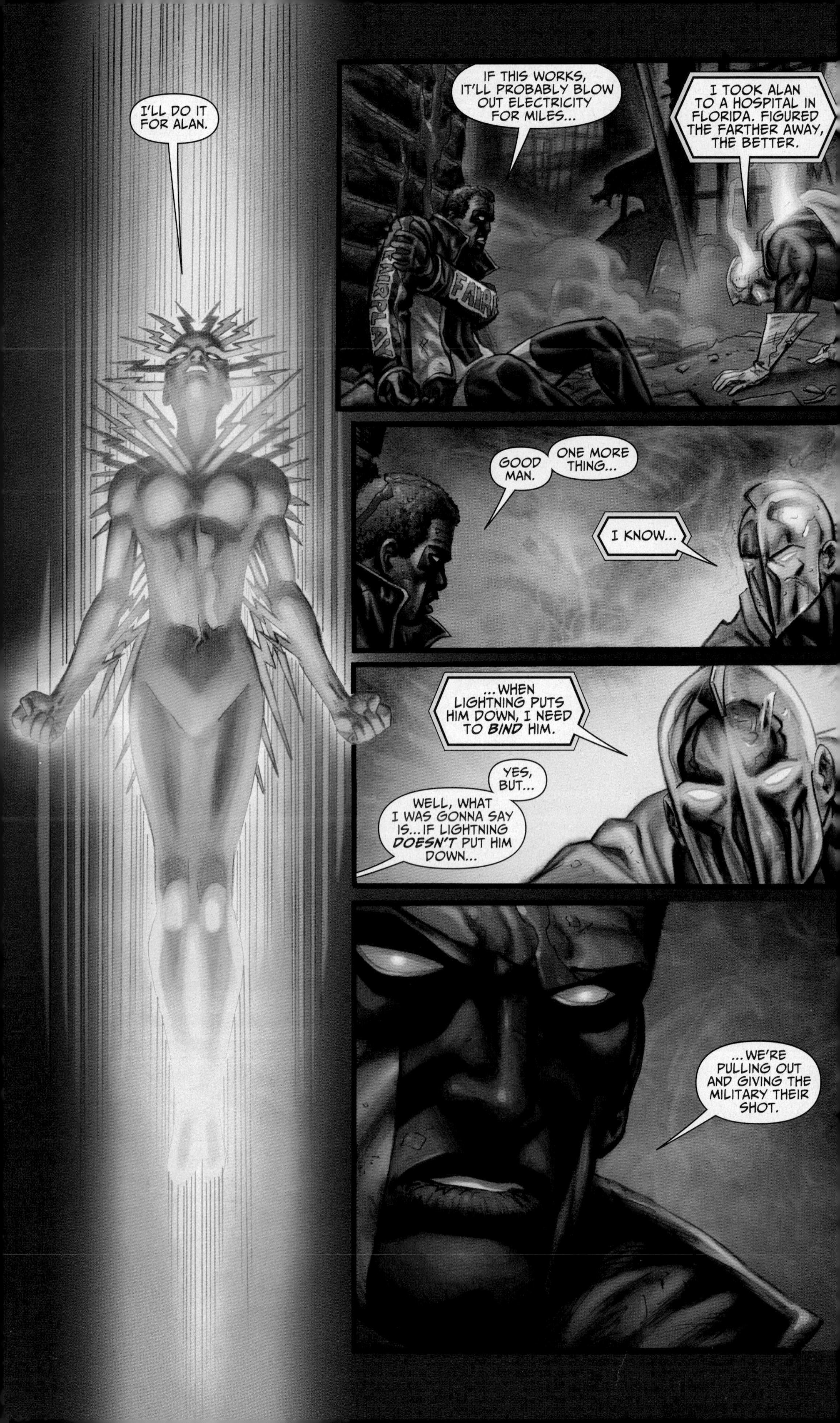
I'LL DO IT FOR ALAN.
IF THIS WORKS, IT'LL PROBABLY BLOW OUT ELECTRICITY FOR MILES...
I TOOK ALAN TO A HOSPITAL IN FLORIDA. FIGURED THE FARTHER AWAY, THE BETTER.
GOOD MAN.
ONE MORE THING...
I KNOW...
...WHEN LIGHTNING PUTS HIM DOWN, I NEED TO **BIND** HIM.
YES, BUT...
WELL, WHAT I WAS GONNA SAY IS...IF LIGHTNING **DOESN'T** PUT HIM DOWN...
...WE'RE PULLING OUT AND GIVING THE MILITARY THEIR SHOT.

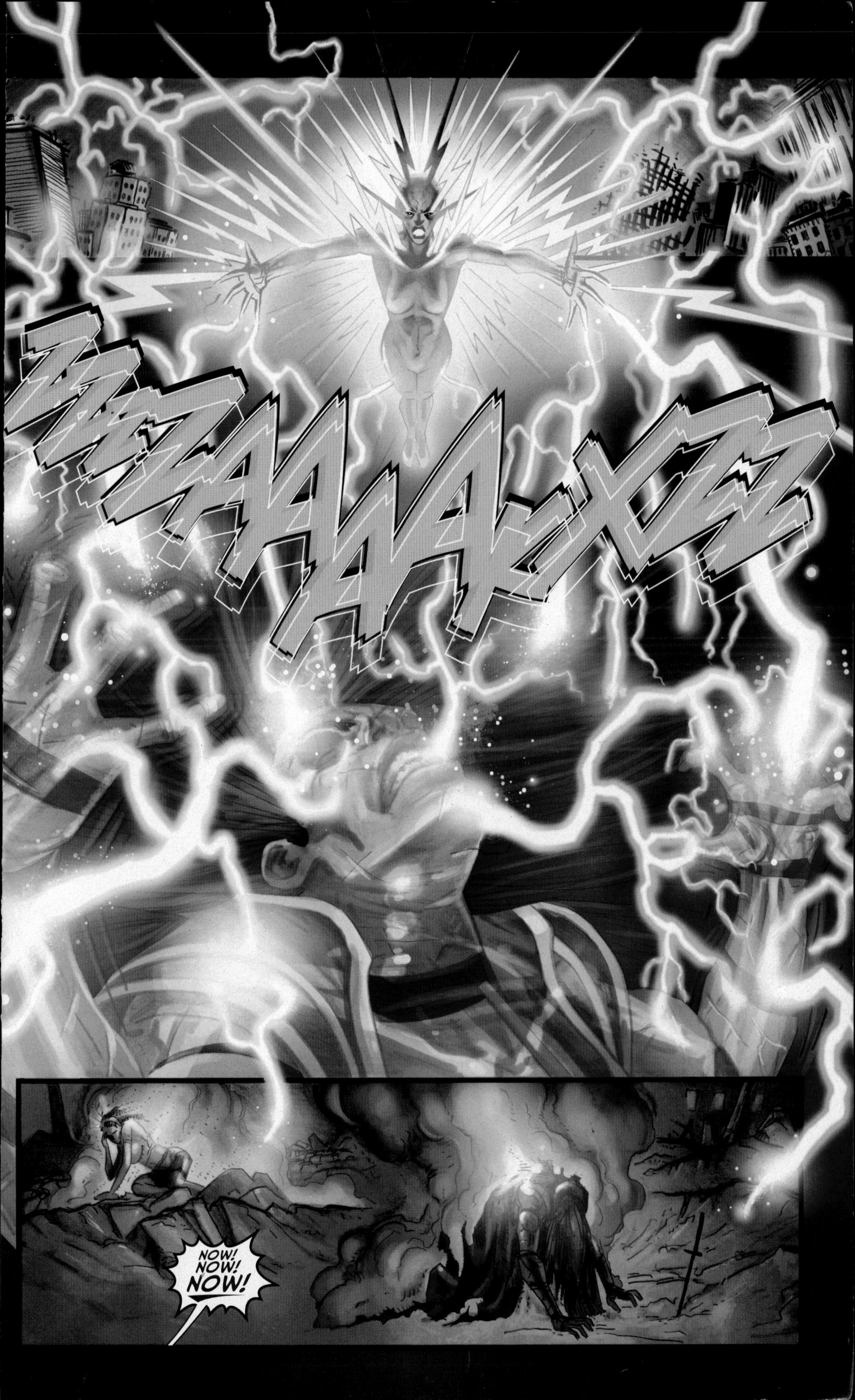
NOW! NOW! NOW!

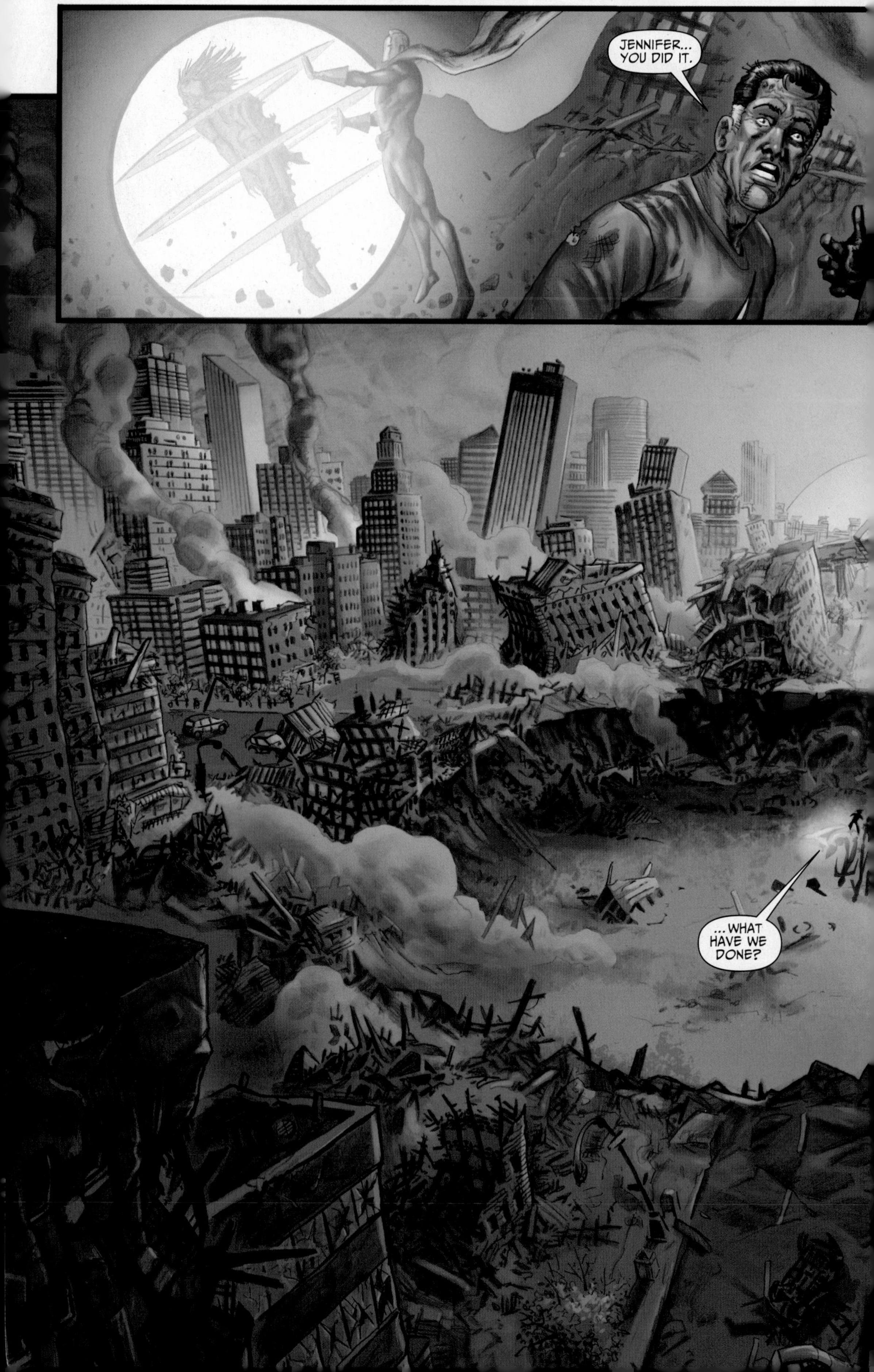
JENNIFER... YOU DID IT.
...WHAT HAVE WE DONE?

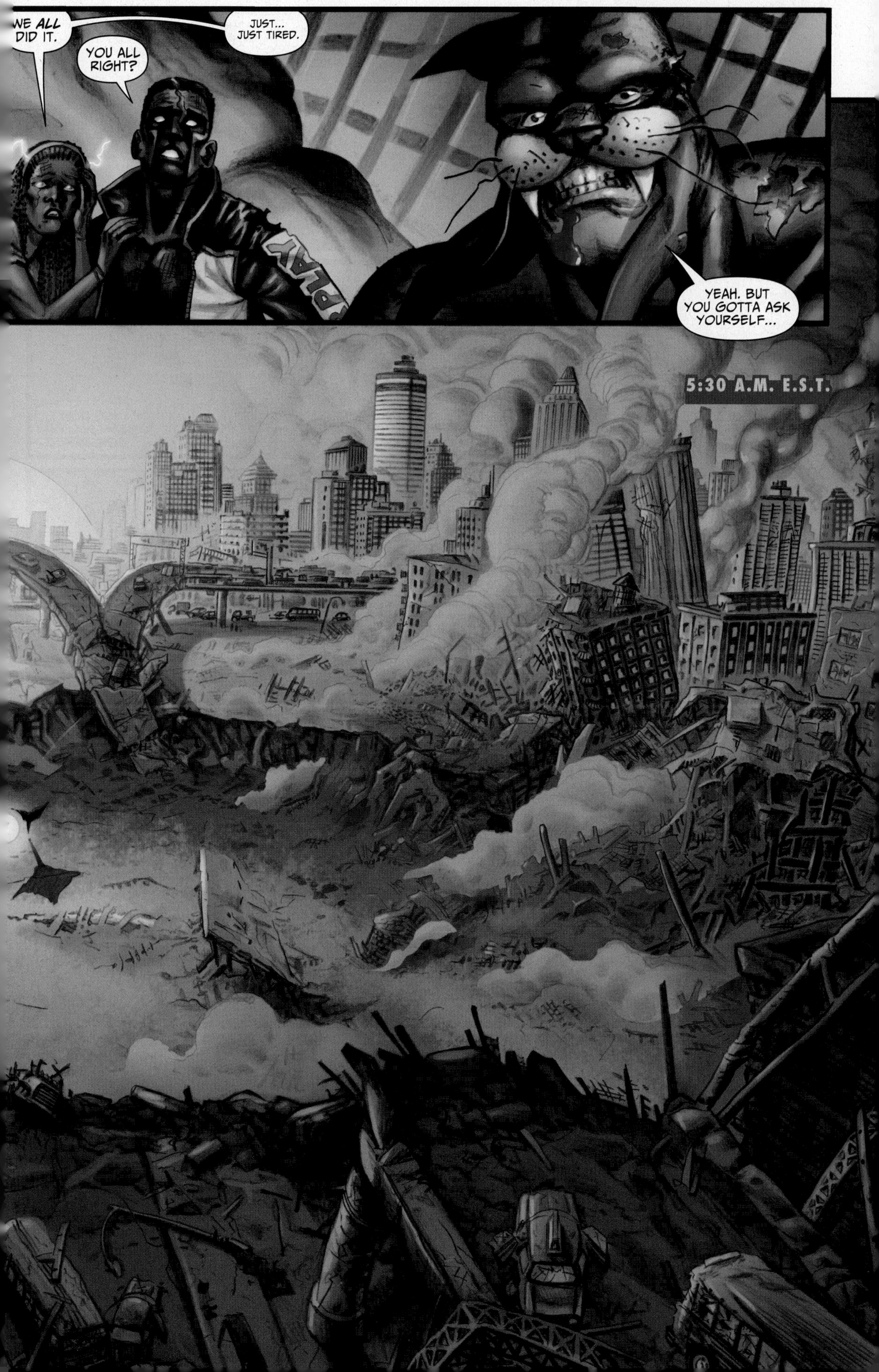
WE ALL DID IT.
YOU ALL RIGHT?
JUST... JUST TIRED.
PLAY
YEAH. BUT YOU GOTTA ASK YOURSELF...
5:30 A.M. E.S.T.

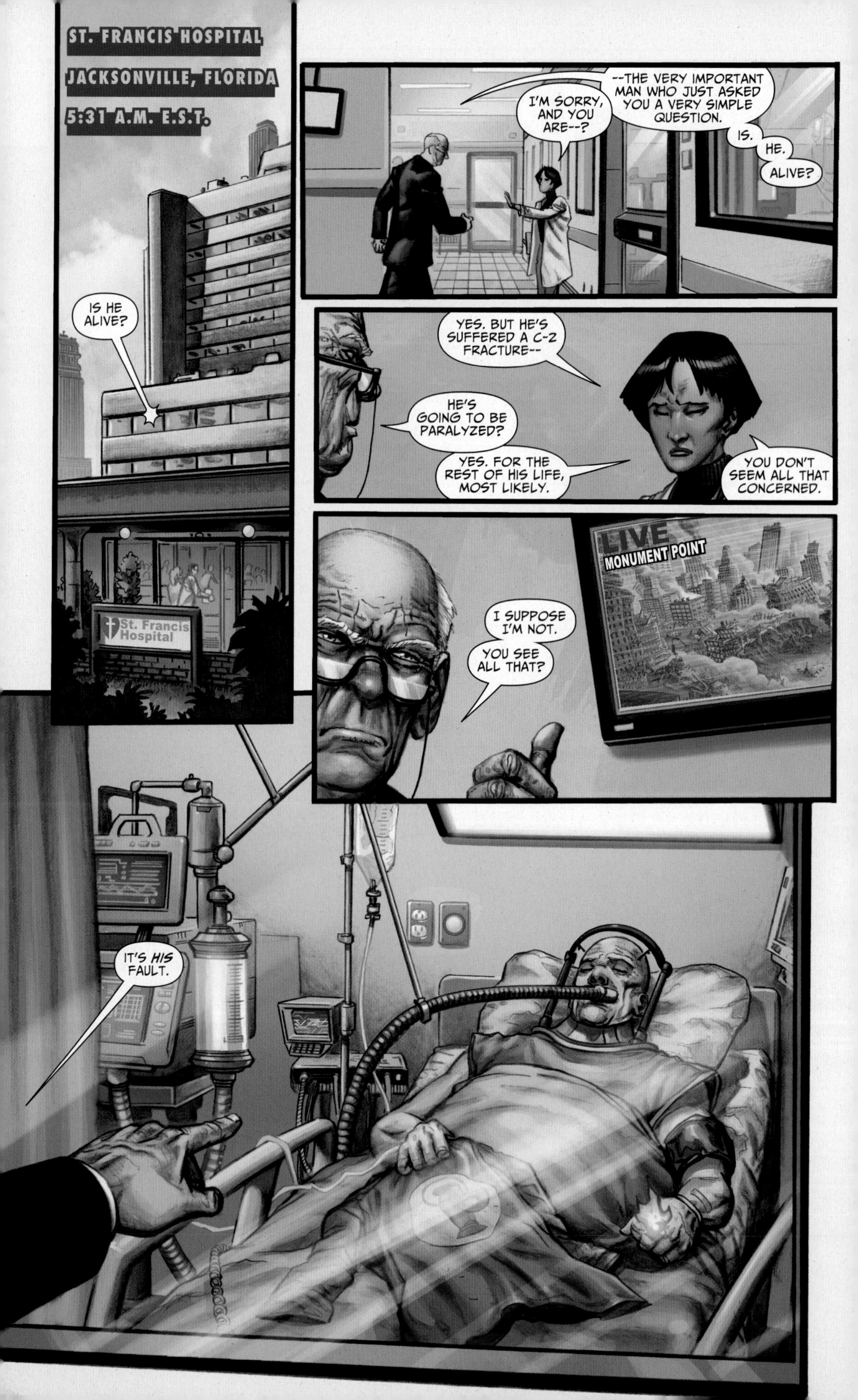
ST. FRANCIS HOSPITAL
JACKSONVILLE, FLORIDA
5:31 A.M. E.S.T.
IS HE ALIVE?
St. Francis Hospital
I'M SORRY, AND YOU ARE--?
--THE VERY IMPORTANT MAN WHO JUST ASKED YOU A VERY SIMPLE QUESTION.
IS.
HE.
ALIVE?
YES. BUT HE'S SUFFERED A C-2 FRACTURE--
HE'S GOING TO BE PARALYZED?
YES. FOR THE REST OF HIS LIFE, MOST LIKELY.
YOU DON'T SEEM ALL THAT CONCERNED.
LIVE
MONUMENT POINT
I SUPPOSE I'M NOT.
YOU SEE ALL THAT?
IT'S HIS FAULT.

SUPERTOWN Part Two

Cover by SHANE DAVIS & SANDRA HOPE
with BARBARA CIARDO

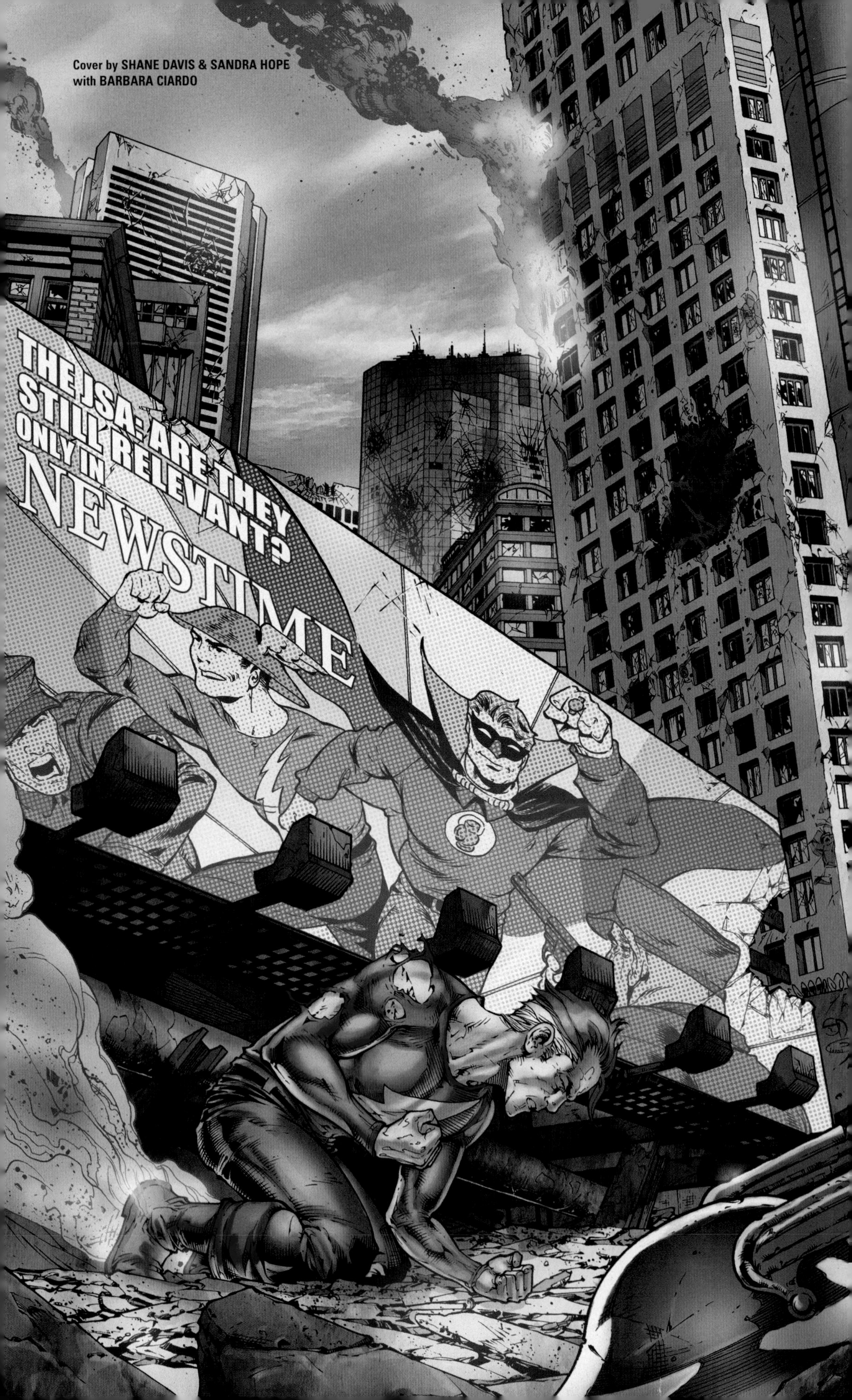
THE JSA: ARE THEY STILL RELEVANT?
ONLY IN
NEWSTIME

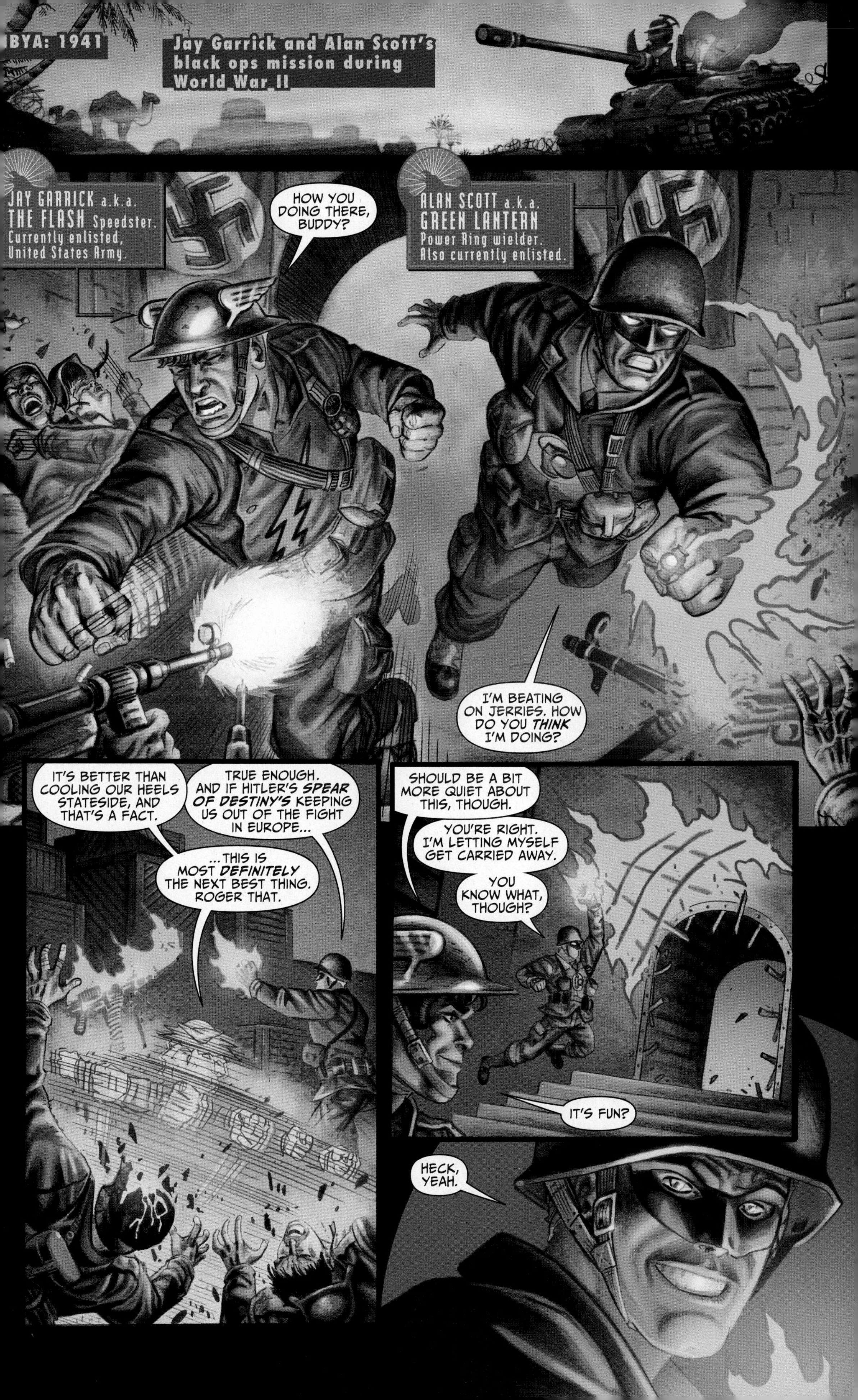
BYA: 1941
Jay Garrick and Alan Scott's black ops mission during World War II
JAY GARRICK a.k.a. THE FLASH Speedster. Currently enlisted, United States Army.
HOW YOU DOING THERE, BUDDY?
ALAN SCOTT a.k.a. GREEN LANTERN Power Ring wielder. Also currently enlisted.
I'M BEATING ON JERRIES. HOW DO YOU THINK I'M DOING?
IT'S BETTER THAN COOLING OUR HEELS STATESIDE, AND THAT'S A FACT.
TRUE ENOUGH. AND IF HITLER'S SPEAR OF DESTINY'S KEEPING US OUT OF THE FIGHT IN EUROPE...
...THIS IS MOST DEFINITELY THE NEXT BEST THING. ROGER THAT.
SHOULD BE A BIT MORE QUIET ABOUT THIS, THOUGH.
YOU'RE RIGHT. I'M LETTING MYSELF GET CARRIED AWAY.
YOU KNOW WHAT, THOUGH?
IT'S FUN?
HECK, YEAH.

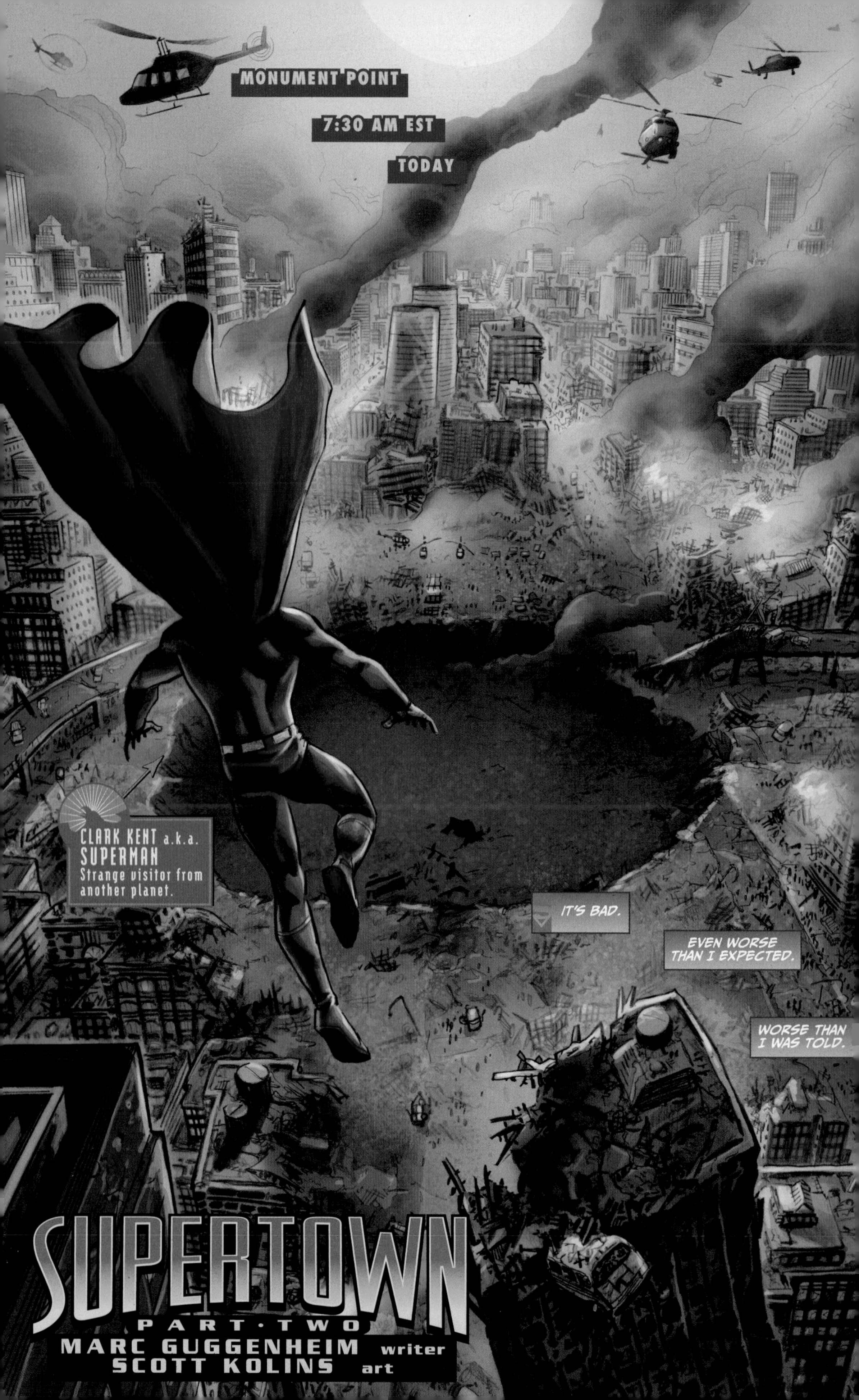
MONUMENT POINT
7:30 AM EST
TODAY
CLARK KENT a.k.a. SUPERMAN
Strange visitor from another planet.
IT'S BAD.
EVEN WORSE THAN I EXPECTED.
WORSE THAN I WAS TOLD.
SUPERTOWN
PART·TWO
MARC GUGGENHEIM writer
SCOTT KOLINS art

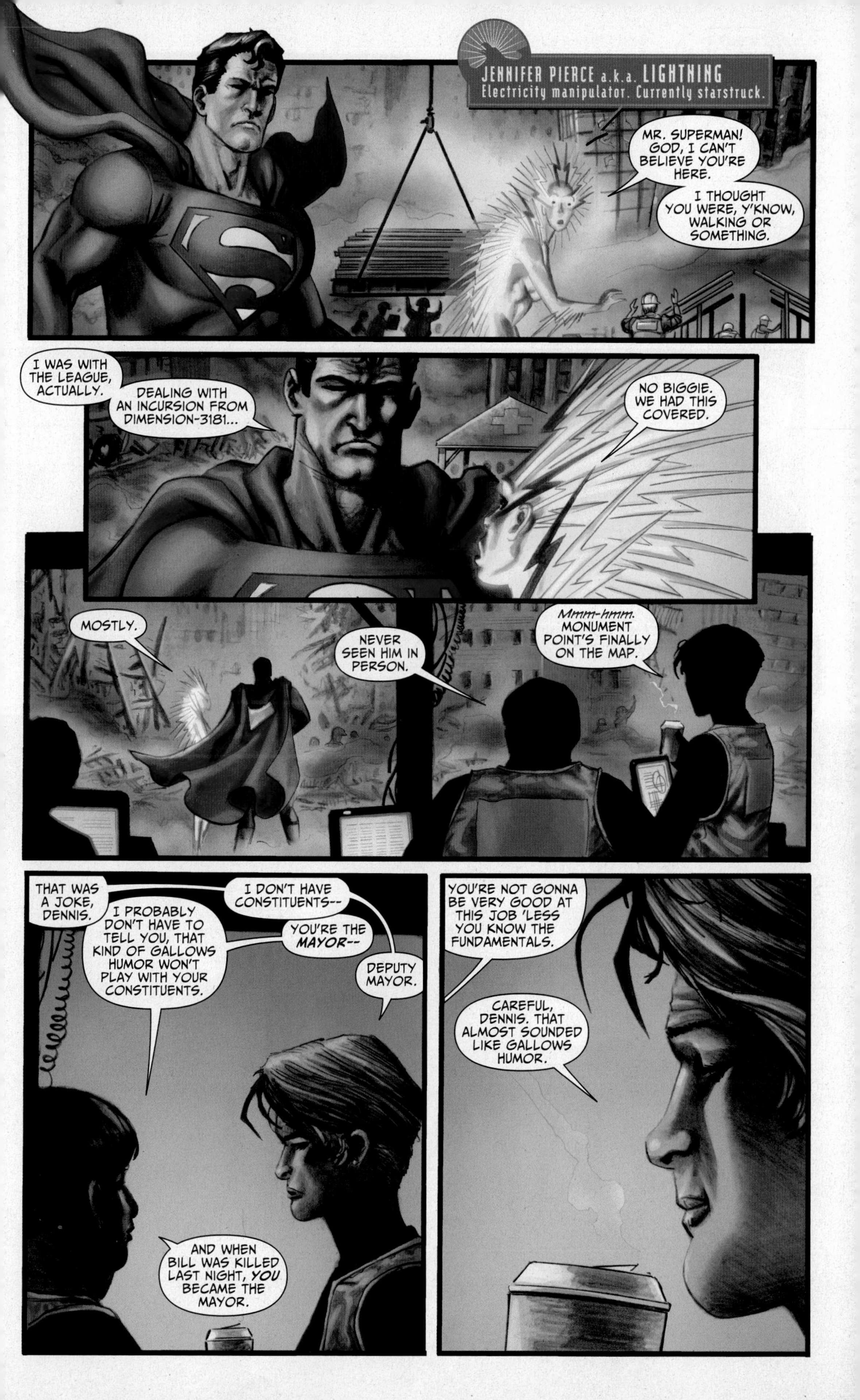
JENNIFER PIERCE a.k.a. LIGHTNING
Electricity manipulator. Currently starstruck.
MR. SUPERMAN! GOD, I CAN'T BELIEVE YOU'RE HERE.
I THOUGHT YOU WERE, Y'KNOW, WALKING OR SOMETHING.
I WAS WITH THE LEAGUE, ACTUALLY.
DEALING WITH AN INCURSION FROM DIMENSION-3181...
NO BIGGIE. WE HAD THIS COVERED.
MOSTLY.
NEVER SEEN HIM IN PERSON.
Mmm-hmm. MONUMENT POINT'S FINALLY ON THE MAP.
THAT WAS A JOKE, DENNIS.
I PROBABLY DON'T HAVE TO TELL YOU, THAT KIND OF GALLOWS HUMOR WON'T PLAY WITH YOUR CONSTITUENTS.
I DON'T HAVE CONSTITUENTS--
YOU'RE THE MAYOR--
DEPUTY MAYOR.
AND WHEN BILL WAS KILLED LAST NIGHT, YOU BECAME THE MAYOR.
YOU'RE NOT GONNA BE VERY GOOD AT THIS JOB 'LESS YOU KNOW THE FUNDAMENTALS.
CAREFUL, DENNIS. THAT ALMOST SOUNDED LIKE GALLOWS HUMOR.

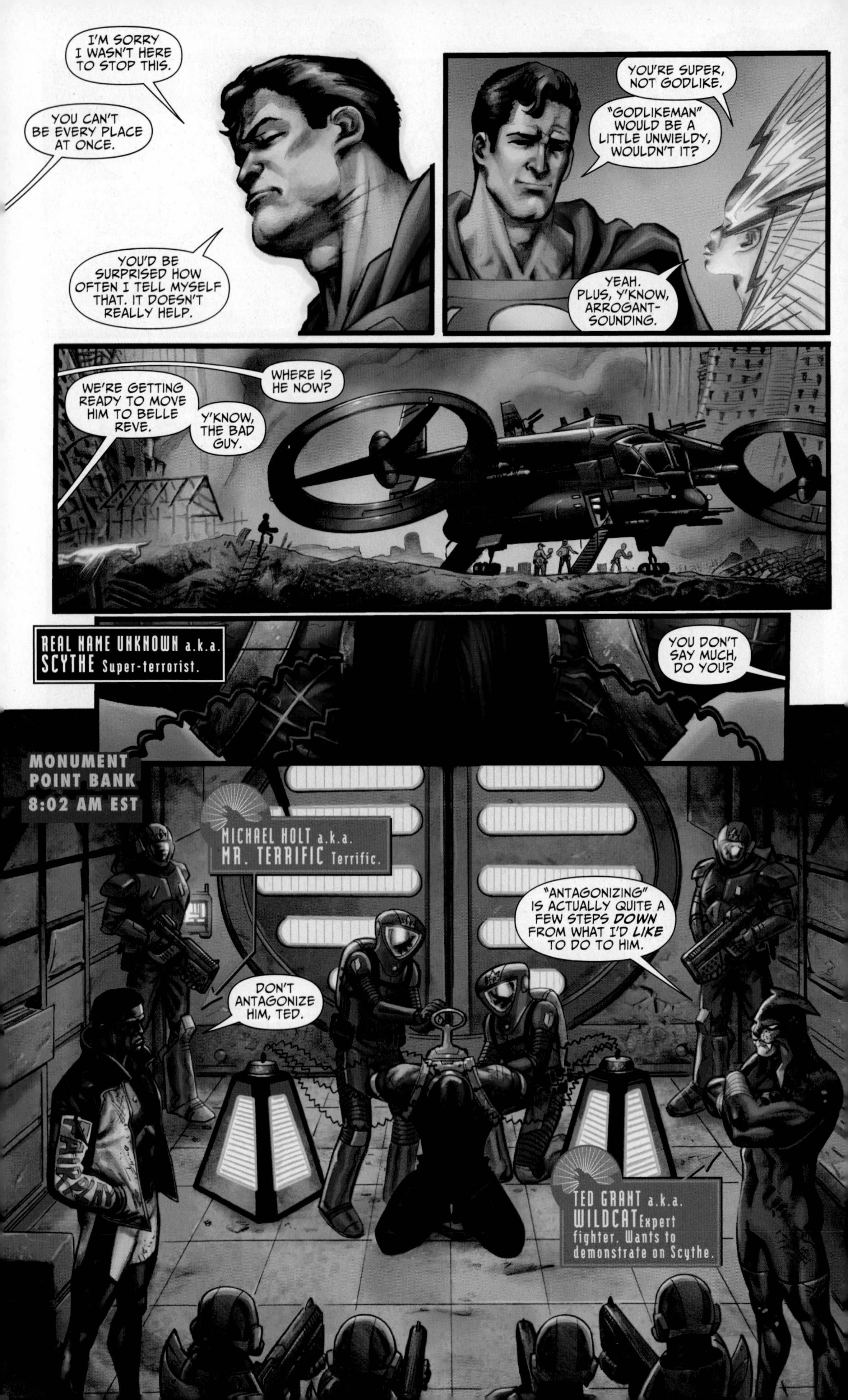
I'M SORRY I WASN'T HERE TO STOP THIS.
YOU CAN'T BE EVERY PLACE AT ONCE.
YOU'D BE SURPRISED HOW OFTEN I TELL MYSELF THAT. IT DOESN'T REALLY HELP.
YOU'RE SUPER, NOT GODLIKE.
"GODLIKEMAN" WOULD BE A LITTLE UNWIELDY, WOULDN'T IT?
YEAH. PLUS, Y'KNOW, ARROGANT-SOUNDING.
WHERE IS HE NOW?
Y'KNOW, THE BAD GUY.
WE'RE GETTING READY TO MOVE HIM TO BELLE REVE.
REAL NAME UNKNOWN a.k.a. SCYTHE Super-terrorist.
YOU DON'T SAY MUCH, DO YOU?
MONUMENT POINT BANK 8:02 AM EST
MICHAEL HOLT a.k.a. MR. TERRIFIC Terrific.
"ANTAGONIZING" IS ACTUALLY QUITE A FEW STEPS *DOWN* FROM WHAT I'D *LIKE* TO DO TO HIM.
DON'T ANTAGONIZE HIM, TED.
TED GRANT a.k.a. WILDCAT Expert fighter. Wants to demonstrate on Scythe.

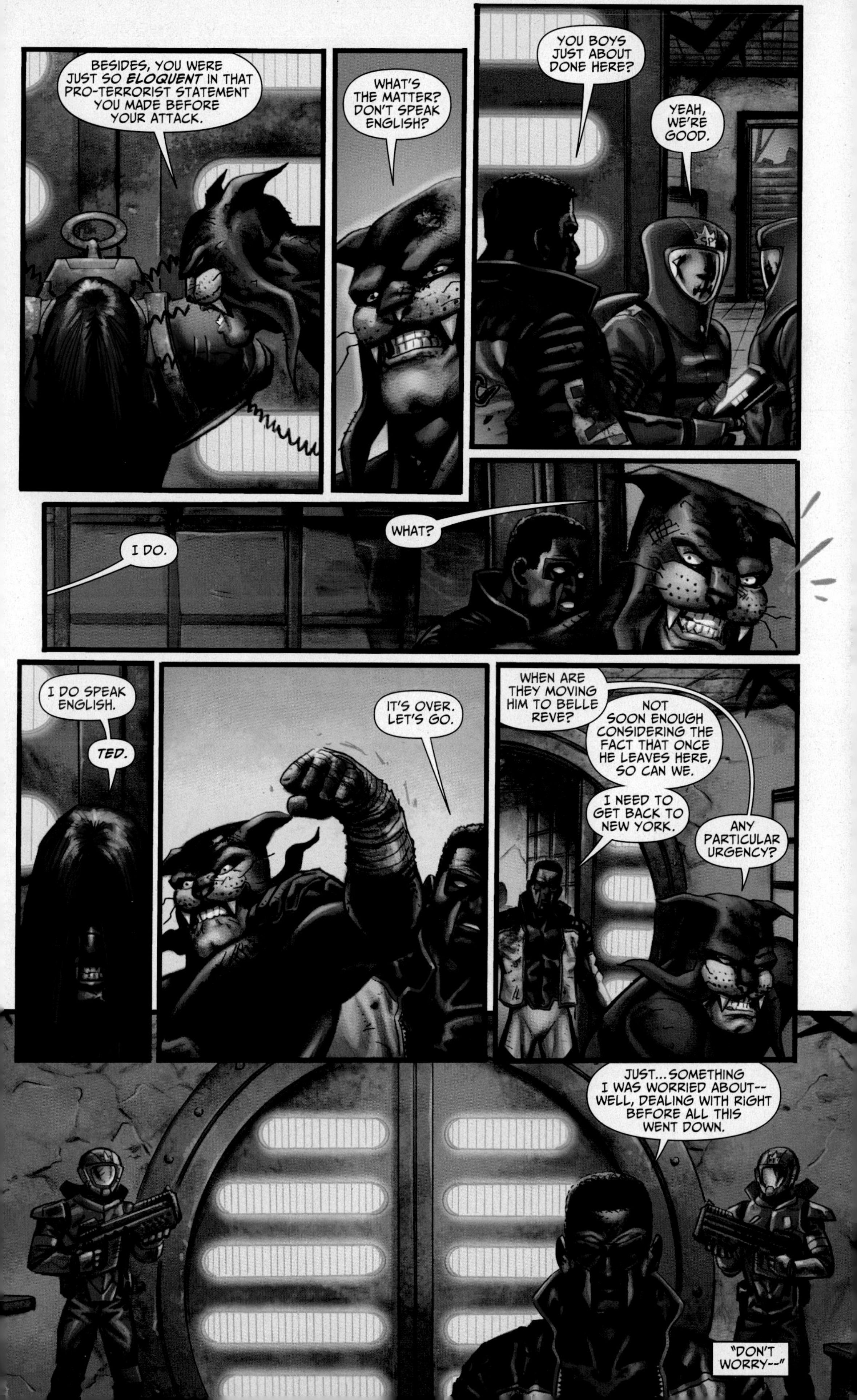
BESIDES, YOU WERE JUST SO ELOQUENT IN THAT PRO-TERRORIST STATEMENT YOU MADE BEFORE YOUR ATTACK.
WHAT'S THE MATTER? DON'T SPEAK ENGLISH?
YOU BOYS JUST ABOUT DONE HERE?
YEAH, WE'RE GOOD.
WHAT?
I DO.
I DO SPEAK ENGLISH.
TED.
IT'S OVER. LET'S GO.
WHEN ARE THEY MOVING HIM TO BELLE REVE?
NOT SOON ENOUGH CONSIDERING THE FACT THAT ONCE HE LEAVES HERE, SO CAN WE.
I NEED TO GET BACK TO NEW YORK.
ANY PARTICULAR URGENCY?
JUST...SOMETHING I WAS WORRIED ABOUT--WELL, DEALING WITH RIGHT BEFORE ALL THIS WENT DOWN.
"DON'T WORRY--"

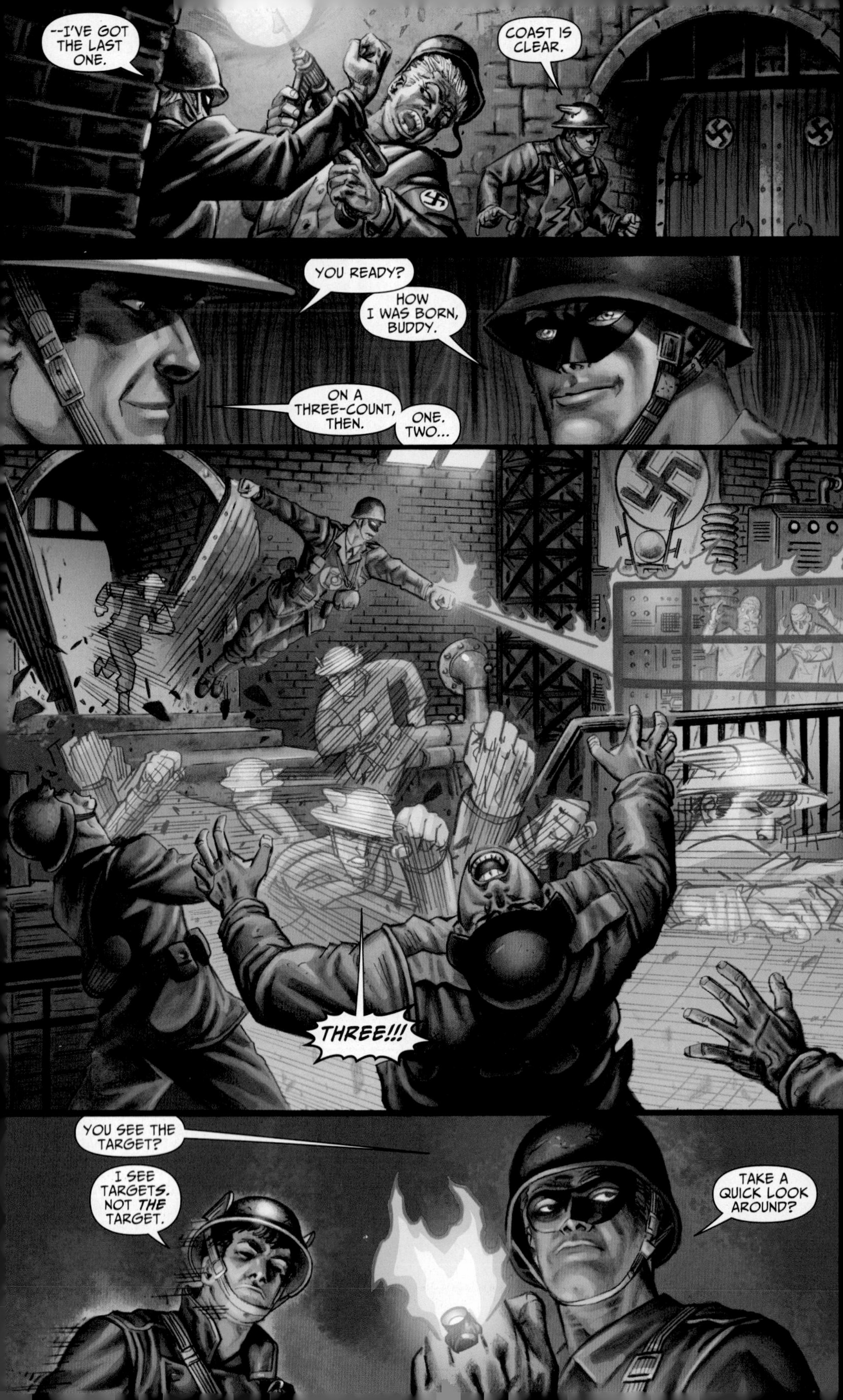
--I'VE GOT THE LAST ONE.
COAST IS CLEAR.
YOU READY?
HOW I WAS BORN, BUDDY.
ON A THREE-COUNT, THEN.
ONE. TWO...
THREE!!!
YOU SEE THE TARGET?
I SEE TARGETS. NOT THE TARGET.
TAKE A QUICK LOOK AROUND?

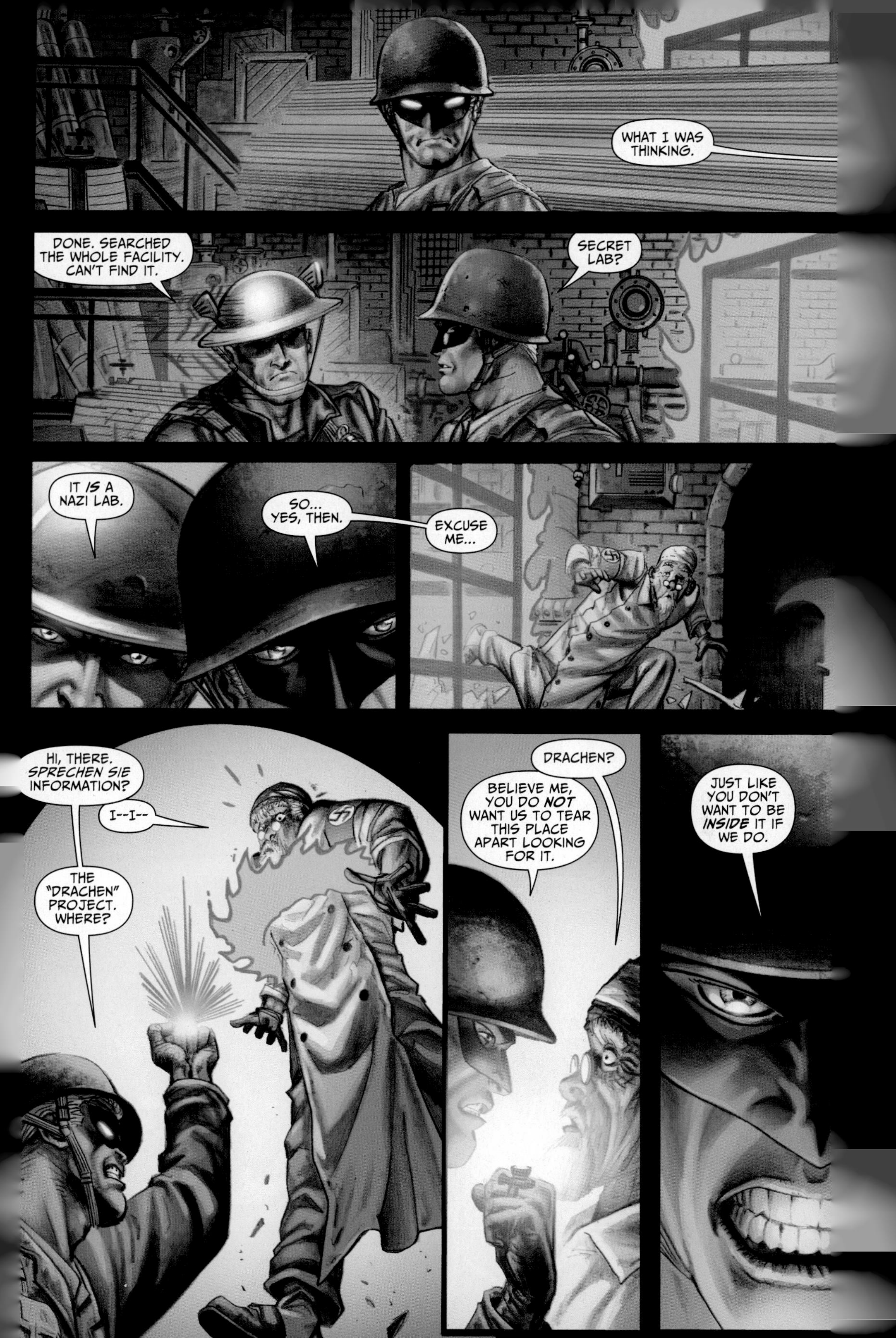
WHAT I WAS THINKING.
DONE. SEARCHED THE WHOLE FACILITY. CAN'T FIND IT.
SECRET LAB?
IT *IS* A NAZI LAB.
SO... YES, THEN.
EXCUSE ME...
HI, THERE. *SPRECHEN SIE* INFORMATION?
I--I--
THE "DRACHEN" PROJECT. WHERE?
DRACHEN?
BELIEVE ME, YOU DO ***NOT*** WANT US TO TEAR THIS PLACE APART LOOKING FOR IT.
JUST LIKE YOU DON'T WANT TO BE ***INSIDE*** IT IF WE DO.

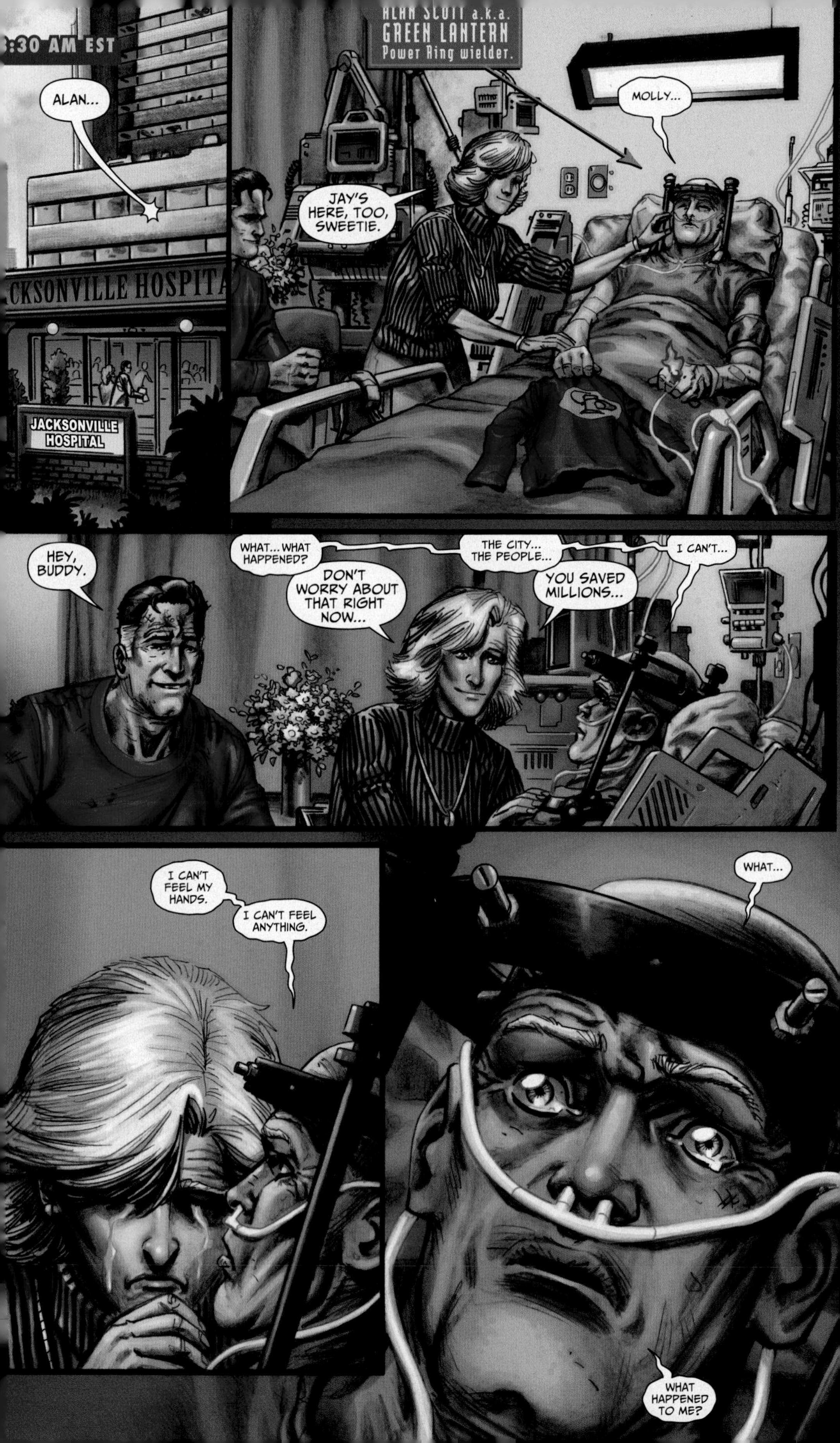

:30 AM EST
ALAN...
JACKSONVILLE HOSPITAL
ALAN SCOTT a.k.a. GREEN LANTERN Power Ring wielder.
JAY'S HERE, TOO, SWEETIE.
MOLLY...
HEY, BUDDY.
WHAT...WHAT HAPPENED?
DON'T WORRY ABOUT THAT RIGHT NOW...
THE CITY... THE PEOPLE...
YOU SAVED MILLIONS...
I CAN'T...
I CAN'T FEEL MY HANDS.
I CAN'T FEEL ANYTHING.
WHAT...
WHAT HAPPENED TO ME?

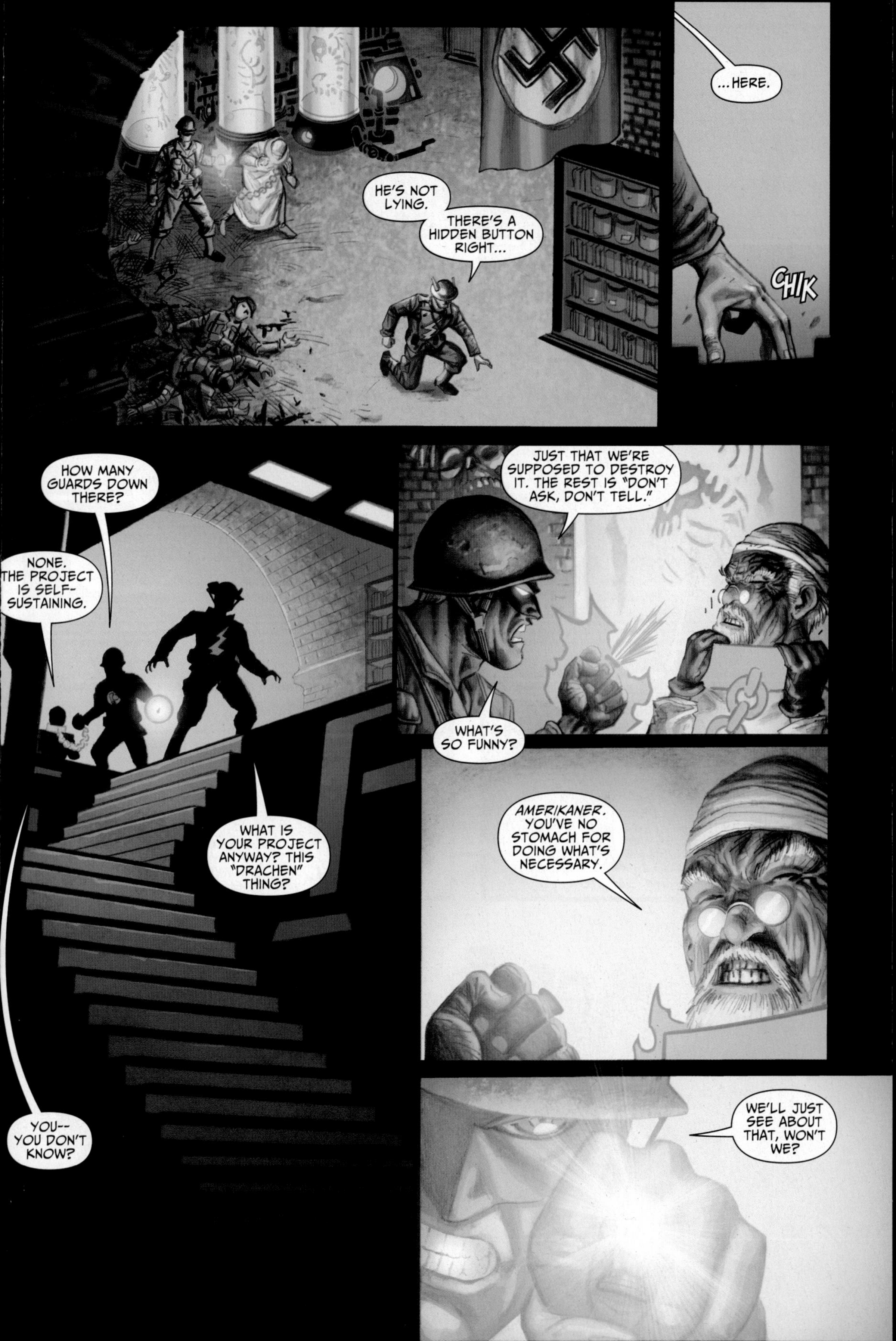
HE'S NOT LYING.
THERE'S A HIDDEN BUTTON RIGHT...
...HERE.
CHIK
HOW MANY GUARDS DOWN THERE?
NONE. THE PROJECT IS SELF-SUSTAINING.
WHAT IS YOUR PROJECT ANYWAY? THIS "DRACHEN" THING?
YOU-- YOU DON'T KNOW?
JUST THAT WE'RE SUPPOSED TO DESTROY IT. THE REST IS "DON'T ASK, DON'T TELL."
WHAT'S SO FUNNY?
AMERIKANER. YOU'VE NO STOMACH FOR DOING WHAT'S NECESSARY.
WE'LL JUST SEE ABOUT THAT, WON'T WE?

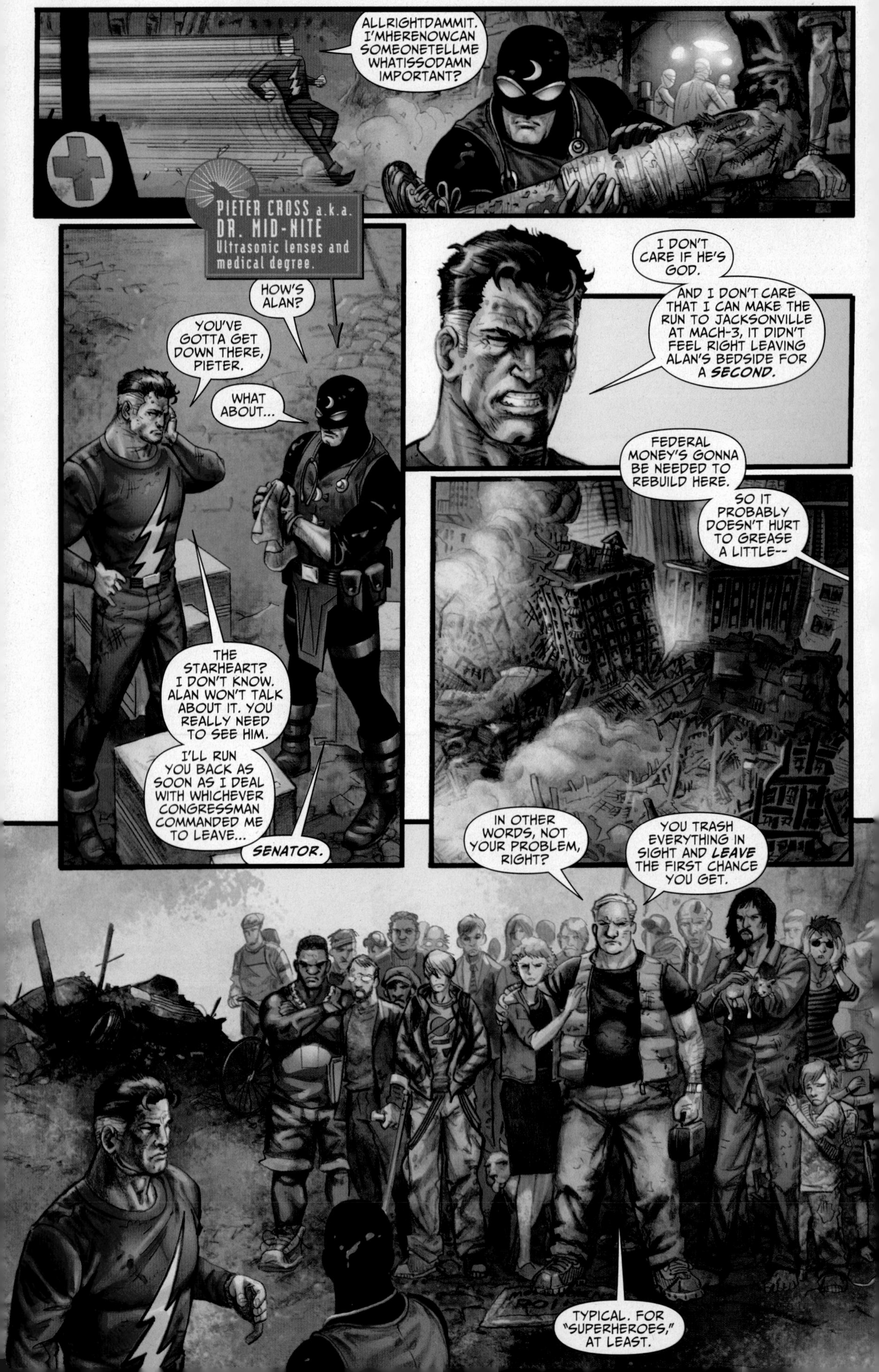
ALLRIGHTDAMMIT. I'MHERENOWCAN SOMEONETELLME WHATISSODAMN IMPORTANT?
PIETER CROSS a.k.a. DR. MID-NITE
Ultrasonic lenses and medical degree.
HOW'S ALAN?
YOU'VE GOTTA GET DOWN THERE, PIETER.
WHAT ABOUT...
THE STARHEART? I DON'T KNOW. ALAN WON'T TALK ABOUT IT. YOU REALLY NEED TO SEE HIM.
I'LL RUN YOU BACK AS SOON AS I DEAL WITH WHICHEVER CONGRESSMAN COMMANDED ME TO LEAVE...
SENATOR.
I DON'T CARE IF HE'S GOD.
AND I DON'T CARE THAT I CAN MAKE THE RUN TO JACKSONVILLE AT MACH-3, IT DIDN'T FEEL RIGHT LEAVING ALAN'S BEDSIDE FOR A SECOND.
FEDERAL MONEY'S GONNA BE NEEDED TO REBUILD HERE.
SO IT PROBABLY DOESN'T HURT TO GREASE A LITTLE--
IN OTHER WORDS, NOT YOUR PROBLEM, RIGHT?
YOU TRASH EVERYTHING IN SIGHT AND LEAVE THE FIRST CHANCE YOU GET.
TYPICAL. FOR "SUPERHEROES," AT LEAST.

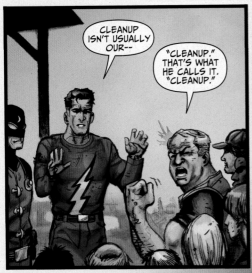

CLEANUP ISN'T USUALLY OUR--

"CLEANUP." THAT'S WHAT HE CALLS IT. "CLEANUP."

WE LOST OUR CITY. WE LOST OUR HOMES.

THEY WERE RESPONDING TO AN ATTACK, A *TERRORIST ATTACK*--

RIGHT. *RIGHT.* BUT ANSWER ME ONE QUESTION. JUST ONE...

WHEN YOU WERE FIGHTING THIS GUY, DID YOU--AT *ANY* POINT-- DID YOU EVEN *THINK* ABOUT WHAT YOU WERE DOING TO OUR CITY?

WHEN YOU WERE THROWING CARS OR PUSHING OVER BUILDINGS...

...DID YOU EVER *CARE?*

NO. NO, THEY *DIDN'T.*

THESE SUPER-TYPES NEVER DO.

NOW REASONABLE MINDS MAY DISAGREE ON WHETHER THEY *SHOULD.*

BUT THAT, I THINK, IS A DEBATE FOR ANOTHER TIME.

JAY, THIS IS SENATOR EAGIN--

I KNOW WHO HE IS.

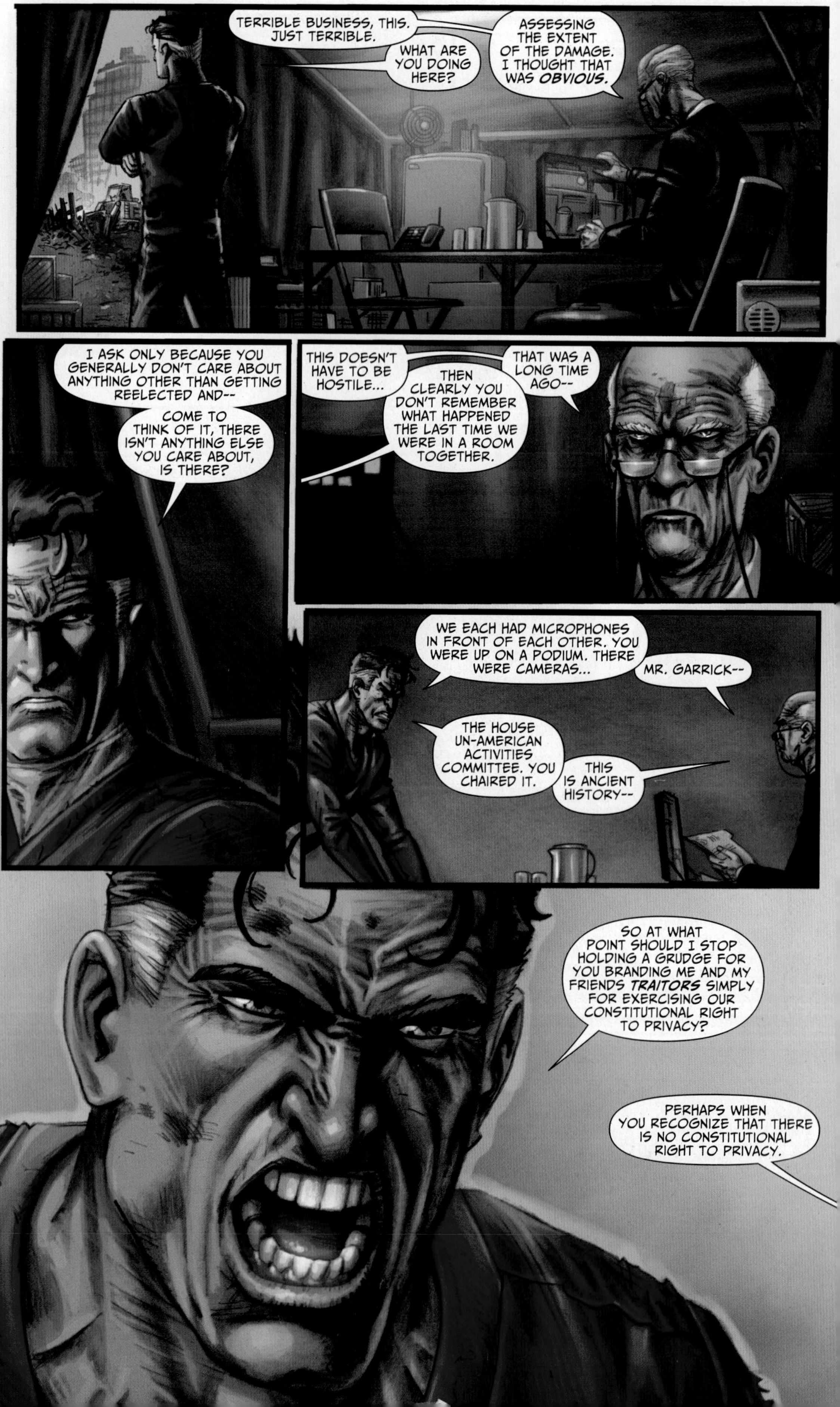
TERRIBLE BUSINESS, THIS. JUST TERRIBLE.
WHAT ARE YOU DOING HERE?
ASSESSING THE EXTENT OF THE DAMAGE. I THOUGHT THAT WAS OBVIOUS.
I ASK ONLY BECAUSE YOU GENERALLY DON'T CARE ABOUT ANYTHING OTHER THAN GETTING REELECTED AND--
COME TO THINK OF IT, THERE ISN'T ANYTHING ELSE YOU CARE ABOUT, IS THERE?
THIS DOESN'T HAVE TO BE HOSTILE...
THEN CLEARLY YOU DON'T REMEMBER WHAT HAPPENED THE LAST TIME WE WERE IN A ROOM TOGETHER.
THAT WAS A LONG TIME AGO--
WE EACH HAD MICROPHONES IN FRONT OF EACH OTHER. YOU WERE UP ON A PODIUM. THERE WERE CAMERAS...
MR. GARRICK--
THE HOUSE UN-AMERICAN ACTIVITIES COMMITTEE. YOU CHAIRED IT.
THIS IS ANCIENT HISTORY--
SO AT WHAT POINT SHOULD I STOP HOLDING A GRUDGE FOR YOU BRANDING ME AND MY FRIENDS TRAITORS SIMPLY FOR EXERCISING OUR CONSTITUTIONAL RIGHT TO PRIVACY?
PERHAPS WHEN YOU RECOGNIZE THAT THERE IS NO CONSTITUTIONAL RIGHT TO PRIVACY.

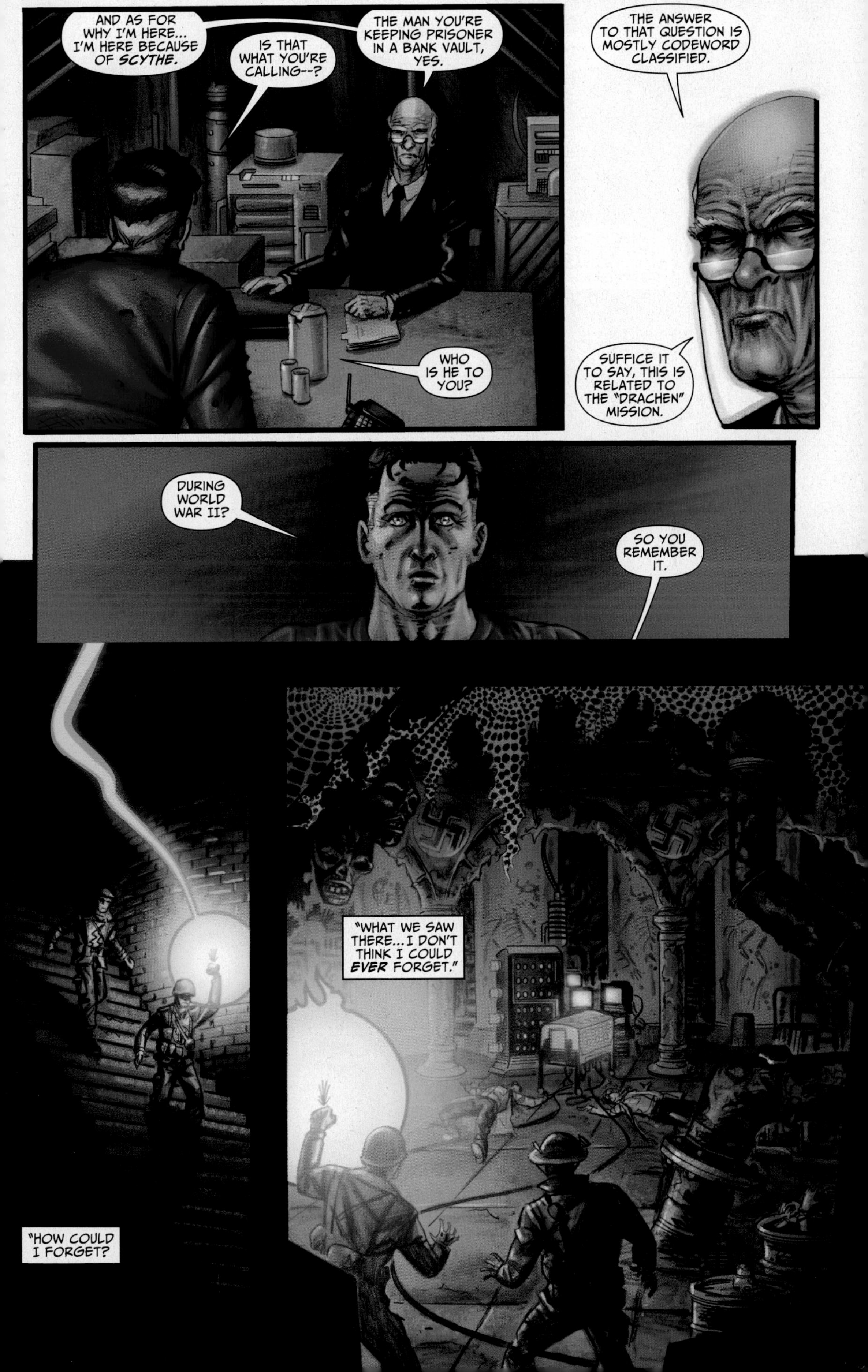
AND AS FOR WHY I'M HERE... I'M HERE BECAUSE OF SCYTHE.
IS THAT WHAT YOU'RE CALLING--?
THE MAN YOU'RE KEEPING PRISONER IN A BANK VAULT, YES.
WHO IS HE TO YOU?
THE ANSWER TO THAT QUESTION IS MOSTLY CODEWORD CLASSIFIED.
SUFFICE IT TO SAY, THIS IS RELATED TO THE "DRACHEN" MISSION.
DURING WORLD WAR II?
SO YOU REMEMBER IT.
"HOW COULD I FORGET?
"WHAT WE SAW THERE...I DON'T THINK I COULD EVER FORGET."

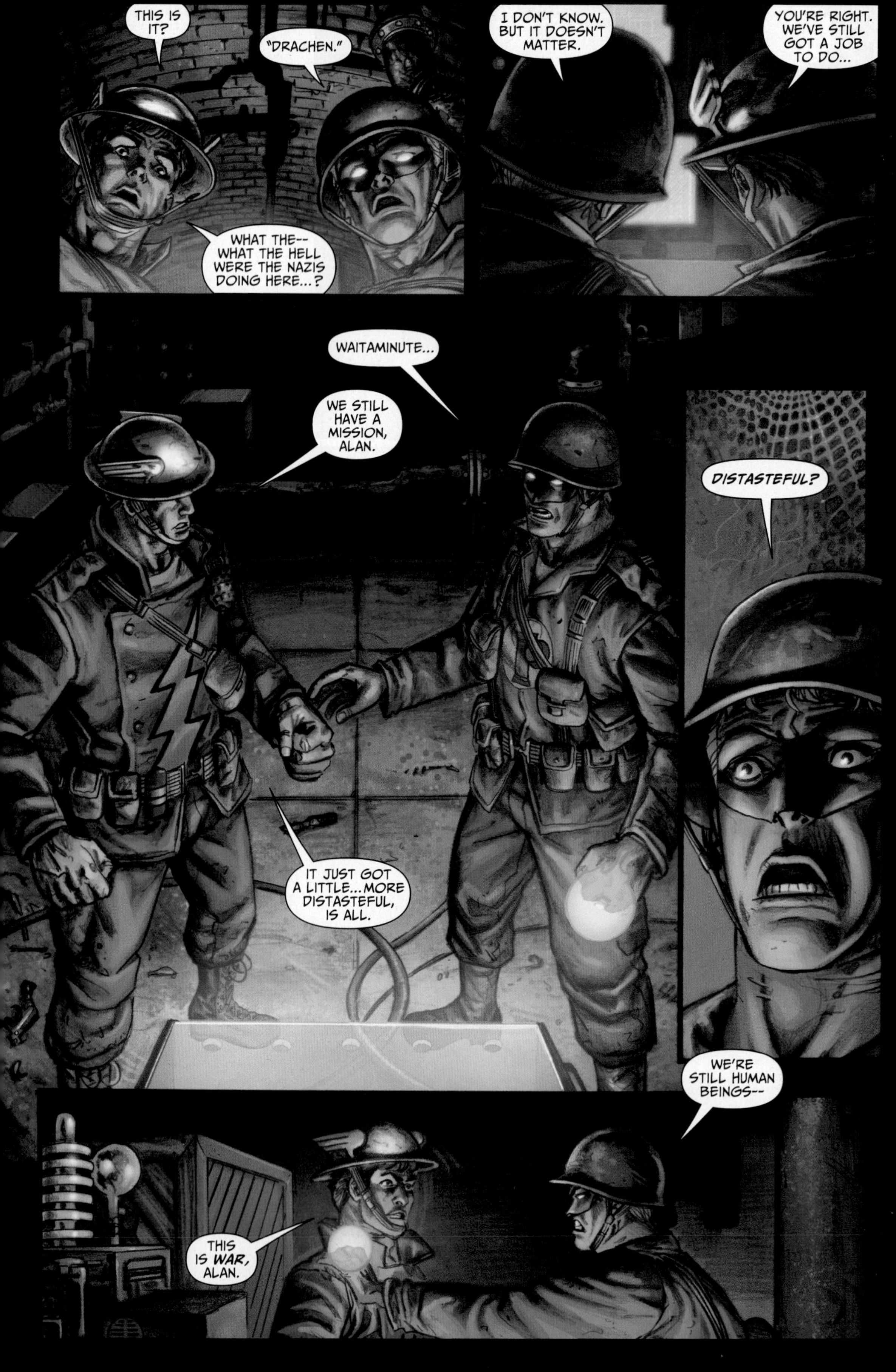
THIS IS IT?
"DRACHEN."
WHAT THE-- WHAT THE HELL WERE THE NAZIS DOING HERE...?
I DON'T KNOW. BUT IT DOESN'T MATTER.
YOU'RE RIGHT. WE'VE STILL GOT A JOB TO DO...
WAITAMINUTE...
WE STILL HAVE A MISSION, ALAN.
IT JUST GOT A LITTLE... MORE DISTASTEFUL, IS ALL.
DISTASTEFUL?
WE'RE STILL HUMAN BEINGS--
THIS IS WAR, ALAN.

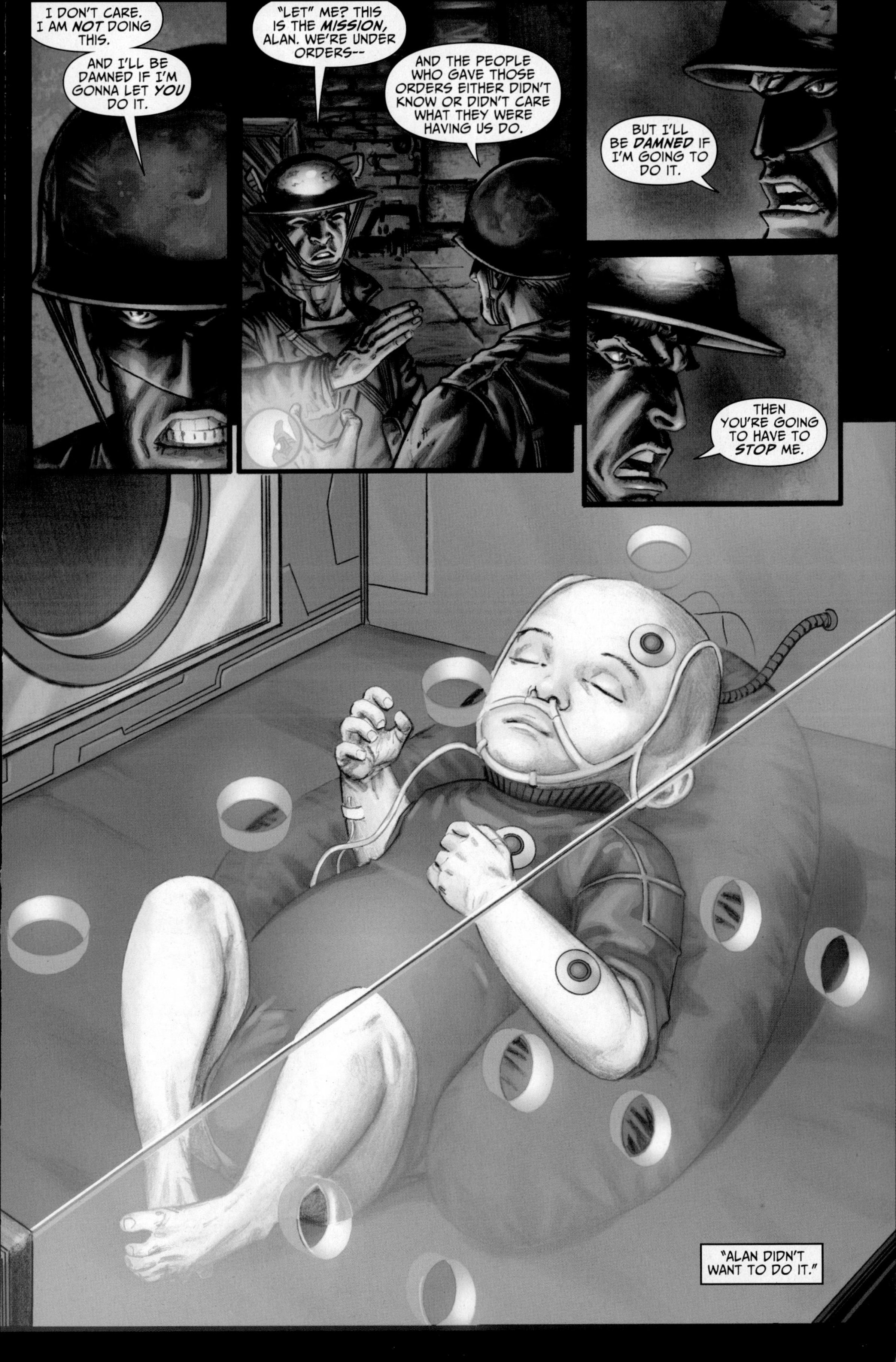
I DON'T CARE. I AM NOT DOING THIS.
AND I'LL BE DAMNED IF I'M GONNA LET YOU DO IT.
"LET" ME? THIS IS THE MISSION, ALAN. WE'RE UNDER ORDERS--
AND THE PEOPLE WHO GAVE THOSE ORDERS EITHER DIDN'T KNOW OR DIDN'T CARE WHAT THEY WERE HAVING US DO.
BUT I'LL BE DAMNED IF I'M GOING TO DO IT.
THEN YOU'RE GOING TO HAVE TO STOP ME.
"ALAN DIDN'T WANT TO DO IT."

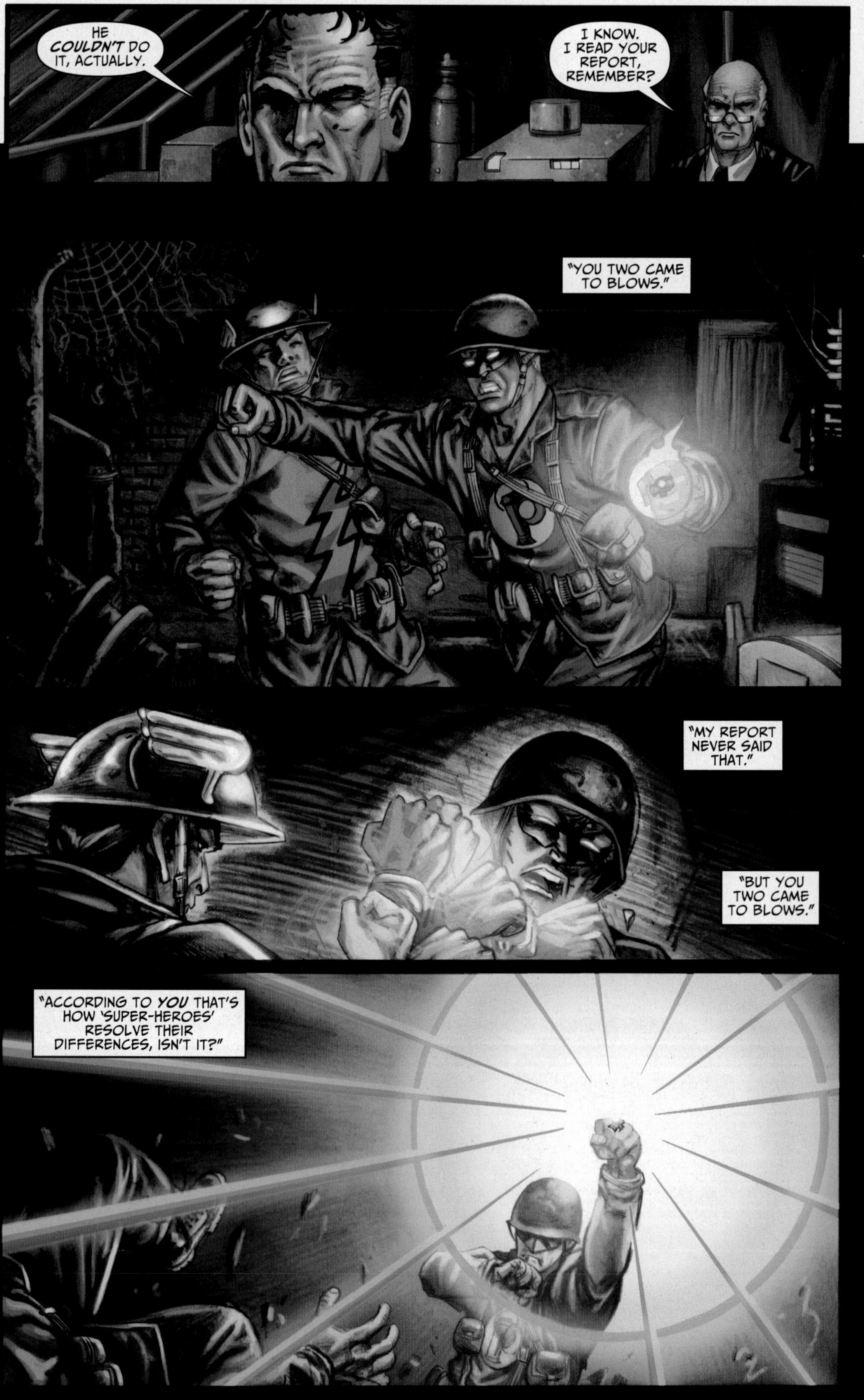
HE COULDN'T DO IT, ACTUALLY.
I KNOW. I READ YOUR REPORT, REMEMBER?
"YOU TWO CAME TO BLOWS."
"MY REPORT NEVER SAID THAT."
"BUT YOU TWO CAME TO BLOWS."
"ACCORDING TO YOU THAT'S HOW 'SUPER-HEROES' RESOLVE THEIR DIFFERENCES, ISN'T IT?"

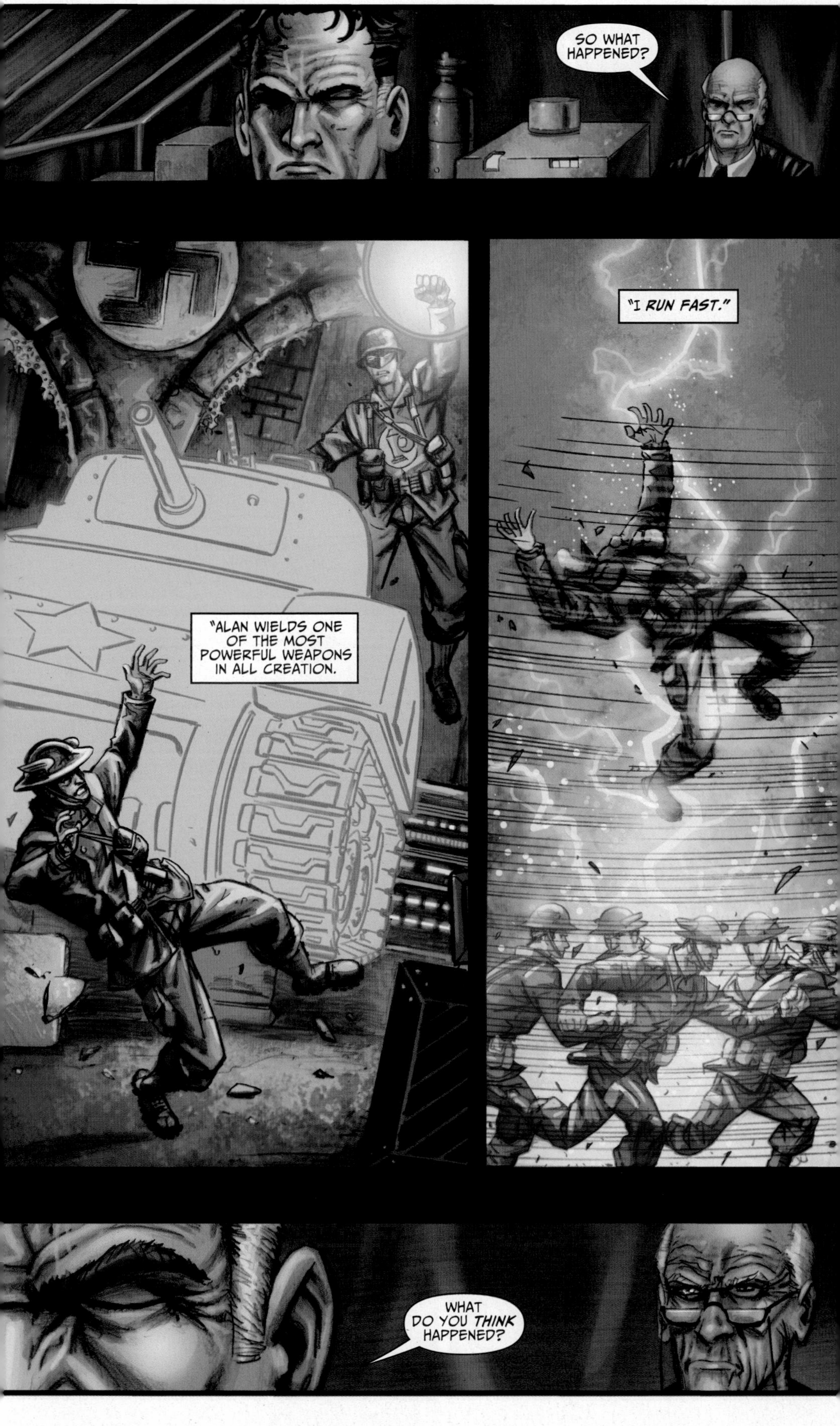
SO WHAT HAPPENED?
"ALAN WIELDS ONE OF THE MOST POWERFUL WEAPONS IN ALL CREATION.
"I RUN FAST."
WHAT DO YOU THINK HAPPENED?

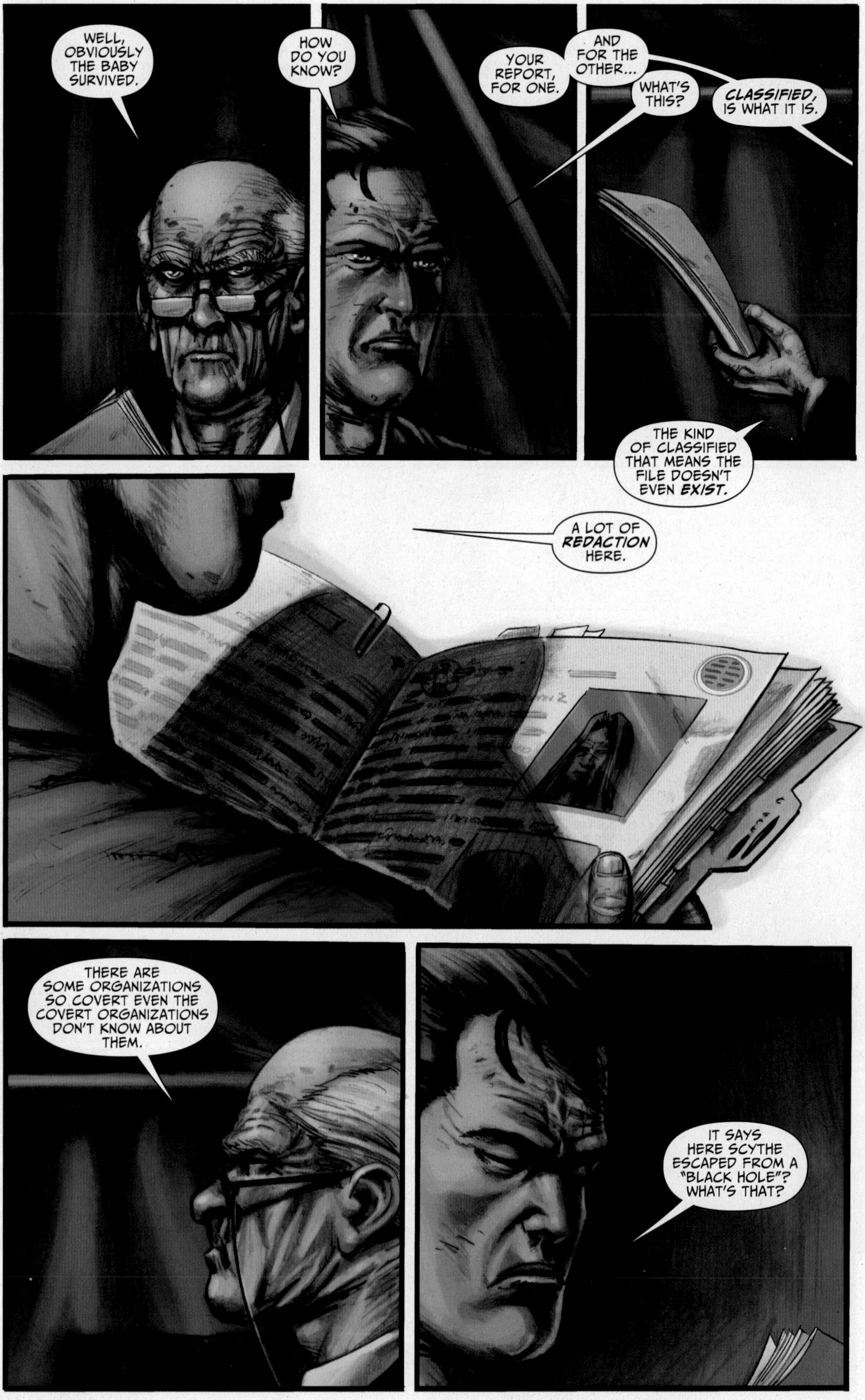
WELL, OBVIOUSLY THE BABY SURVIVED.
HOW DO YOU KNOW?
YOUR REPORT, FOR ONE.
AND FOR THE OTHER...
WHAT'S THIS?
CLASSIFIED, IS WHAT IT IS.
THE KIND OF CLASSIFIED THAT MEANS THE FILE DOESN'T EVEN *EXIST.*
A LOT OF *REDACTION* HERE.
THERE ARE SOME ORGANIZATIONS SO COVERT EVEN THE COVERT ORGANIZATIONS DON'T KNOW ABOUT THEM.
IT SAYS HERE SCYTHE ESCAPED FROM A "BLACK HOLE"? WHAT'S THAT?

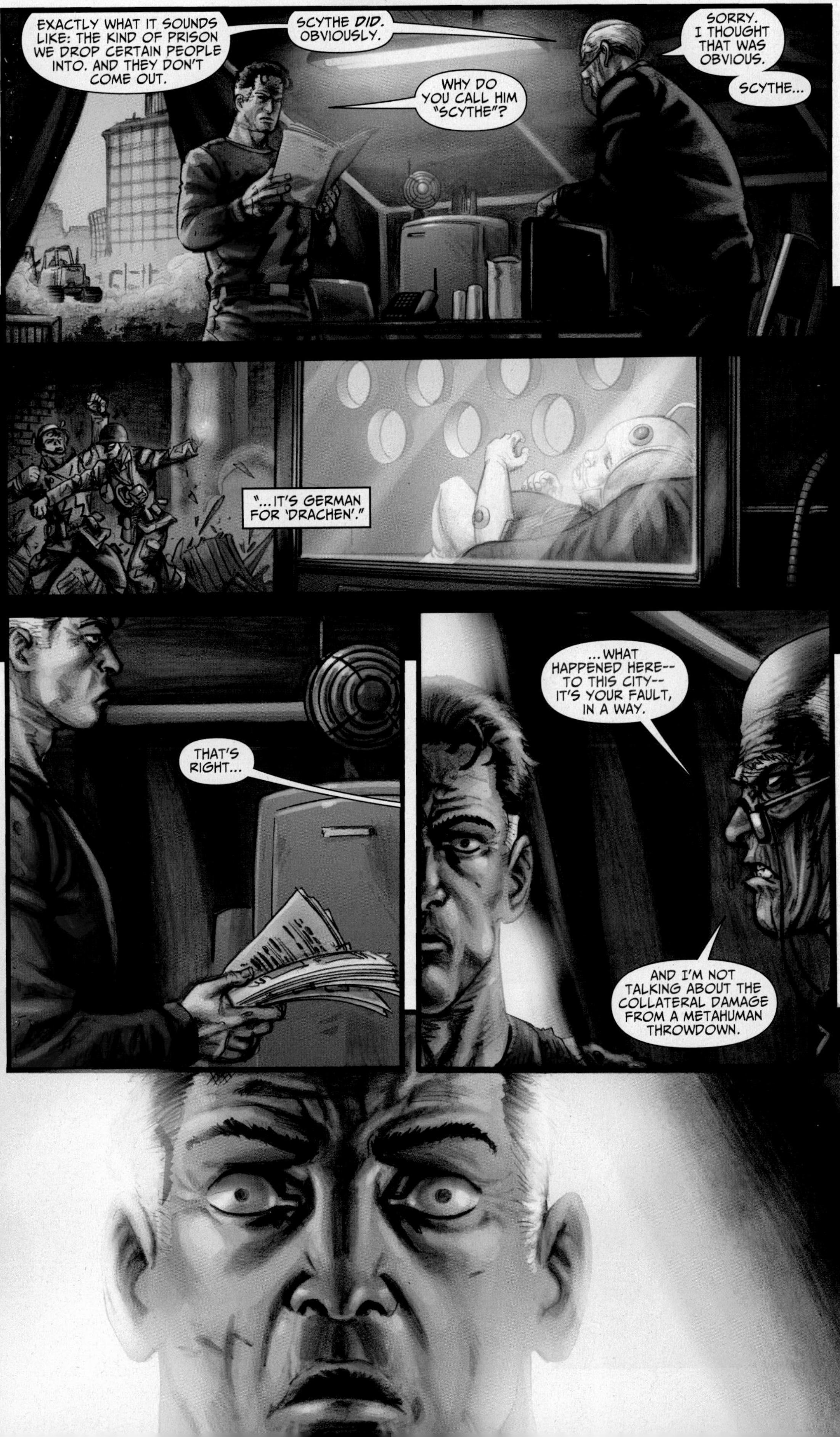
EXACTLY WHAT IT SOUNDS LIKE: THE KIND OF PRISON WE DROP CERTAIN PEOPLE INTO. AND THEY DON'T COME OUT.
SCYTHE *DID.* OBVIOUSLY.
SORRY. I THOUGHT THAT WAS OBVIOUS.
WHY DO YOU CALL HIM "SCYTHE"?
SCYTHE...
"...IT'S GERMAN FOR 'DRACHEN'."
THAT'S RIGHT...
...WHAT HAPPENED HERE-- TO THIS CITY-- IT'S YOUR FAULT, IN A WAY.
AND I'M NOT TALKING ABOUT THE COLLATERAL DAMAGE FROM A METAHUMAN THROWDOWN.

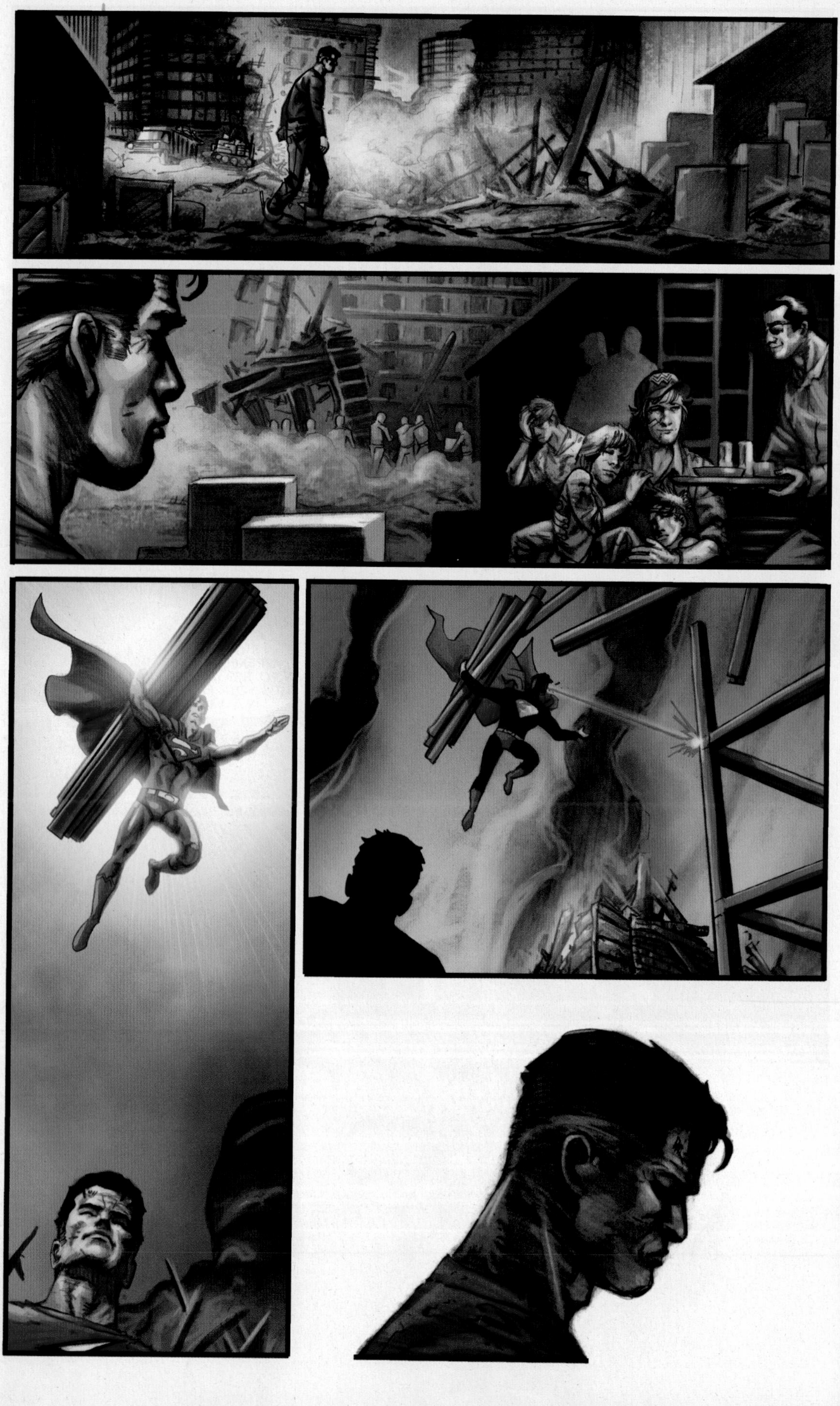

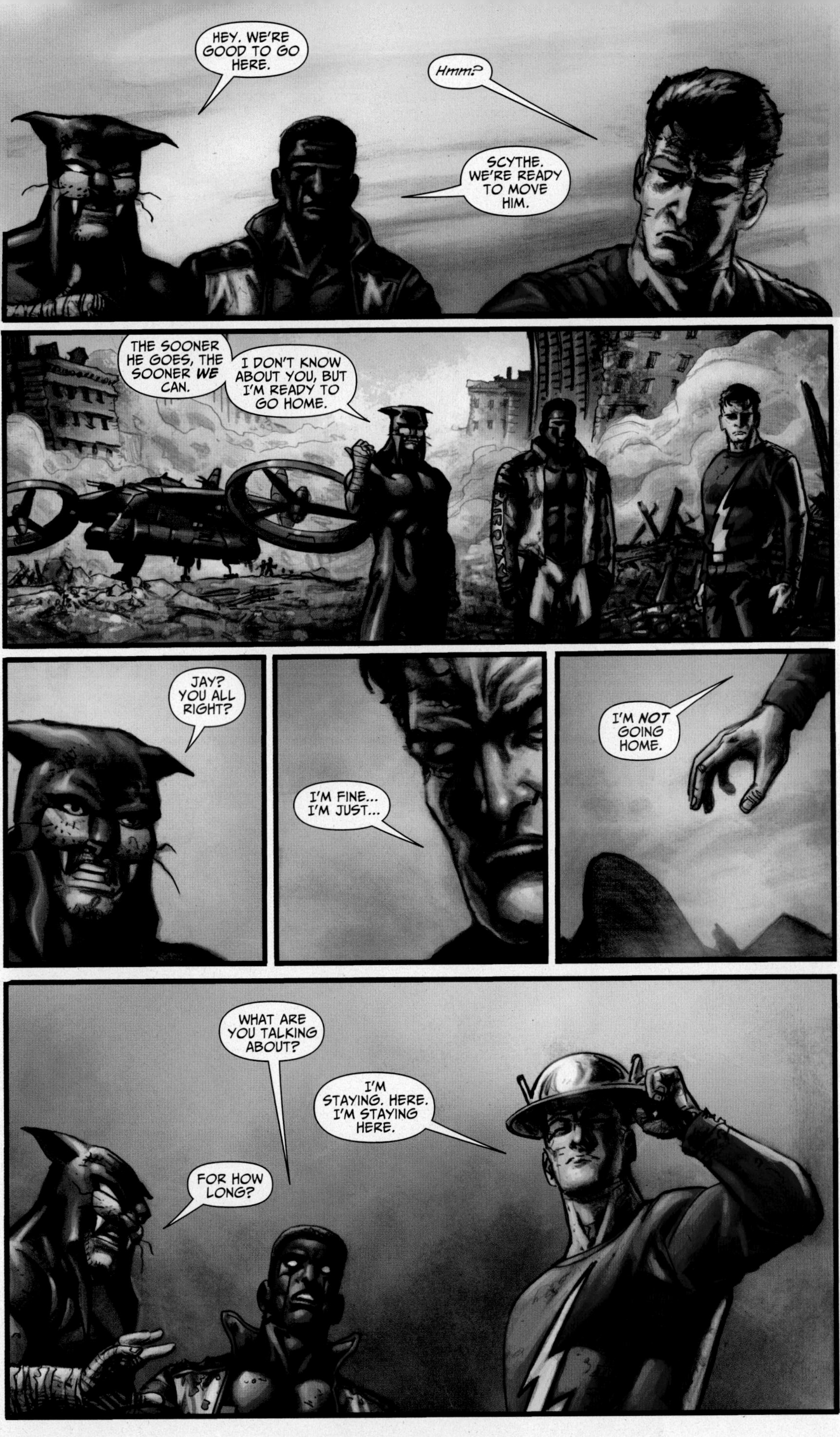
HEY. WE'RE GOOD TO GO HERE.
Hmm?
SCYTHE. WE'RE READY TO MOVE HIM.
THE SOONER HE GOES, THE SOONER WE CAN.
I DON'T KNOW ABOUT YOU, BUT I'M READY TO GO HOME.
JAY? YOU ALL RIGHT?
I'M FINE... I'M JUST...
I'M NOT GOING HOME.
WHAT ARE YOU TALKING ABOUT?
I'M STAYING. HERE. I'M STAYING HERE.
FOR HOW LONG?

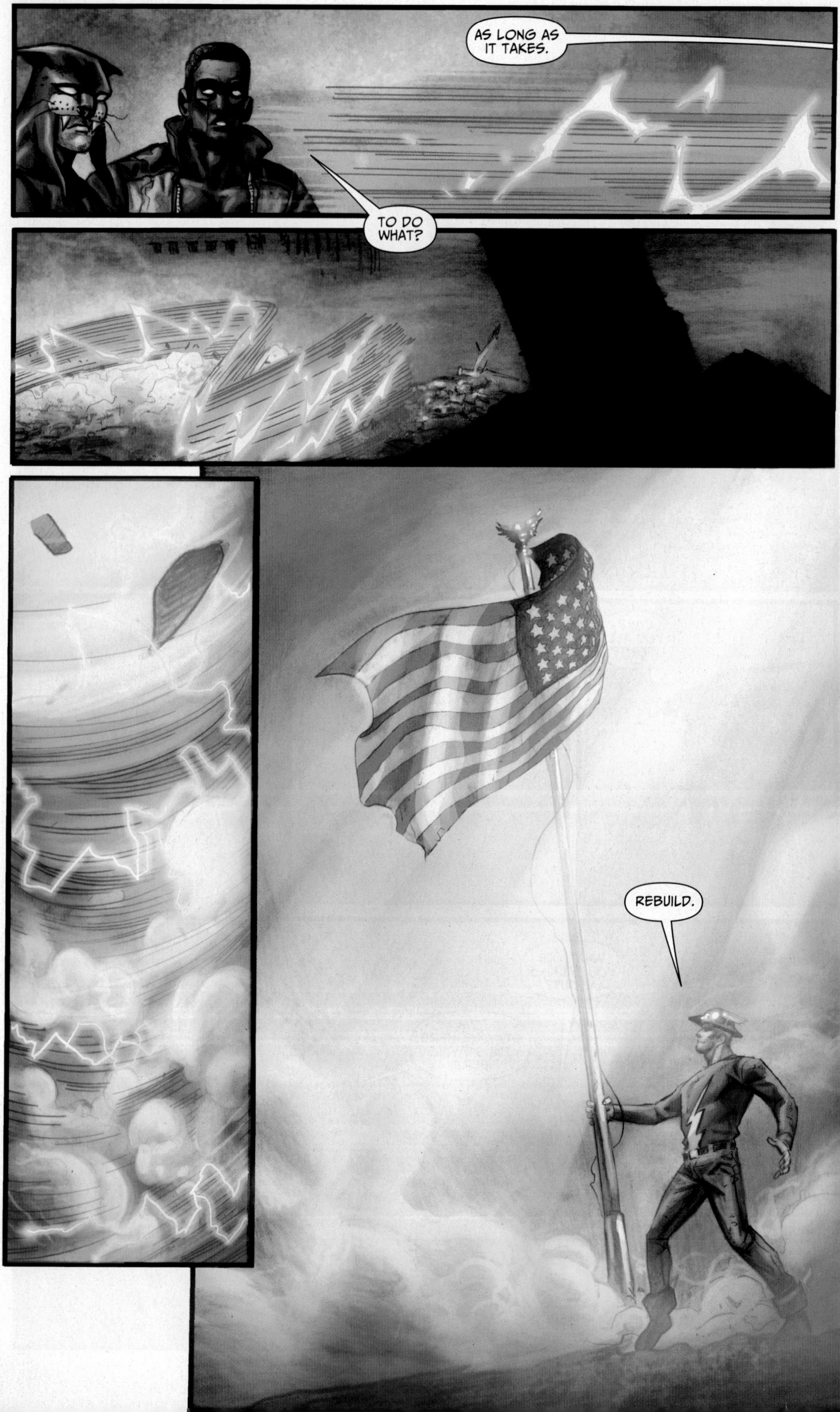
AS LONG AS IT TAKES.
TO DO WHAT?
REBUILD.

SUPERTOWN Part Three

Cover by SHANE DAVIS & SANDRA HOPE
with BARBARA CIARDO

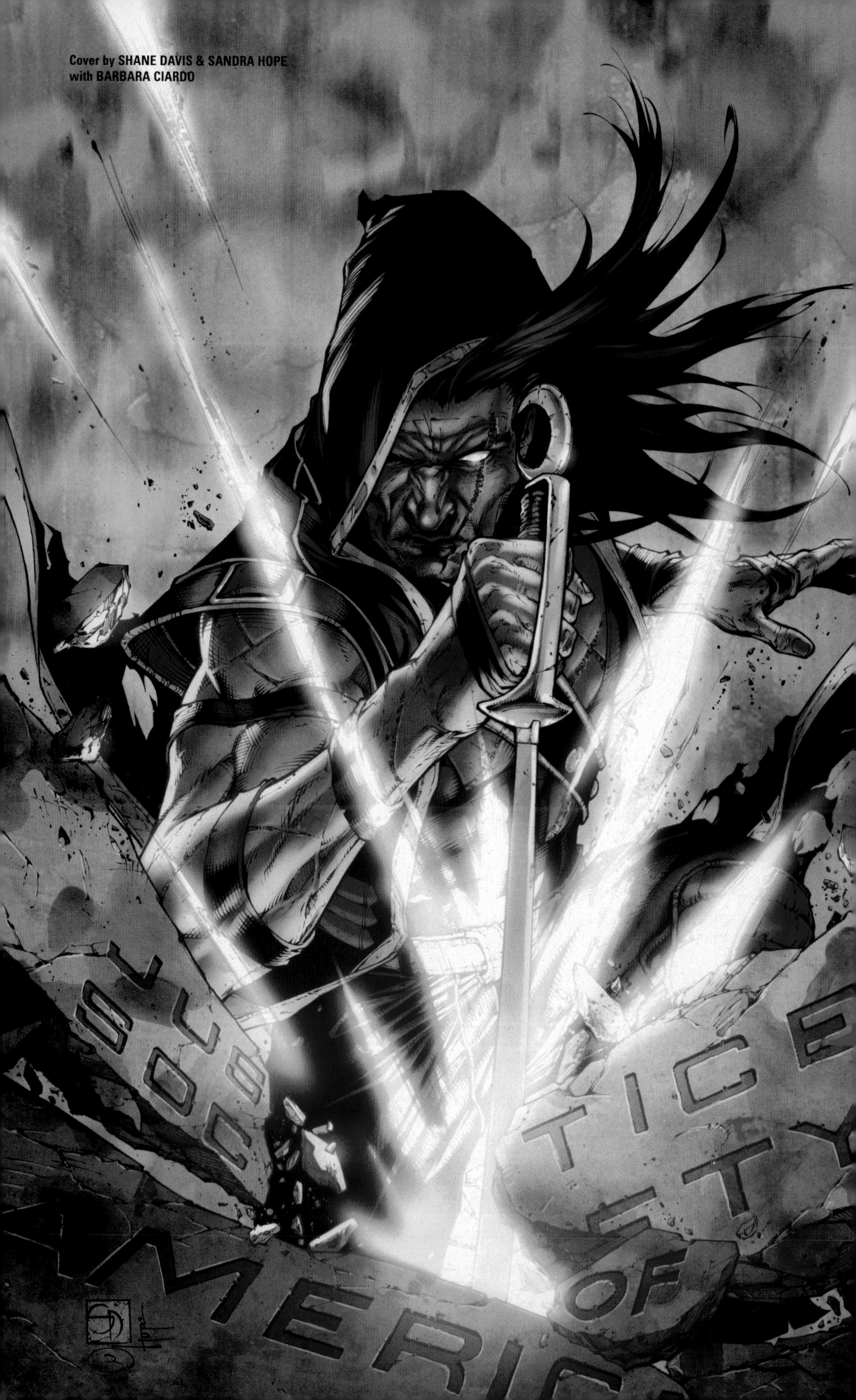
OF

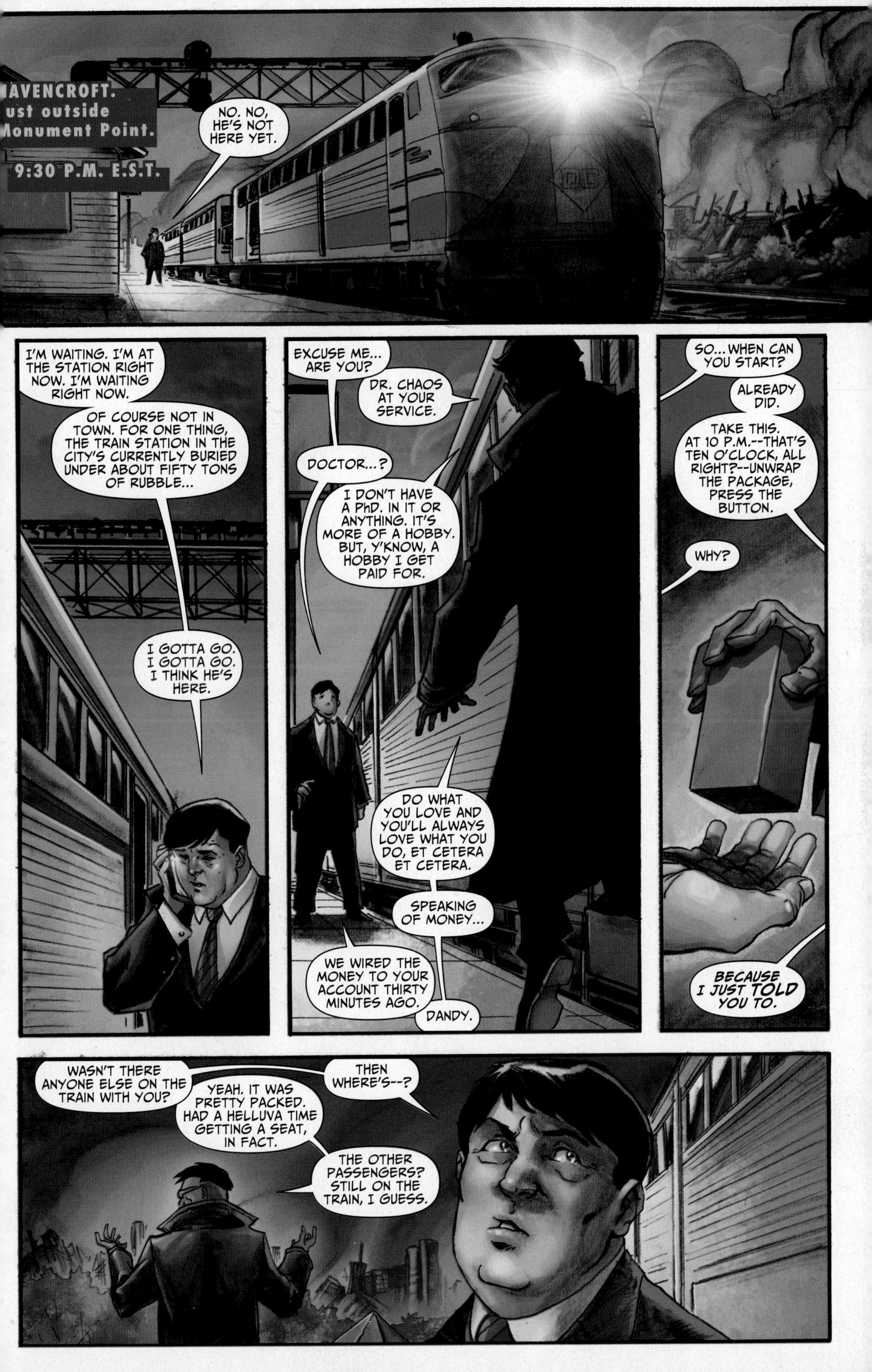
AVENCROFT. ust outside onument Point.
9:30 P.M. E.S.T.
NO. NO, HE'S NOT HERE YET.
I'M WAITING. I'M AT THE STATION RIGHT NOW. I'M WAITING RIGHT NOW.
OF COURSE NOT IN TOWN. FOR ONE THING, THE TRAIN STATION IN THE CITY'S CURRENTLY BURIED UNDER ABOUT FIFTY TONS OF RUBBLE...
I GOTTA GO. I GOTTA GO. I THINK HE'S HERE.
EXCUSE ME... ARE YOU?
DR. CHAOS AT YOUR SERVICE.
DOCTOR...?
I DON'T HAVE A PhD. IN IT OR ANYTHING. IT'S MORE OF A HOBBY. BUT, Y'KNOW, A HOBBY I GET PAID FOR.
DO WHAT YOU LOVE AND YOU'LL ALWAYS LOVE WHAT YOU DO, ET CETERA ET CETERA.
SPEAKING OF MONEY...
WE WIRED THE MONEY TO YOUR ACCOUNT THIRTY MINUTES AGO.
DANDY.
SO... WHEN CAN YOU START?
ALREADY DID.
TAKE THIS. AT 10 P.M.--THAT'S TEN O'CLOCK, ALL RIGHT?--UNWRAP THE PACKAGE, PRESS THE BUTTON.
WHY?
BECAUSE I JUST TOLD YOU TO.
WASN'T THERE ANYONE ELSE ON THE TRAIN WITH YOU?
YEAH. IT WAS PRETTY PACKED. HAD A HELLUVA TIME GETTING A SEAT, IN FACT.
THEN WHERE'S--?
THE OTHER PASSENGERS? STILL ON THE TRAIN, I GUESS.

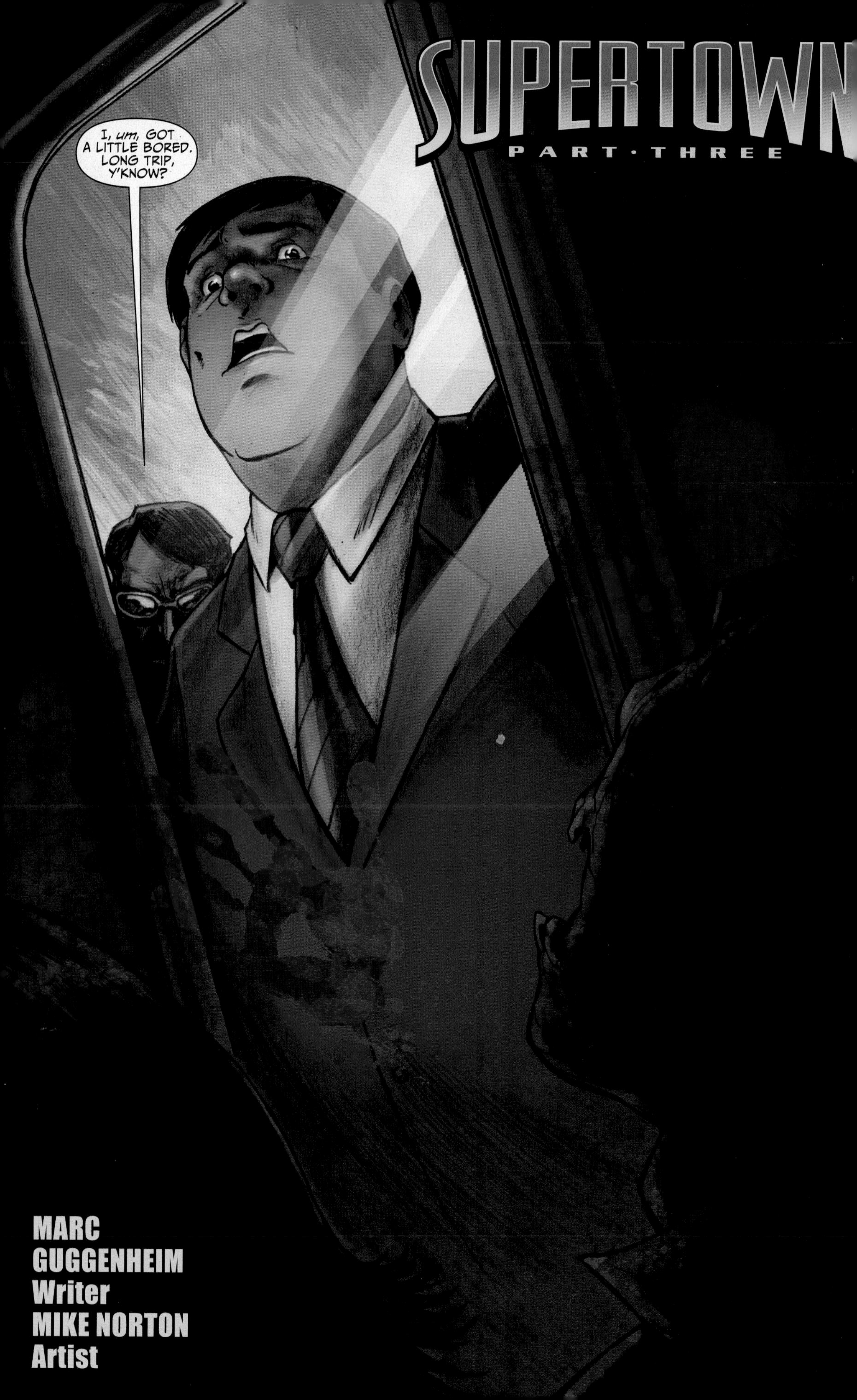
SUPERTOWN
PART·THREE
I, um, GOT A LITTLE BORED. LONG TRIP, Y'KNOW?
MARC GUGGENHEIM Writer
MIKE NORTON Artist

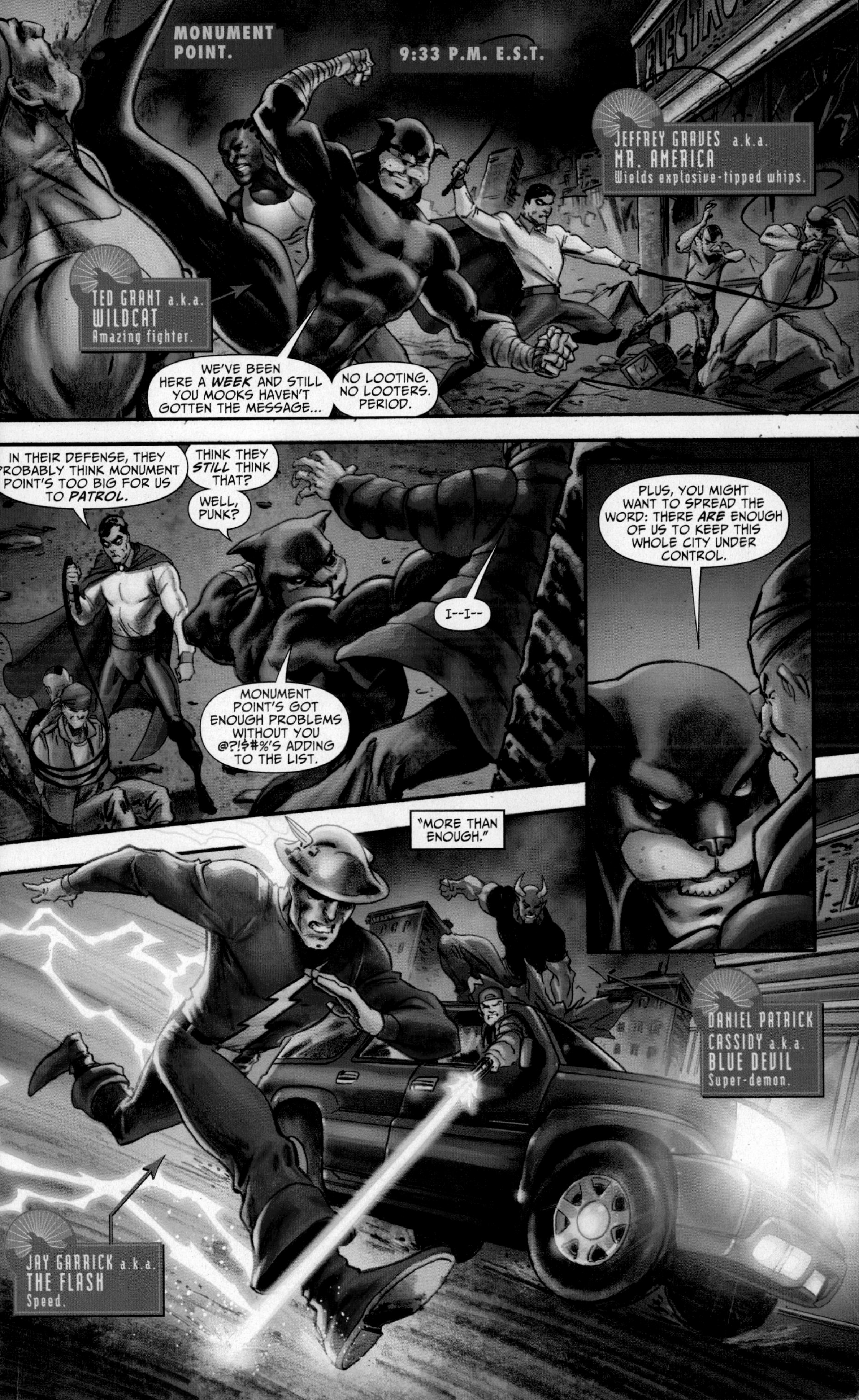
MONUMENT POINT.
9:33 P.M. E.S.T.
JEFFREY GRAVES a.k.a. MR. AMERICA Wields explosive-tipped whips.
TED GRANT a.k.a. WILDCAT Amazing fighter.
WE'VE BEEN HERE A WEEK AND STILL YOU MOOKS HAVEN'T GOTTEN THE MESSAGE...
NO LOOTING. NO LOOTERS. PERIOD.
IN THEIR DEFENSE, THEY PROBABLY THINK MONUMENT POINT'S TOO BIG FOR US TO PATROL.
THINK THEY STILL THINK THAT?
WELL, PUNK?
I--I--
MONUMENT POINT'S GOT ENOUGH PROBLEMS WITHOUT YOU @?!$#%'S ADDING TO THE LIST.
PLUS, YOU MIGHT WANT TO SPREAD THE WORD: THERE ARE ENOUGH OF US TO KEEP THIS WHOLE CITY UNDER CONTROL.
"MORE THAN ENOUGH."
DANIEL PATRICK CASSIDY a.k.a. BLUE DEVIL Super-demon.
JAY GARRICK a.k.a. THE FLASH Speed.

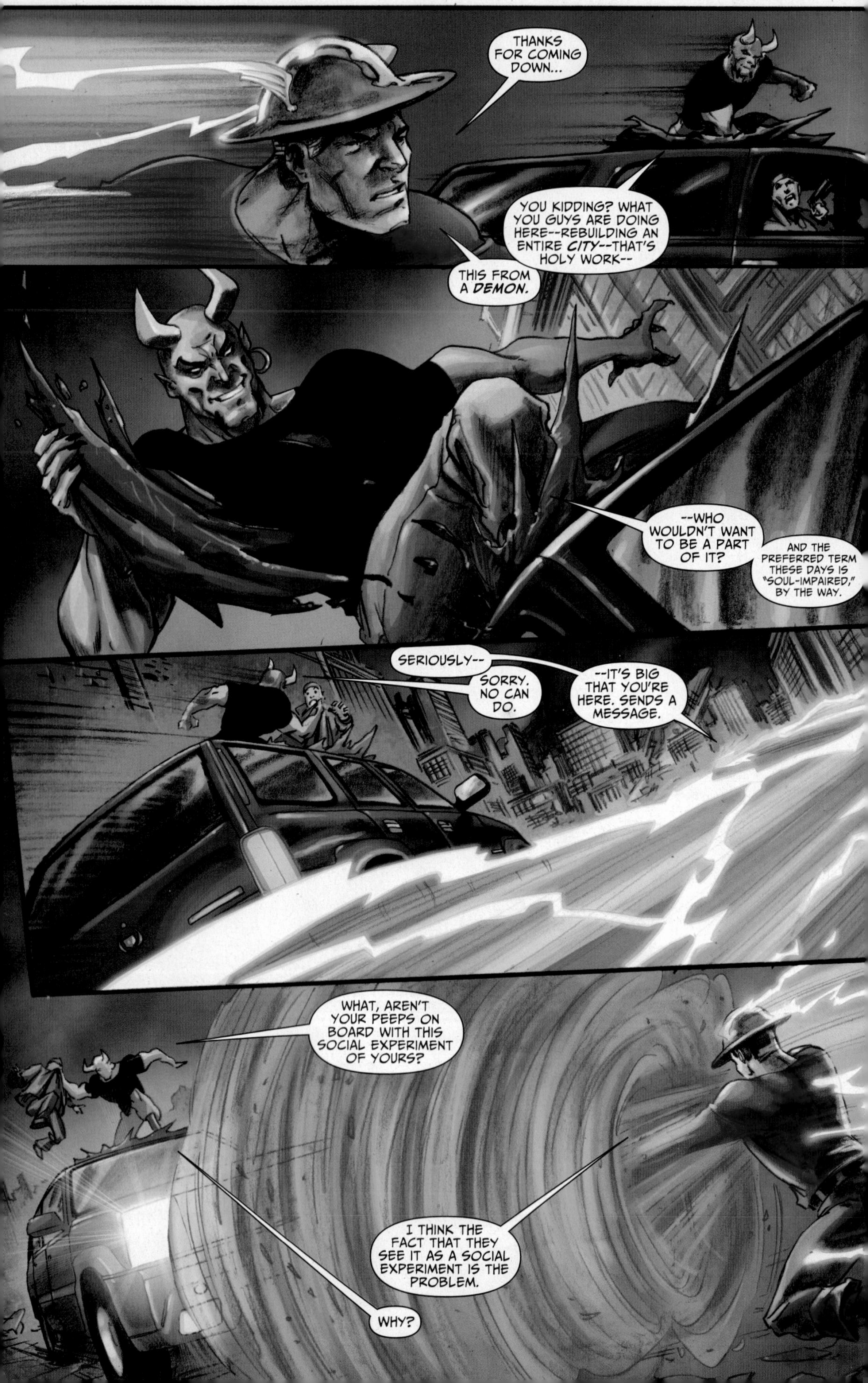
THANKS FOR COMING DOWN...
YOU KIDDING? WHAT YOU GUYS ARE DOING HERE--REBUILDING AN ENTIRE *CITY*--THAT'S HOLY WORK--
THIS FROM A *DEMON.*
--WHO WOULDN'T WANT TO BE A PART OF IT?
AND THE PREFERRED TERM THESE DAYS IS "SOUL-IMPAIRED," BY THE WAY.
SERIOUSLY--
SORRY. NO CAN DO.
--IT'S BIG THAT YOU'RE HERE. SENDS A MESSAGE.
WHAT, AREN'T YOUR PEEPS ON BOARD WITH THIS SOCIAL EXPERIMENT OF YOURS?
I THINK THE FACT THAT THEY SEE IT AS A SOCIAL EXPERIMENT IS THE PROBLEM.
WHY?

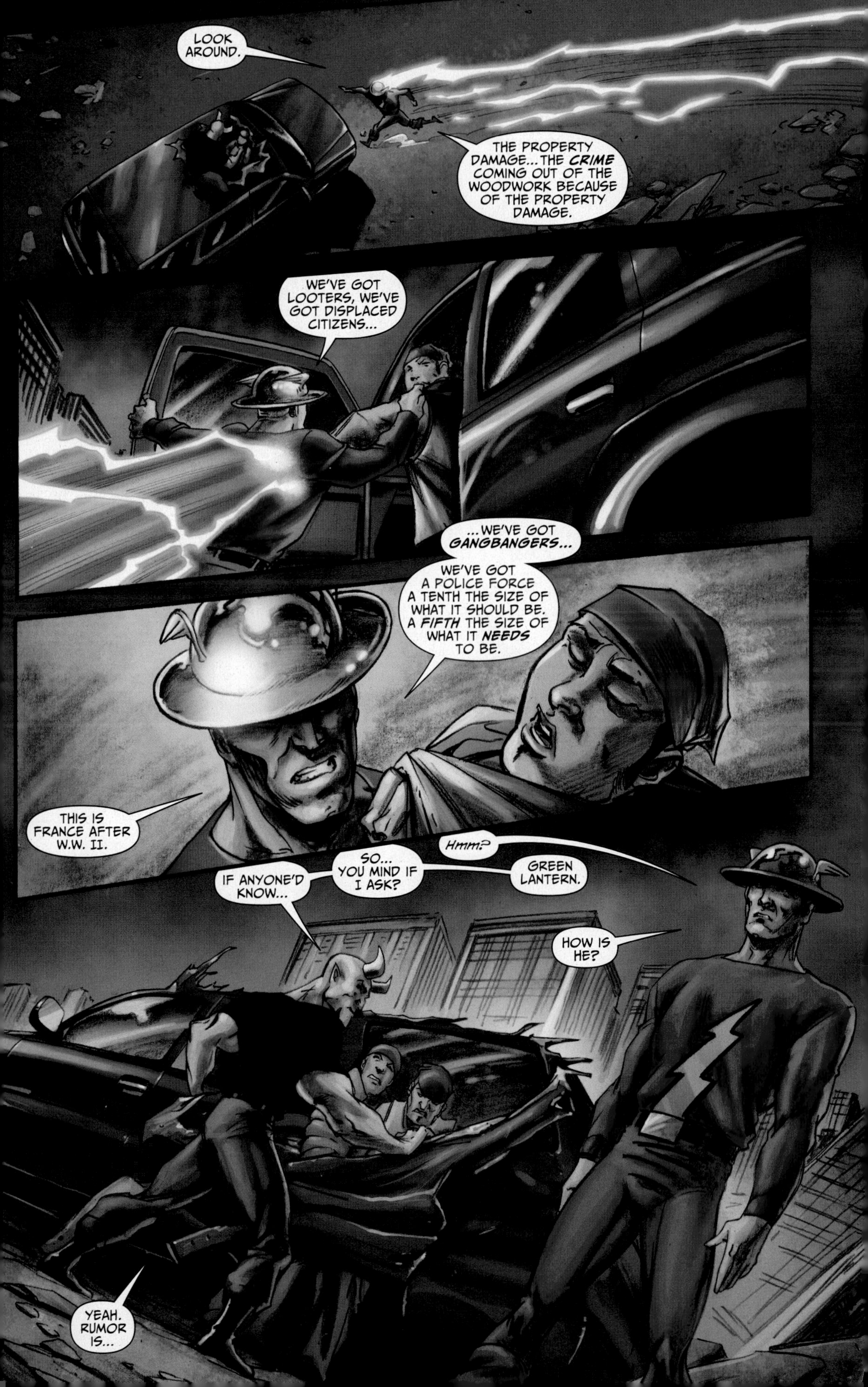
LOOK AROUND.
THE PROPERTY DAMAGE... THE CRIME COMING OUT OF THE WOODWORK BECAUSE OF THE PROPERTY DAMAGE.
WE'VE GOT LOOTERS, WE'VE GOT DISPLACED CITIZENS...
...WE'VE GOT GANGBANGERS...
WE'VE GOT A POLICE FORCE A TENTH THE SIZE OF WHAT IT SHOULD BE. A FIFTH THE SIZE OF WHAT IT NEEDS TO BE.
THIS IS FRANCE AFTER W.W. II.
Hmm?
SO... YOU MIND IF I ASK?
GREEN LANTERN.
HOW IS HE?
IF ANYONE'D KNOW...
YEAH. RUMOR IS...

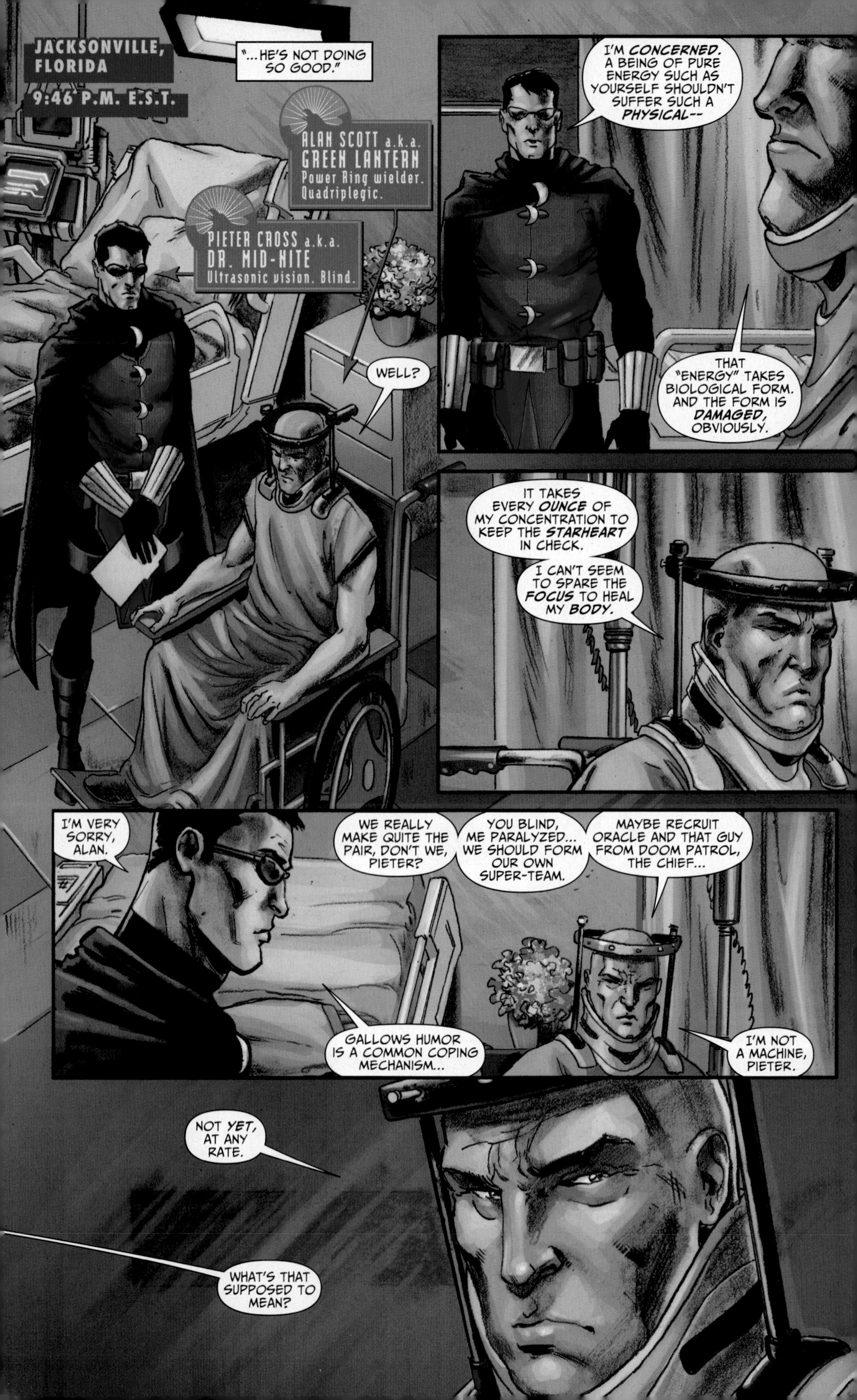
JACKSONVILLE, FLORIDA
9:46 P.M. E.S.T.
"...HE'S NOT DOING SO GOOD."
ALAN SCOTT a.k.a. GREEN LANTERN Power Ring wielder. Quadriplegic.
PIETER CROSS a.k.a. DR. MID-NITE Ultrasonic vision. Blind.
WELL?
I'M CONCERNED. A BEING OF PURE ENERGY SUCH AS YOURSELF SHOULDN'T SUFFER SUCH A PHYSICAL--
THAT "ENERGY" TAKES BIOLOGICAL FORM. AND THE FORM IS DAMAGED, OBVIOUSLY.
IT TAKES EVERY OUNCE OF MY CONCENTRATION TO KEEP THE STARHEART IN CHECK.
I CAN'T SEEM TO SPARE THE FOCUS TO HEAL MY BODY.
I'M VERY SORRY, ALAN.
WE REALLY MAKE QUITE THE PAIR, DON'T WE, PIETER?
YOU BLIND, ME PARALYZED... WE SHOULD FORM OUR OWN SUPER-TEAM.
MAYBE RECRUIT ORACLE AND THAT GUY FROM DOOM PATROL, THE CHIEF...
GALLOWS HUMOR IS A COMMON COPING MECHANISM...
I'M NOT A MACHINE, PIETER.
NOT YET, AT ANY RATE.
WHAT'S THAT SUPPOSED TO MEAN?

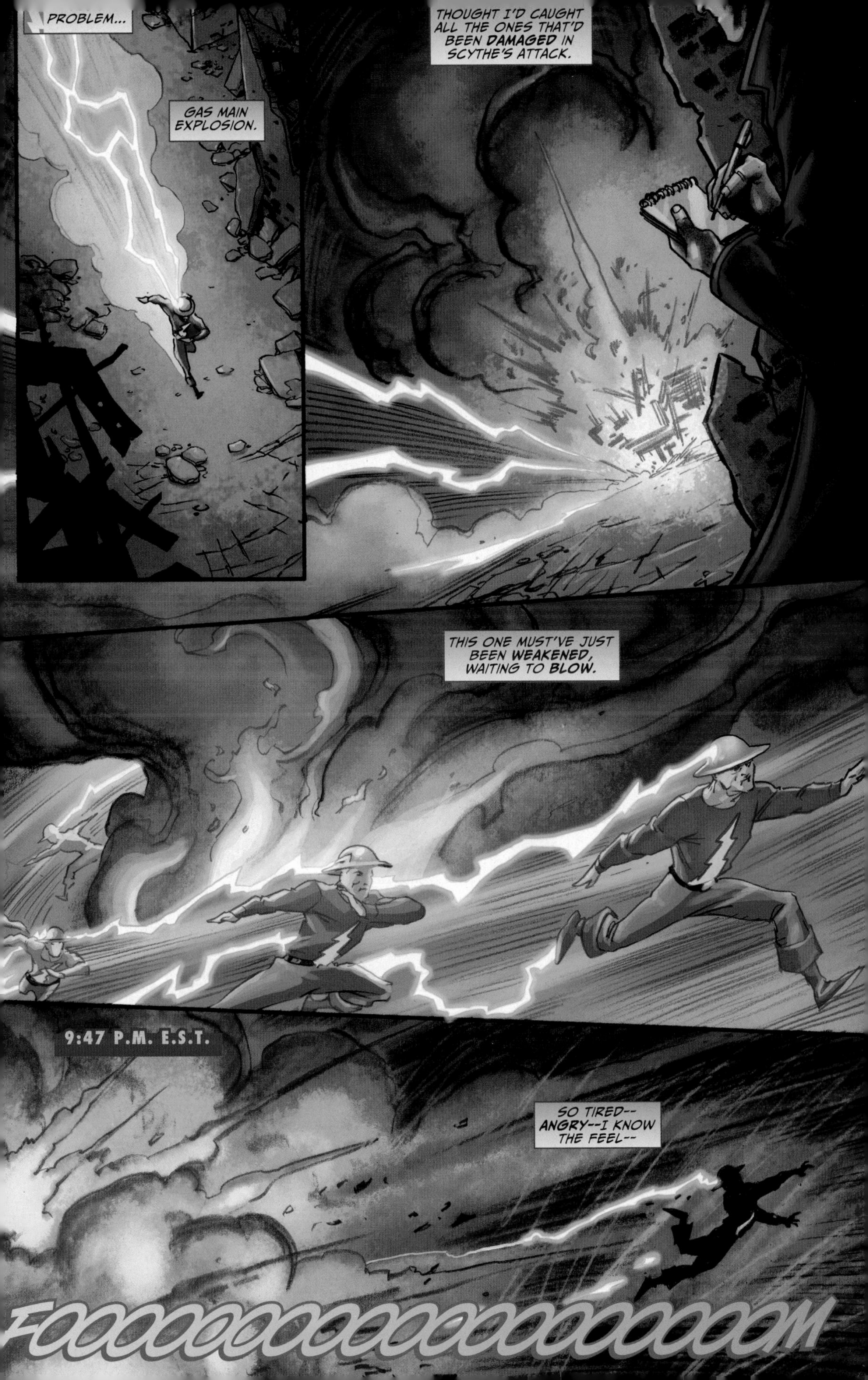
PROBLEM...
GAS MAIN EXPLOSION.
THOUGHT I'D CAUGHT ALL THE ONES THAT'D BEEN DAMAGED IN SCYTHE'S ATTACK.
THIS ONE MUST'VE JUST BEEN WEAKENED, WAITING TO BLOW.
9:47 P.M. E.S.T.
SO TIRED--
ANGRY--I KNOW THE FEEL--
FOOOOOOOOOOOOOOOOOOM

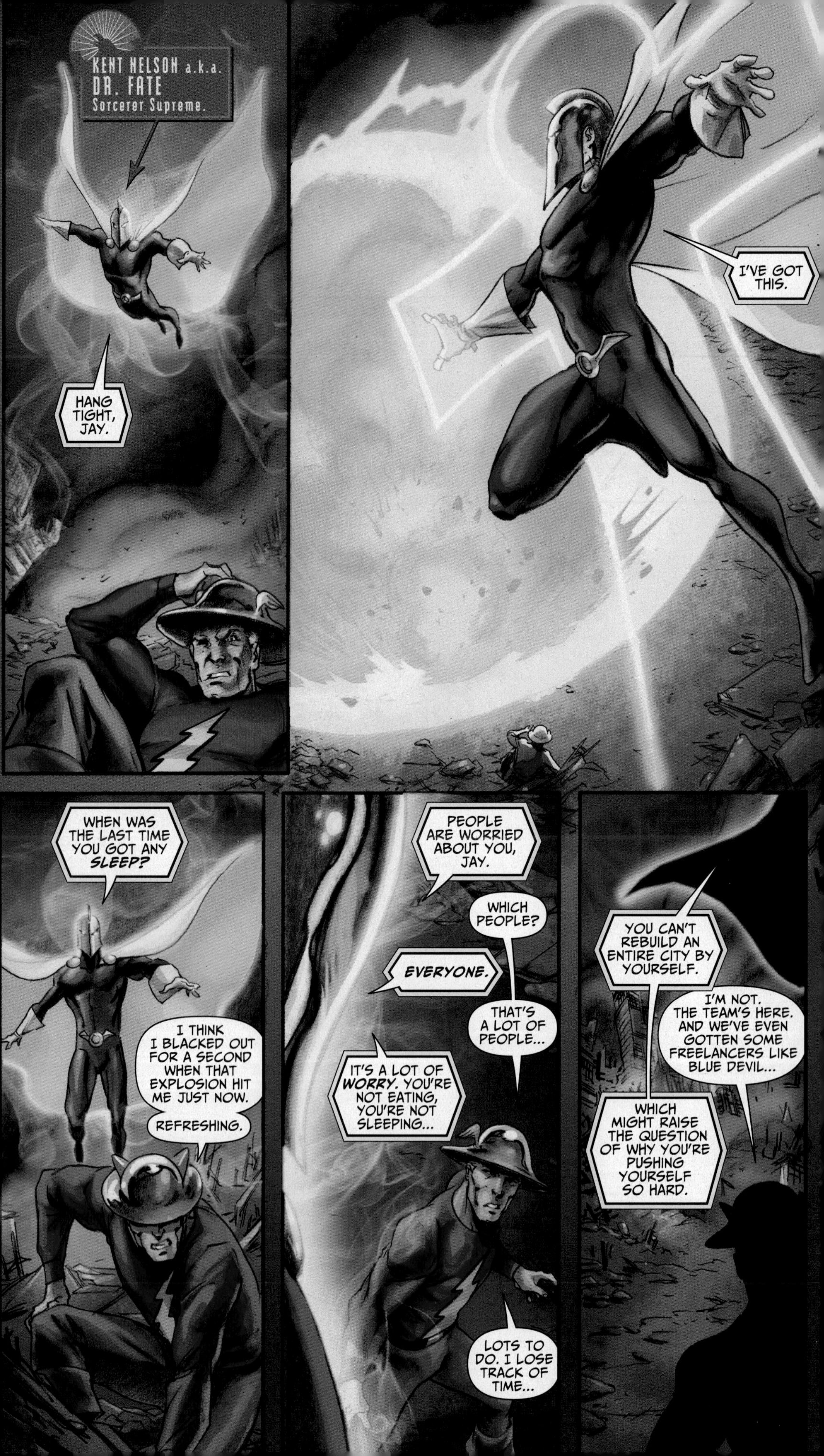
KENT NELSON a.k.a.
DR. FATE
Sorcerer Supreme.
HANG TIGHT, JAY.
I'VE GOT THIS.
WHEN WAS THE LAST TIME YOU GOT ANY SLEEP?
I THINK I BLACKED OUT FOR A SECOND WHEN THAT EXPLOSION HIT ME JUST NOW.
REFRESHING.
PEOPLE ARE WORRIED ABOUT YOU, JAY.
WHICH PEOPLE?
EVERYONE.
THAT'S A LOT OF PEOPLE...
IT'S A LOT OF WORRY. YOU'RE NOT EATING, YOU'RE NOT SLEEPING...
LOTS TO DO. I LOSE TRACK OF TIME...
YOU CAN'T REBUILD AN ENTIRE CITY BY YOURSELF.
I'M NOT. THE TEAM'S HERE. AND WE'VE EVEN GOTTEN SOME FREELANCERS LIKE BLUE DEVIL...
WHICH MIGHT RAISE THE QUESTION OF WHY YOU'RE PUSHING YOURSELF SO HARD.

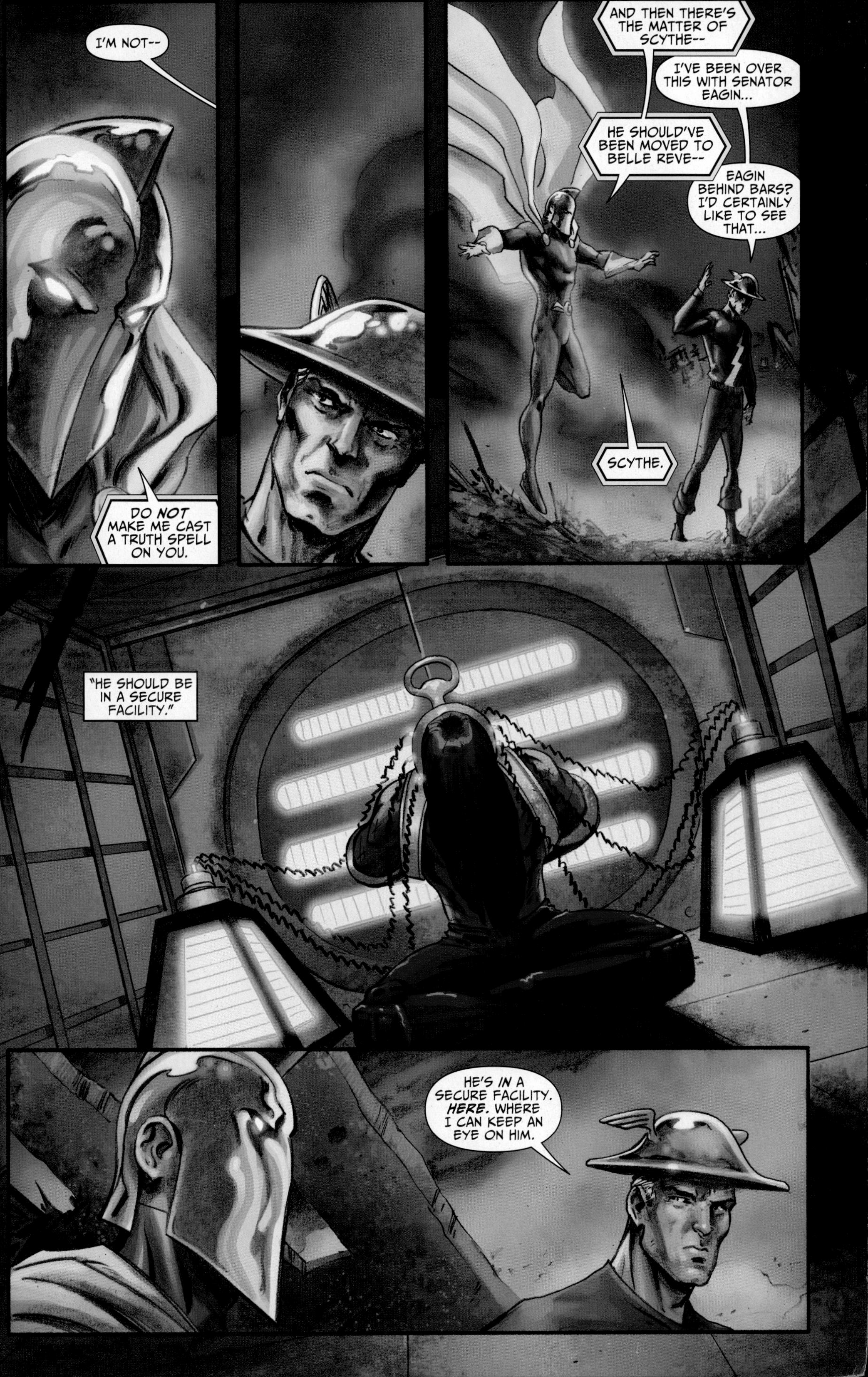
I'M NOT--
DO NOT MAKE ME CAST A TRUTH SPELL ON YOU.
AND THEN THERE'S THE MATTER OF SCYTHE--
HE SHOULD'VE BEEN MOVED TO BELLE REVE--
I'VE BEEN OVER THIS WITH SENATOR EAGIN...
EAGIN BEHIND BARS? I'D CERTAINLY LIKE TO SEE THAT...
SCYTHE.
"HE SHOULD BE IN A SECURE FACILITY."
HE'S IN A SECURE FACILITY. HERE. WHERE I CAN KEEP AN EYE ON HIM.

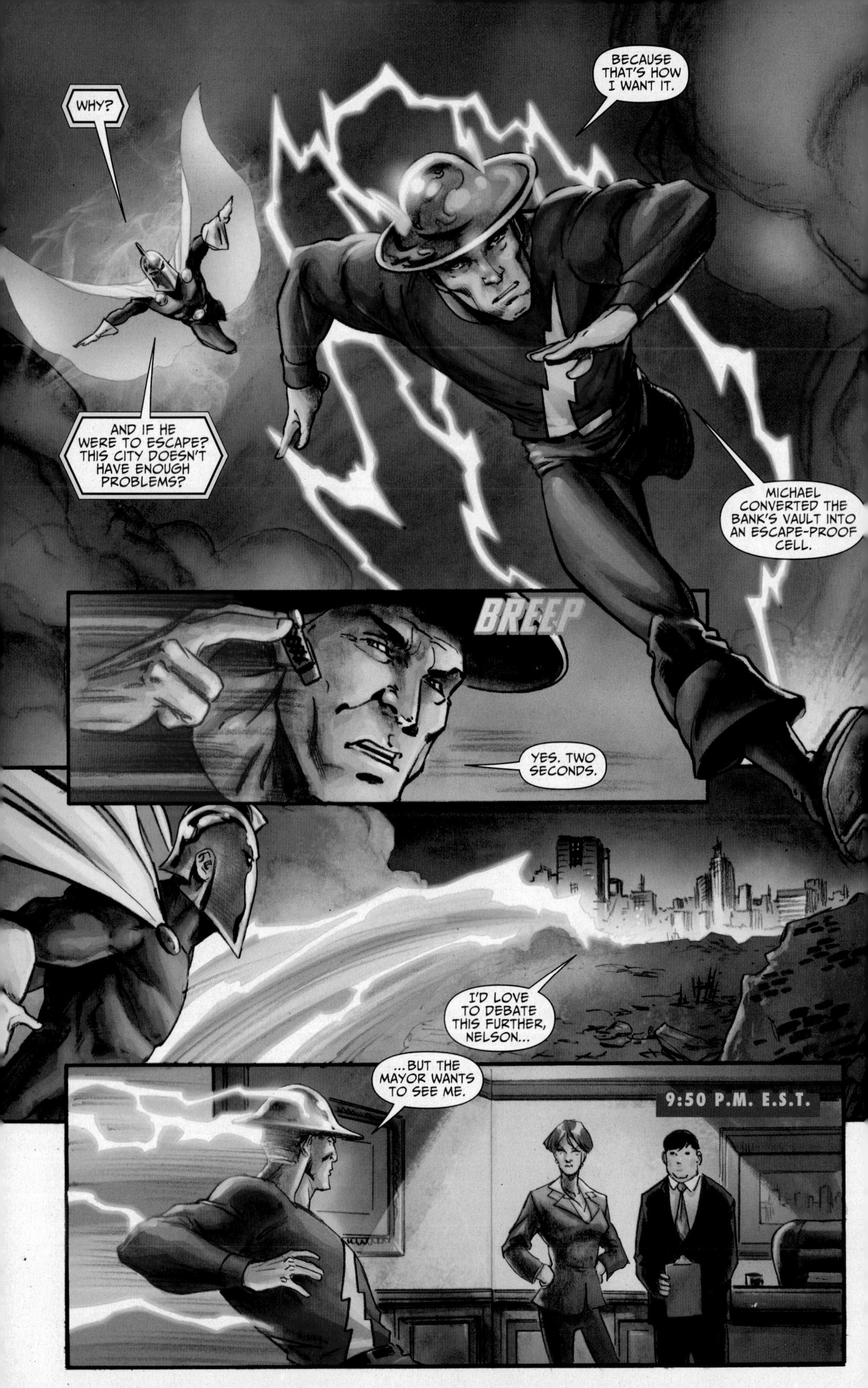
WHY?
BECAUSE THAT'S HOW I WANT IT.
AND IF HE WERE TO ESCAPE? THIS CITY DOESN'T HAVE ENOUGH PROBLEMS?
MICHAEL CONVERTED THE BANK'S VAULT INTO AN ESCAPE-PROOF CELL.
BREEP
YES. TWO SECONDS.
I'D LOVE TO DEBATE THIS FURTHER, NELSON...
...BUT THE MAYOR WANTS TO SEE ME.
9:50 P.M. E.S.T.

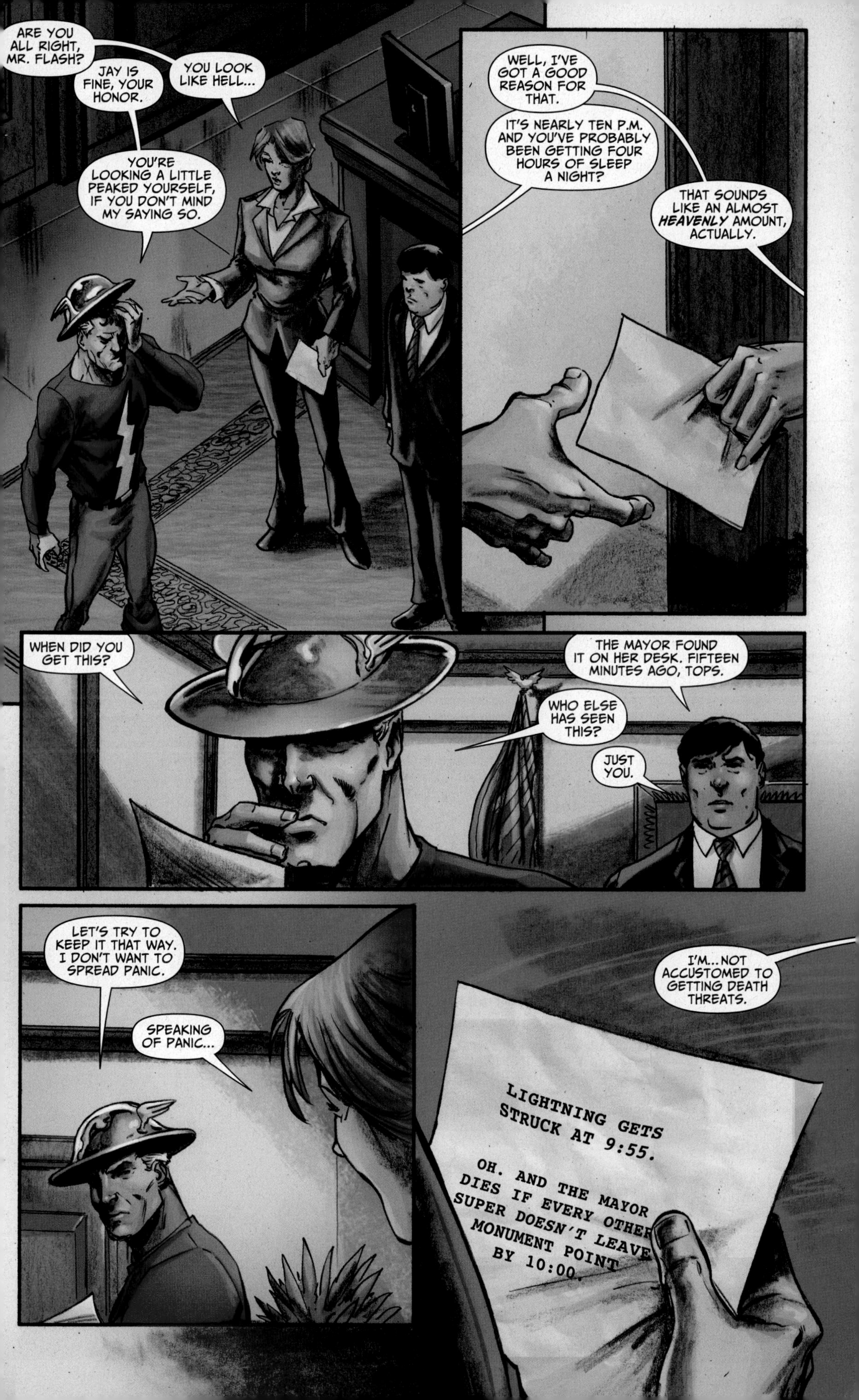
ARE YOU ALL RIGHT, MR. FLASH?
YOU LOOK LIKE HELL...
JAY IS FINE, YOUR HONOR.
YOU'RE LOOKING A LITTLE PEAKED YOURSELF, IF YOU DON'T MIND MY SAYING SO.
WELL, I'VE GOT A GOOD REASON FOR THAT.
IT'S NEARLY TEN P.M. AND YOU'VE PROBABLY BEEN GETTING FOUR HOURS OF SLEEP A NIGHT?
THAT SOUNDS LIKE AN ALMOST HEAVENLY AMOUNT, ACTUALLY.
WHEN DID YOU GET THIS?
THE MAYOR FOUND IT ON HER DESK. FIFTEEN MINUTES AGO, TOPS.
WHO ELSE HAS SEEN THIS?
JUST YOU.
LET'S TRY TO KEEP IT THAT WAY. I DON'T WANT TO SPREAD PANIC.
SPEAKING OF PANIC...
I'M...NOT ACCUSTOMED TO GETTING DEATH THREATS.
LIGHTNING GETS STRUCK AT 9:55.
OH. AND THE MAYOR DIES IF EVERY OTHER SUPER DOESN'T LEAVE MONUMENT POINT BY 10:00.

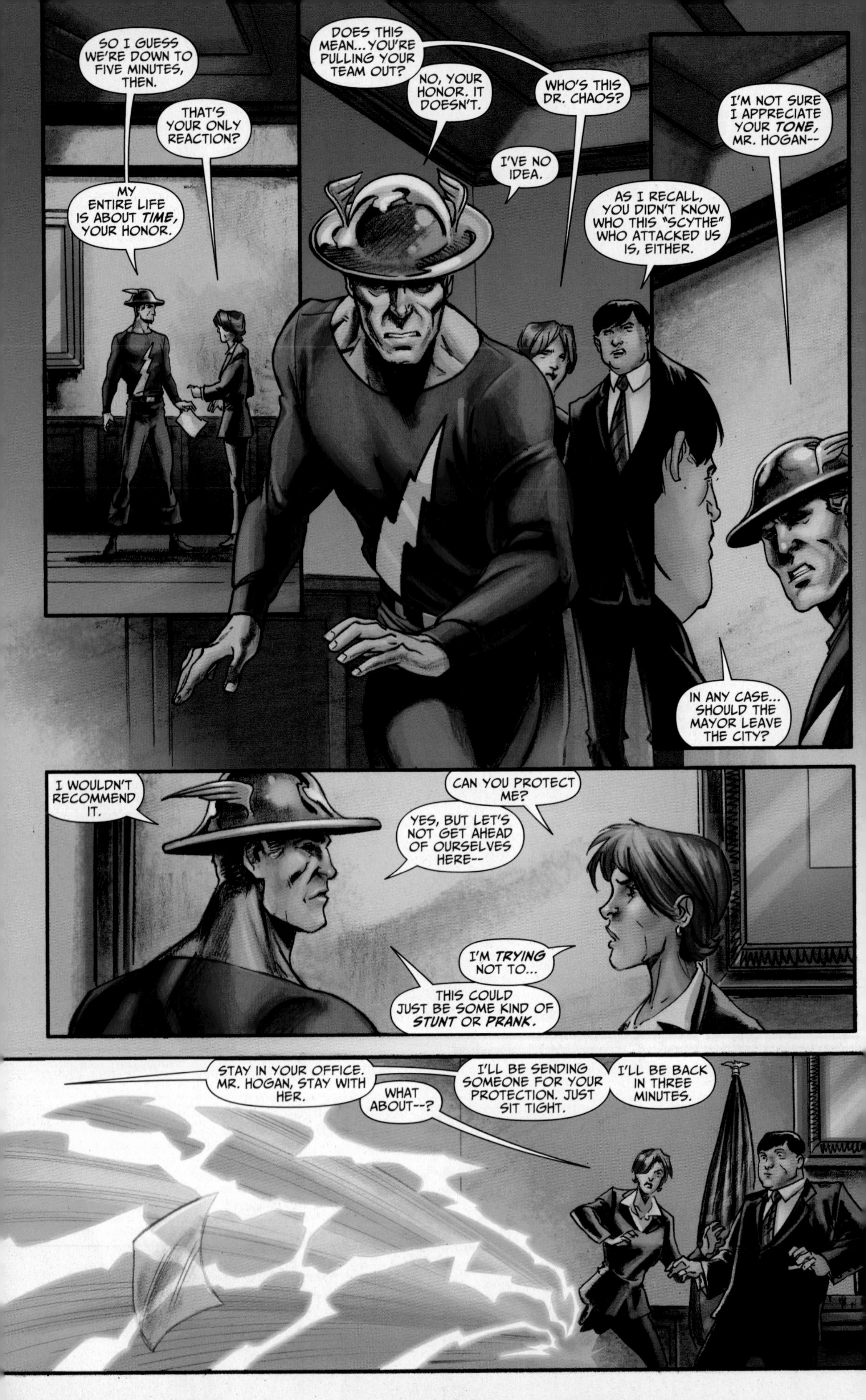
SO I GUESS WE'RE DOWN TO FIVE MINUTES, THEN.
THAT'S YOUR ONLY REACTION?
MY ENTIRE LIFE IS ABOUT *TIME,* YOUR HONOR.
DOES THIS MEAN...YOU'RE PULLING YOUR TEAM OUT?
NO, YOUR HONOR. IT DOESN'T.
WHO'S THIS DR. CHAOS?
I'VE NO IDEA.
I'M NOT SURE I APPRECIATE YOUR *TONE,* MR. HOGAN--
AS I RECALL, YOU DIDN'T KNOW WHO THIS "SCYTHE" WHO ATTACKED US IS, EITHER.
IN ANY CASE... SHOULD THE MAYOR LEAVE THE CITY?
I WOULDN'T RECOMMEND IT.
CAN YOU PROTECT ME?
YES, BUT LET'S NOT GET AHEAD OF OURSELVES HERE--
I'M *TRYING* NOT TO...
THIS COULD JUST BE SOME KIND OF *STUNT* OR *PRANK.*
STAY IN YOUR OFFICE. MR. HOGAN, STAY WITH HER.
WHAT ABOUT--?
I'LL BE SENDING SOMEONE FOR YOUR PROTECTION. JUST SIT TIGHT.
I'LL BE BACK IN THREE MINUTES.

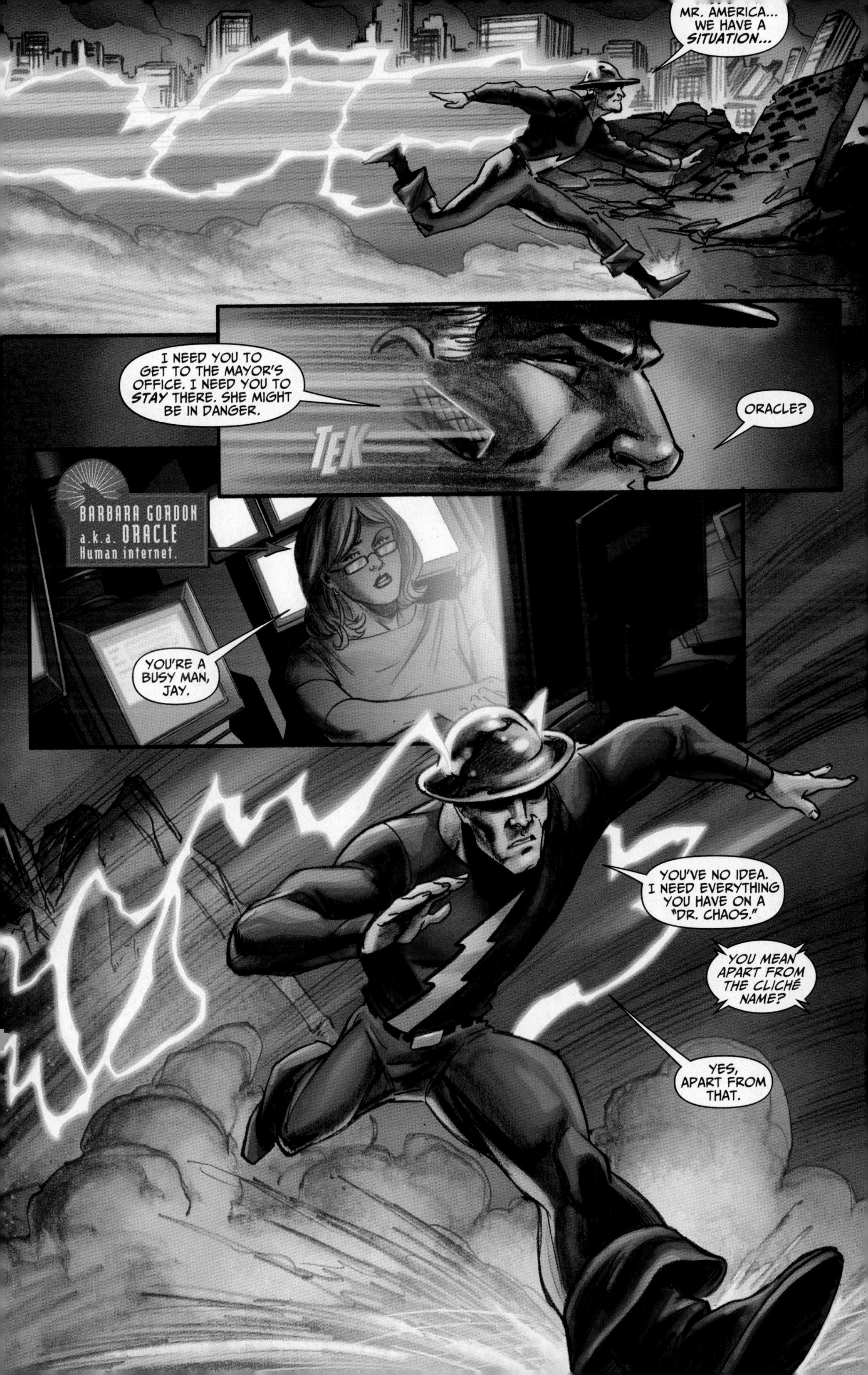
MR. AMERICA... WE HAVE A SITUATION...
I NEED YOU TO GET TO THE MAYOR'S OFFICE. I NEED YOU TO STAY THERE. SHE MIGHT BE IN DANGER.
TEK
ORACLE?
BARBARA GORDON a.k.a. ORACLE Human internet.
YOU'RE A BUSY MAN, JAY.
YOU'VE NO IDEA. I NEED EVERYTHING YOU HAVE ON A "DR. CHAOS."
YOU MEAN APART FROM THE CLICHÉ NAME?
YES, APART FROM THAT.

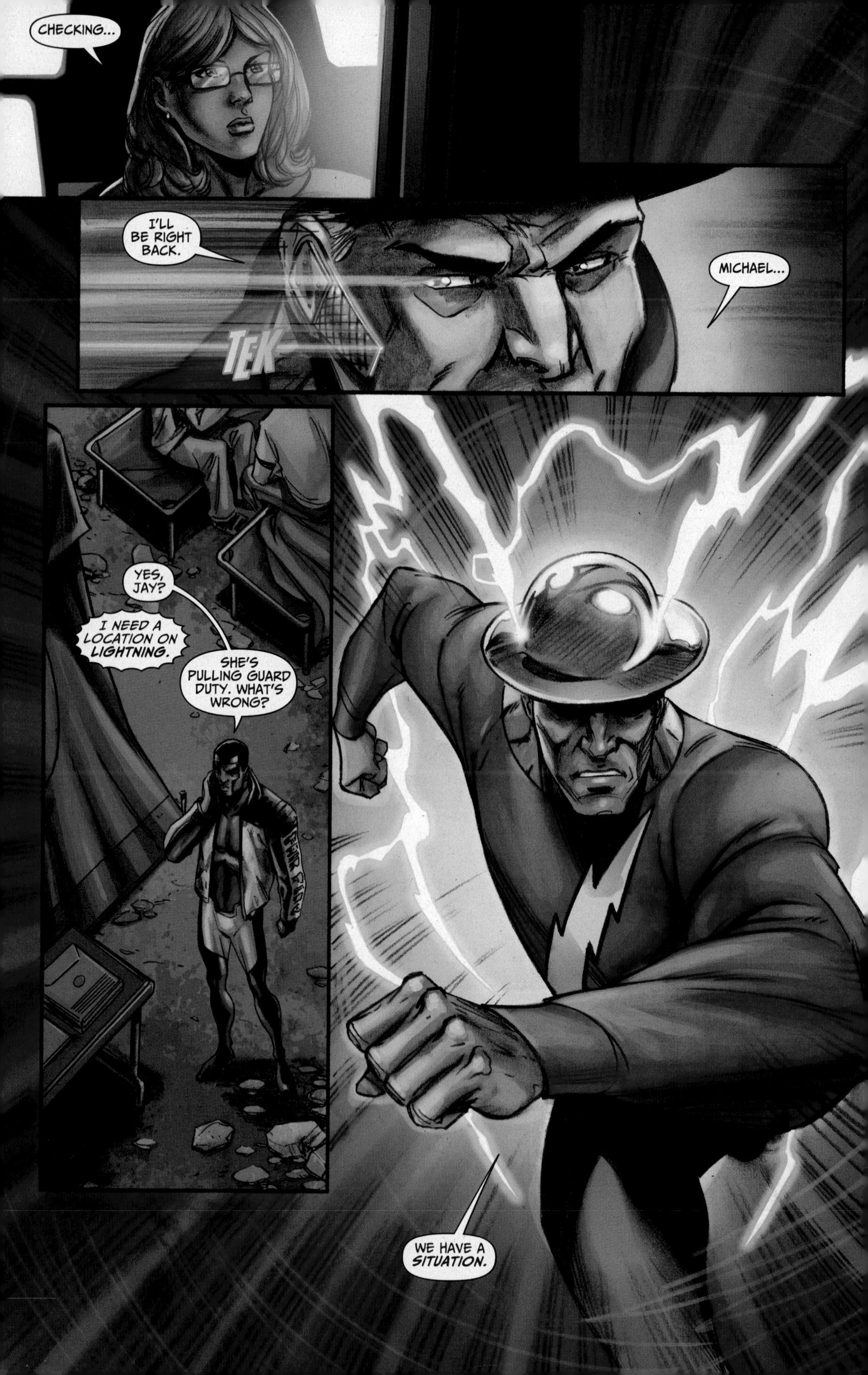
CHECKING...
I'LL BE RIGHT BACK.
TEK
MICHAEL...
YES, JAY?
I NEED A LOCATION ON LIGHTNING.
SHE'S PULLING GUARD DUTY. WHAT'S WRONG?
WE HAVE A SITUATION.

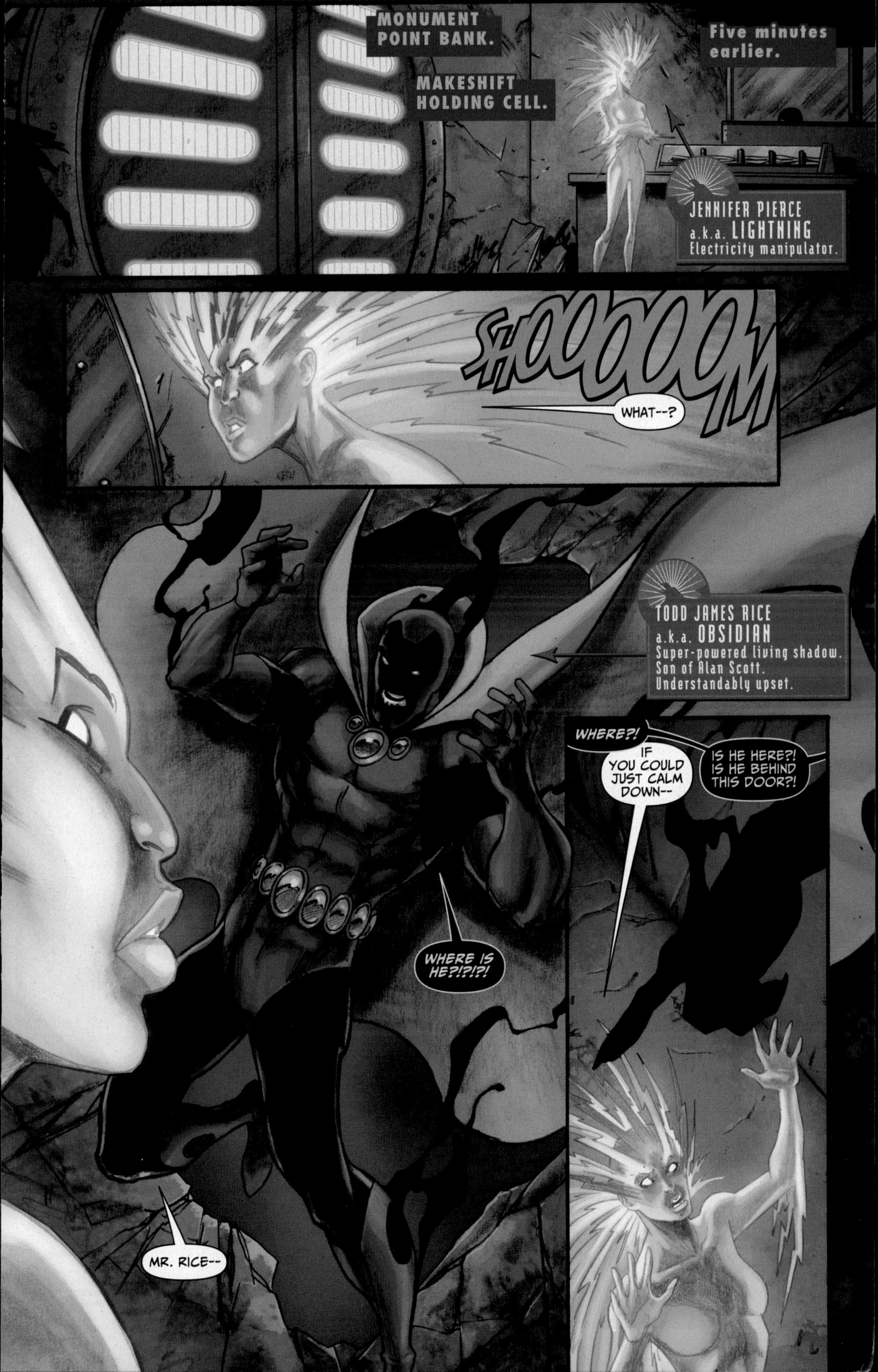
MONUMENT POINT BANK.
MAKESHIFT HOLDING CELL.
Five minutes earlier.
JENNIFER PIERCE a.k.a. LIGHTNING Electricity manipulator.
SHOOOOOM
WHAT--?
TODD JAMES RICE a.k.a. OBSIDIAN Super-powered living shadow. Son of Alan Scott. Understandably upset.
WHERE IS HE?!?!?!
MR. RICE--
WHERE?!
IF YOU COULD JUST CALM DOWN--
IS HE HERE?! IS HE BEHIND THIS DOOR?!

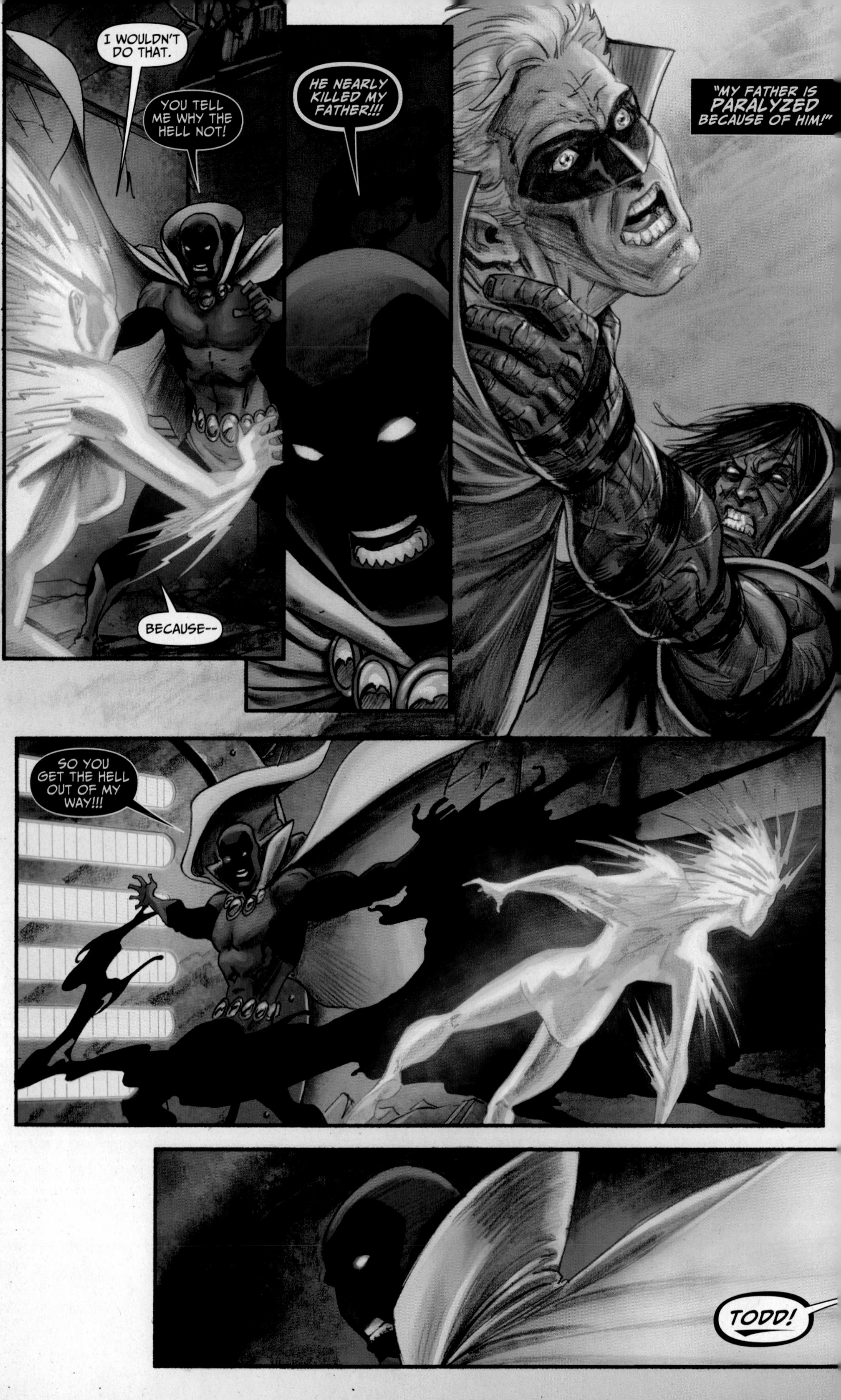
I WOULDN'T DO THAT.
YOU TELL ME WHY THE HELL NOT!
BECAUSE--
HE NEARLY KILLED MY FATHER!!!
"MY FATHER IS PARALYZED BECAUSE OF HIM!"
SO YOU GET THE HELL OUT OF MY WAY!!!
TODD!

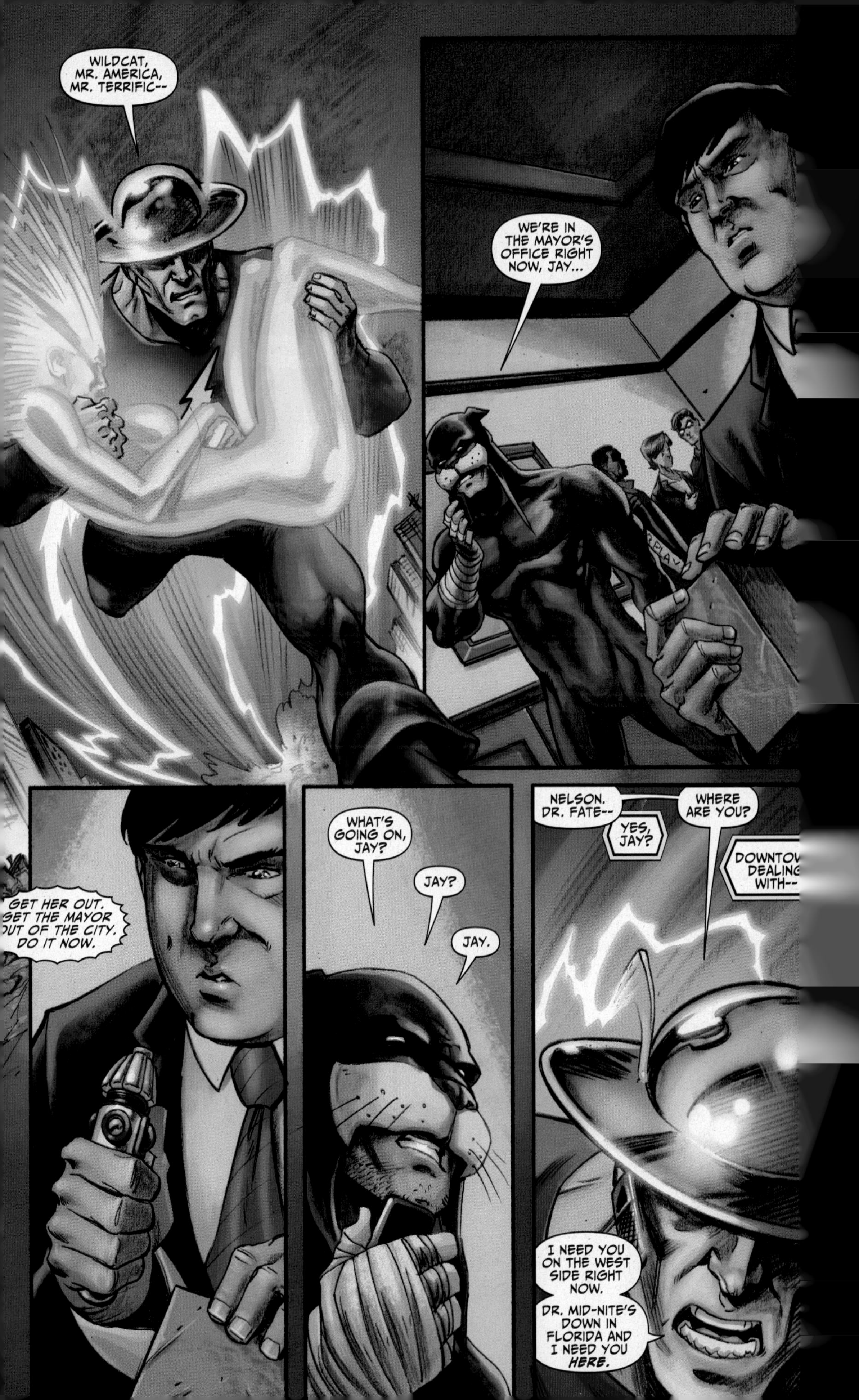
WILDCAT, MR. AMERICA, MR. TERRIFIC--
WE'RE IN THE MAYOR'S OFFICE RIGHT NOW, JAY...
GET HER OUT. GET THE MAYOR OUT OF THE CITY. DO IT NOW.
WHAT'S GOING ON, JAY?
JAY?
JAY.
NELSON. DR. FATE--
YES, JAY?
WHERE ARE YOU?
I NEED YOU ON THE WEST SIDE RIGHT NOW.
DR. MID-NITE'S DOWN IN FLORIDA AND I NEED YOU HERE.

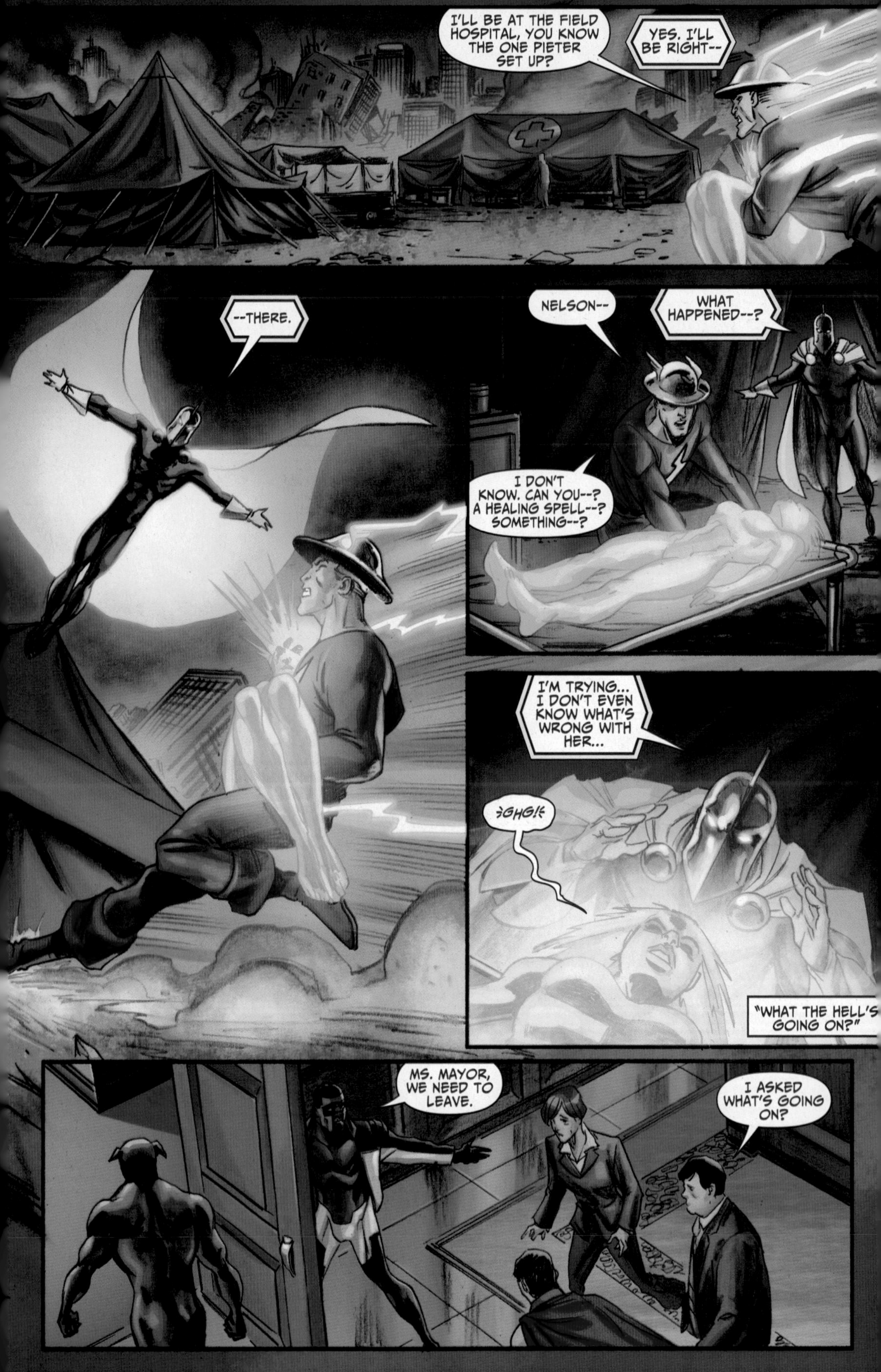
I'LL BE AT THE FIELD HOSPITAL, YOU KNOW THE ONE PIETER SET UP?
YES. I'LL BE RIGHT--
--THERE.
NELSON--
WHAT HAPPENED--?
I DON'T KNOW. CAN YOU--? A HEALING SPELL--? SOMETHING--?
I'M TRYING... I DON'T EVEN KNOW WHAT'S WRONG WITH HER...
GHG!
"WHAT THE HELL'S GOING ON?"
MS. MAYOR, WE NEED TO LEAVE.
I ASKED WHAT'S GOING ON?

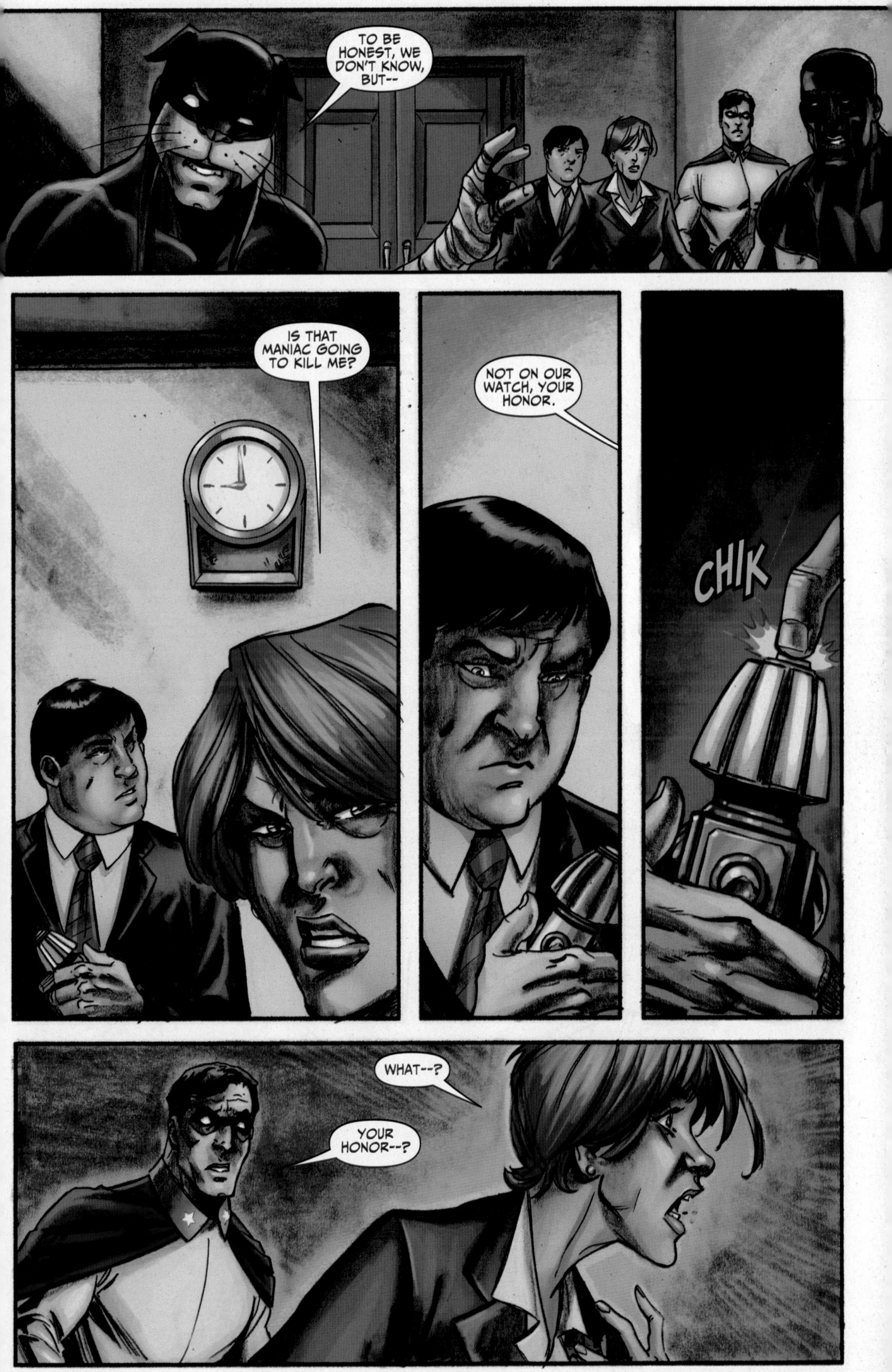
TO BE HONEST, WE DON'T KNOW, BUT--
IS THAT MANIAC GOING TO KILL ME?
NOT ON OUR WATCH, YOUR HONOR.
CHIK
WHAT--?
YOUR HONOR--?

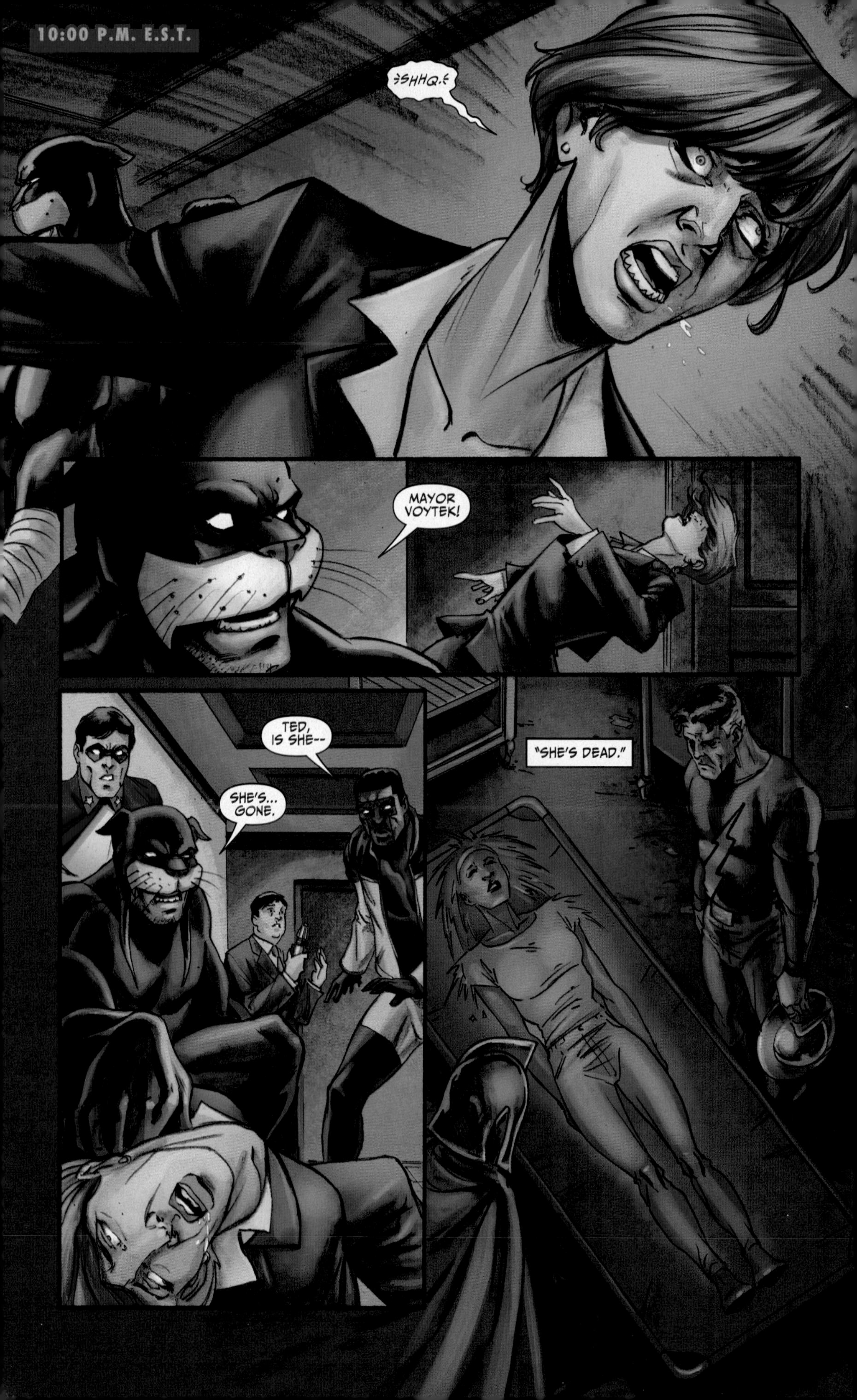
10:00 P.M. E.S.T.
SHHQ.
MAYOR VOYTEK!
TED, IS SHE--
SHE'S... GONE.
"SHE'S DEAD."

SUPERTOWN Part Four

Cover by SHANE DAVIS & SANDRA HOPE
with BARBARA CIARDO

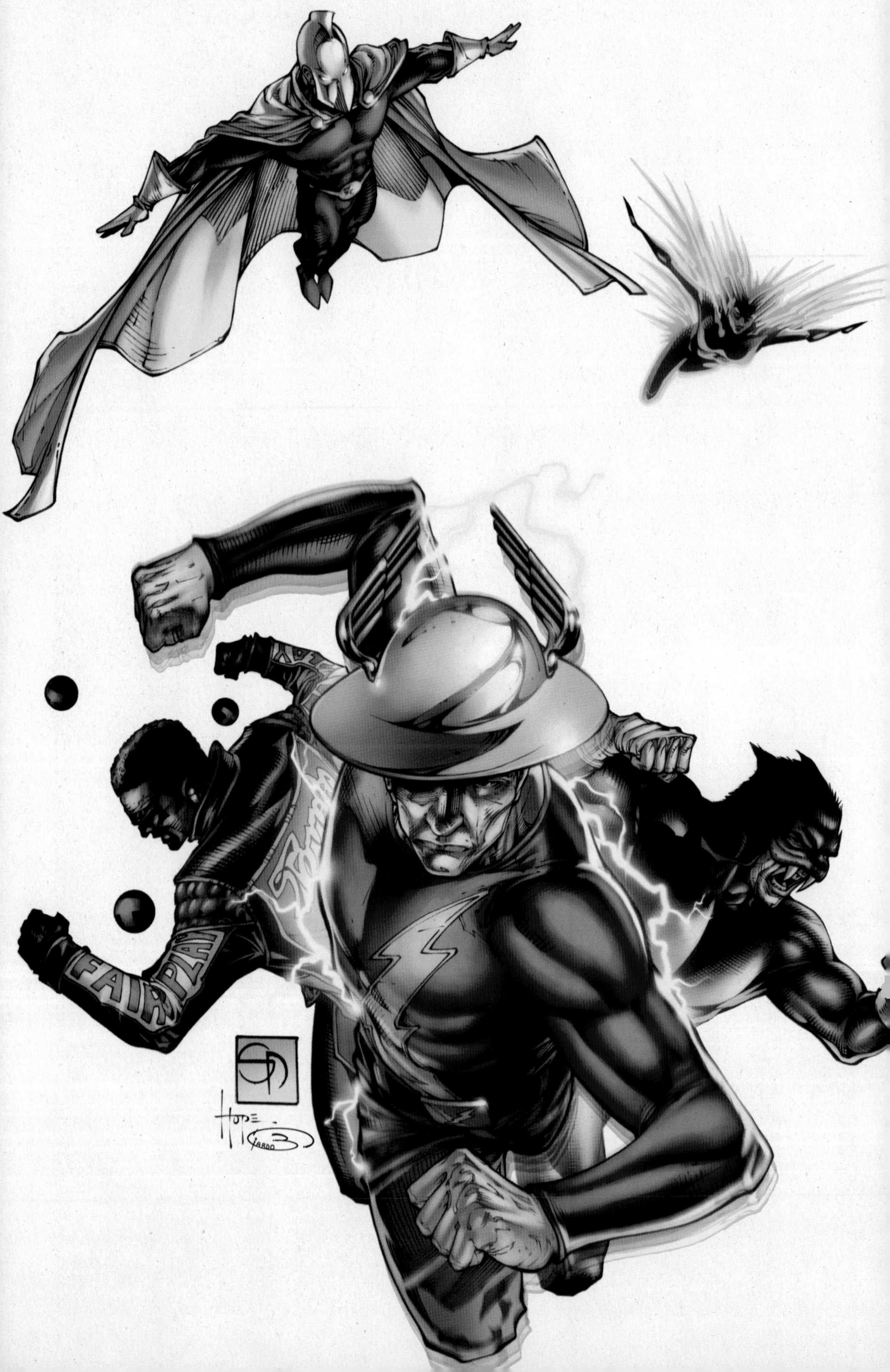

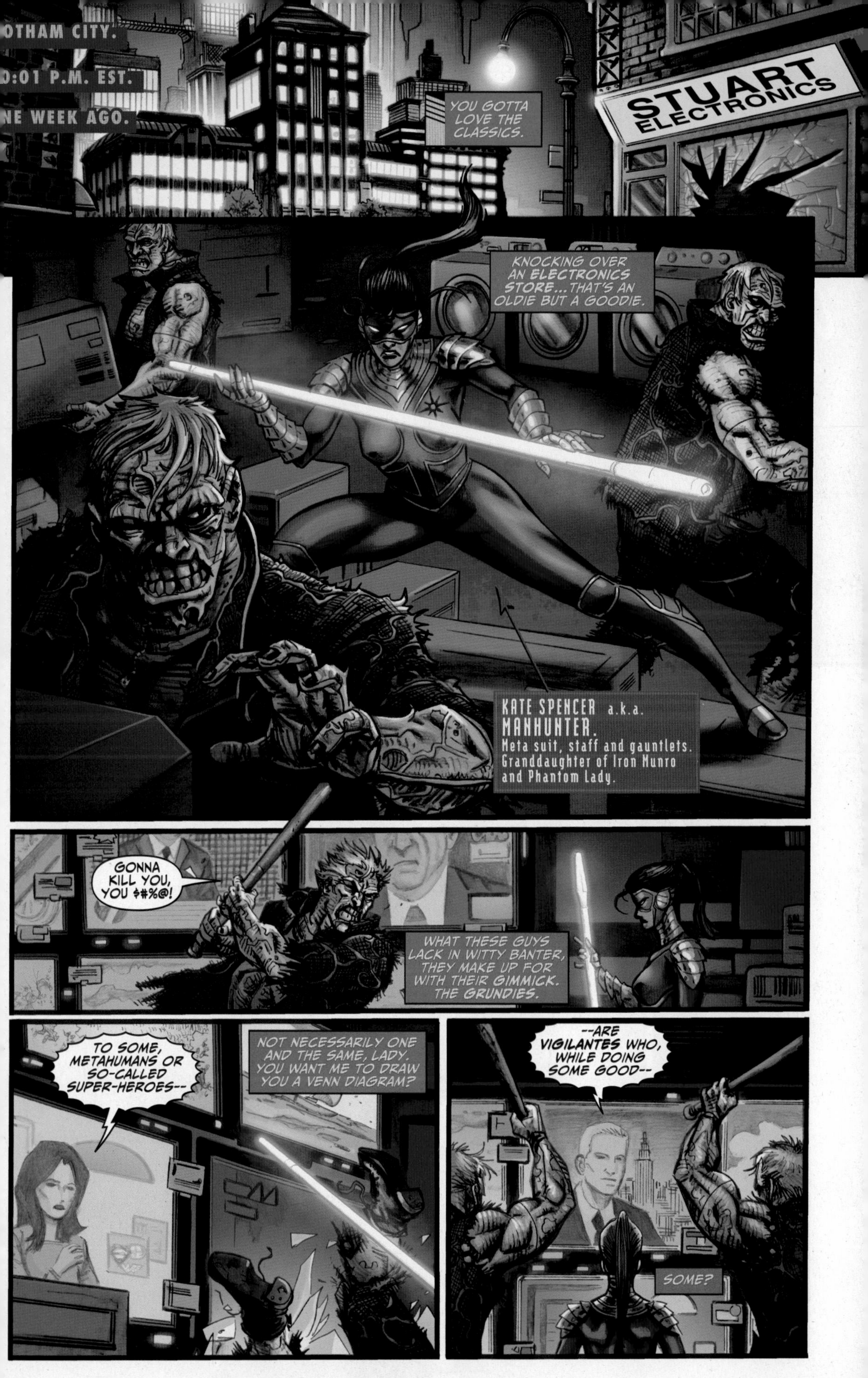

OTHAM CITY.
0:01 P.M. EST.
NE WEEK AGO.
YOU GOTTA LOVE THE CLASSICS.
STUART ELECTRONICS
KNOCKING OVER AN ELECTRONICS STORE...THAT'S AN OLDIE BUT A GOODIE.
KATE SPENCER a.k.a. MANHUNTER.
Meta suit, staff and gauntlets. Granddaughter of Iron Munro and Phantom Lady.
GONNA KILL YOU, YOU $#%@!
WHAT THESE GUYS LACK IN WITTY BANTER, THEY MAKE UP FOR WITH THEIR GIMMICK. THE GRUNDIES.
TO SOME, METAHUMANS OR SO-CALLED SUPER-HEROES--
NOT NECESSARILY ONE AND THE SAME, LADY. YOU WANT ME TO DRAW YOU A VENN DIAGRAM?
--ARE VIGILANTES WHO, WHILE DOING SOME GOOD--
SOME?

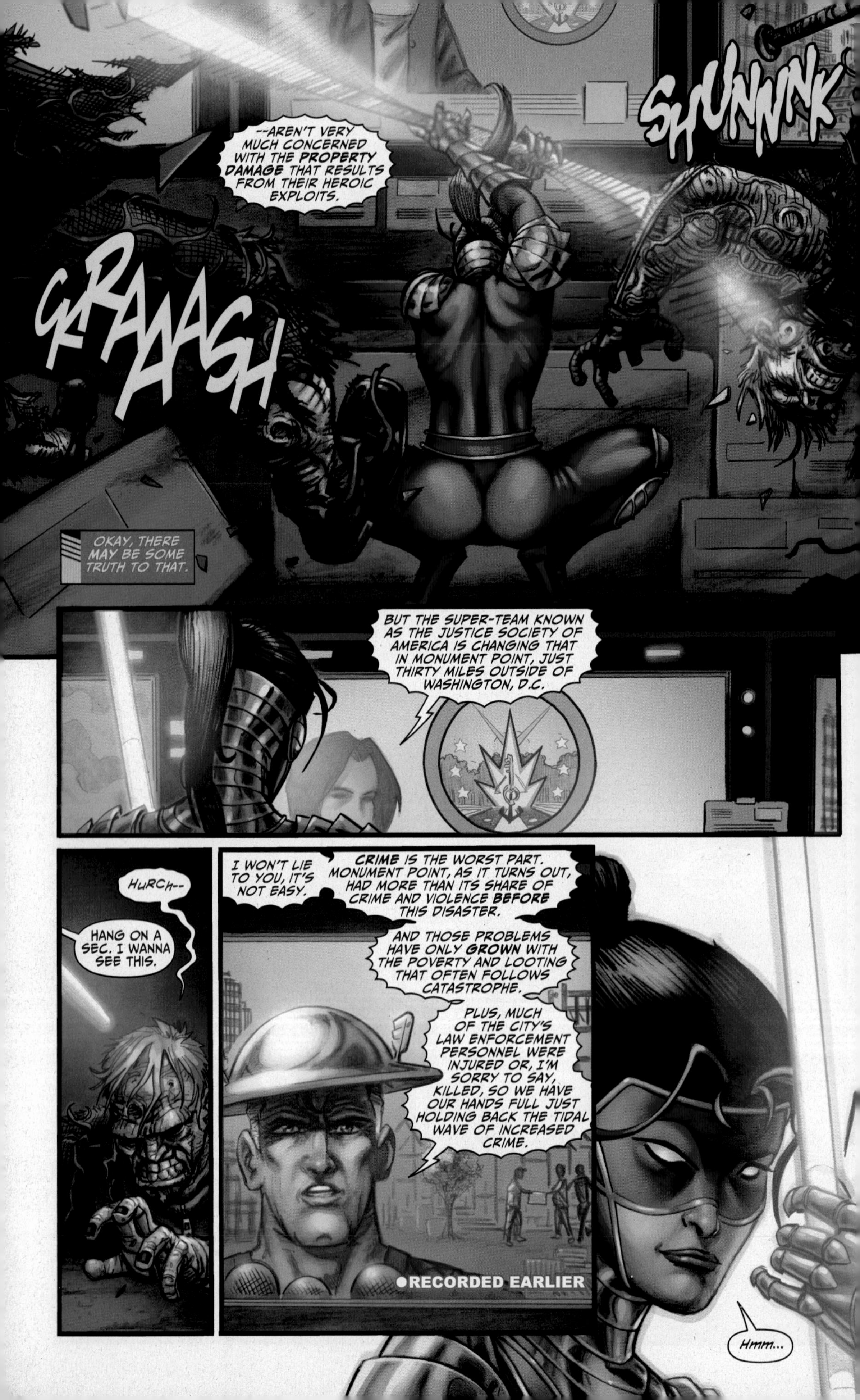
--AREN'T VERY MUCH CONCERNED WITH THE **PROPERTY DAMAGE** THAT RESULTS FROM THEIR HEROIC EXPLOITS.
SHUNNK
GKRAAASH
OKAY, THERE MAY BE SOME TRUTH TO THAT.
BUT THE SUPER-TEAM KNOWN AS THE JUSTICE SOCIETY OF AMERICA IS CHANGING THAT IN MONUMENT POINT, JUST THIRTY MILES OUTSIDE OF WASHINGTON, D.C.
HURCH--
HANG ON A SEC. I WANNA SEE THIS.
I WON'T LIE TO YOU, IT'S NOT EASY.
CRIME IS THE WORST PART. MONUMENT POINT, AS IT TURNS OUT, HAD MORE THAN ITS SHARE OF CRIME AND VIOLENCE **BEFORE** THIS DISASTER.
AND THOSE PROBLEMS HAVE ONLY **GROWN** WITH THE POVERTY AND LOOTING THAT OFTEN FOLLOWS CATASTROPHE.
PLUS, MUCH OF THE CITY'S LAW ENFORCEMENT PERSONNEL WERE INJURED OR, I'M SORRY TO SAY, KILLED, SO WE HAVE OUR HANDS FULL JUST HOLDING BACK THE TIDAL WAVE OF INCREASED CRIME.
RECORDED EARLIER
Hmm...

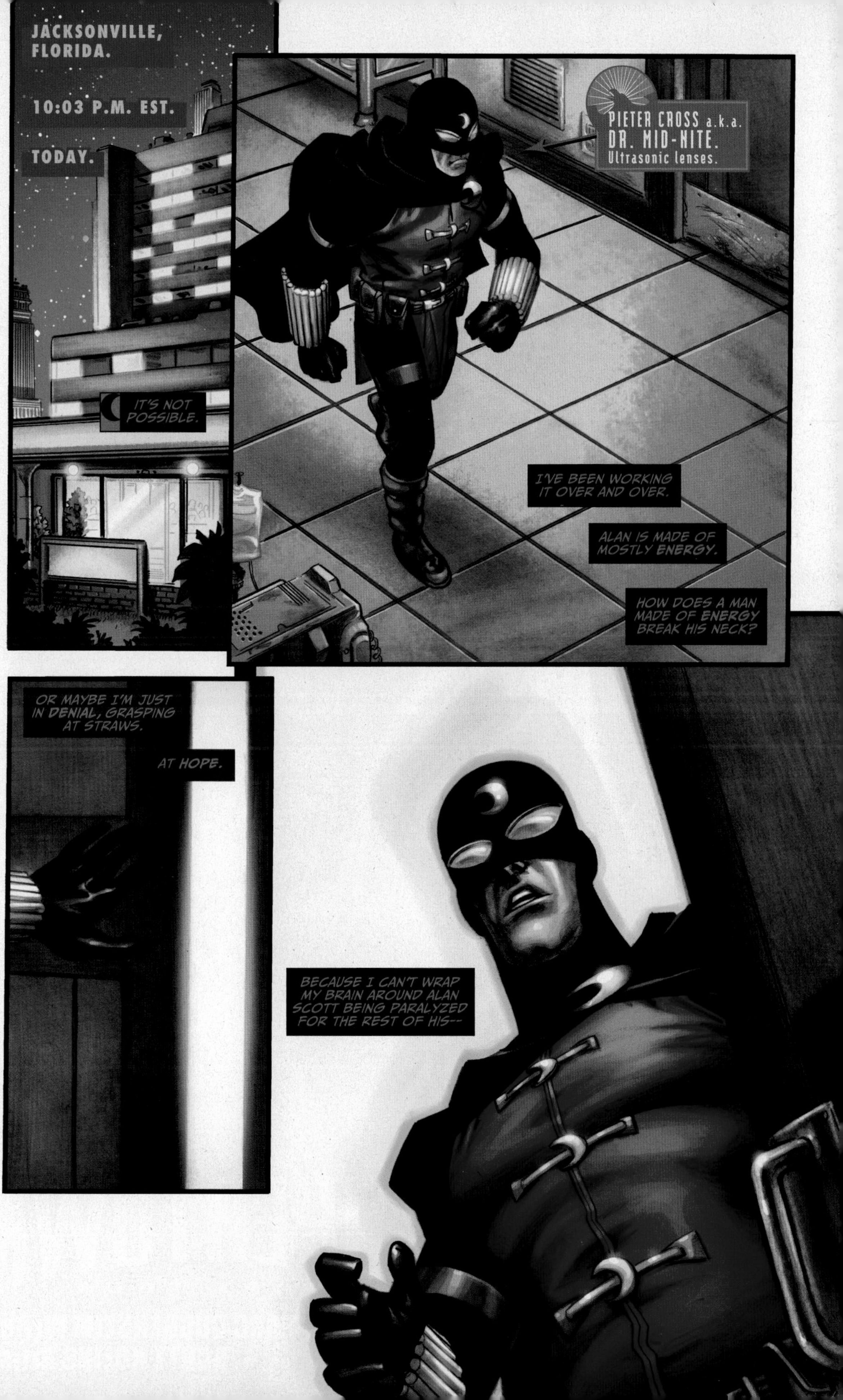
JACKSONVILLE, FLORIDA.
10:03 P.M. EST.
TODAY.
IT'S NOT POSSIBLE.
PIETER CROSS a.k.a. DR. MID-NITE. Ultrasonic lenses.
I'VE BEEN WORKING IT OVER AND OVER.
ALAN IS MADE OF MOSTLY ENERGY.
HOW DOES A MAN MADE OF ENERGY BREAK HIS NECK?
OR MAYBE I'M JUST IN DENIAL, GRASPING AT STRAWS.
AT HOPE.
BECAUSE I CAN'T WRAP MY BRAIN AROUND ALAN SCOTT BEING PARALYZED FOR THE REST OF HIS--

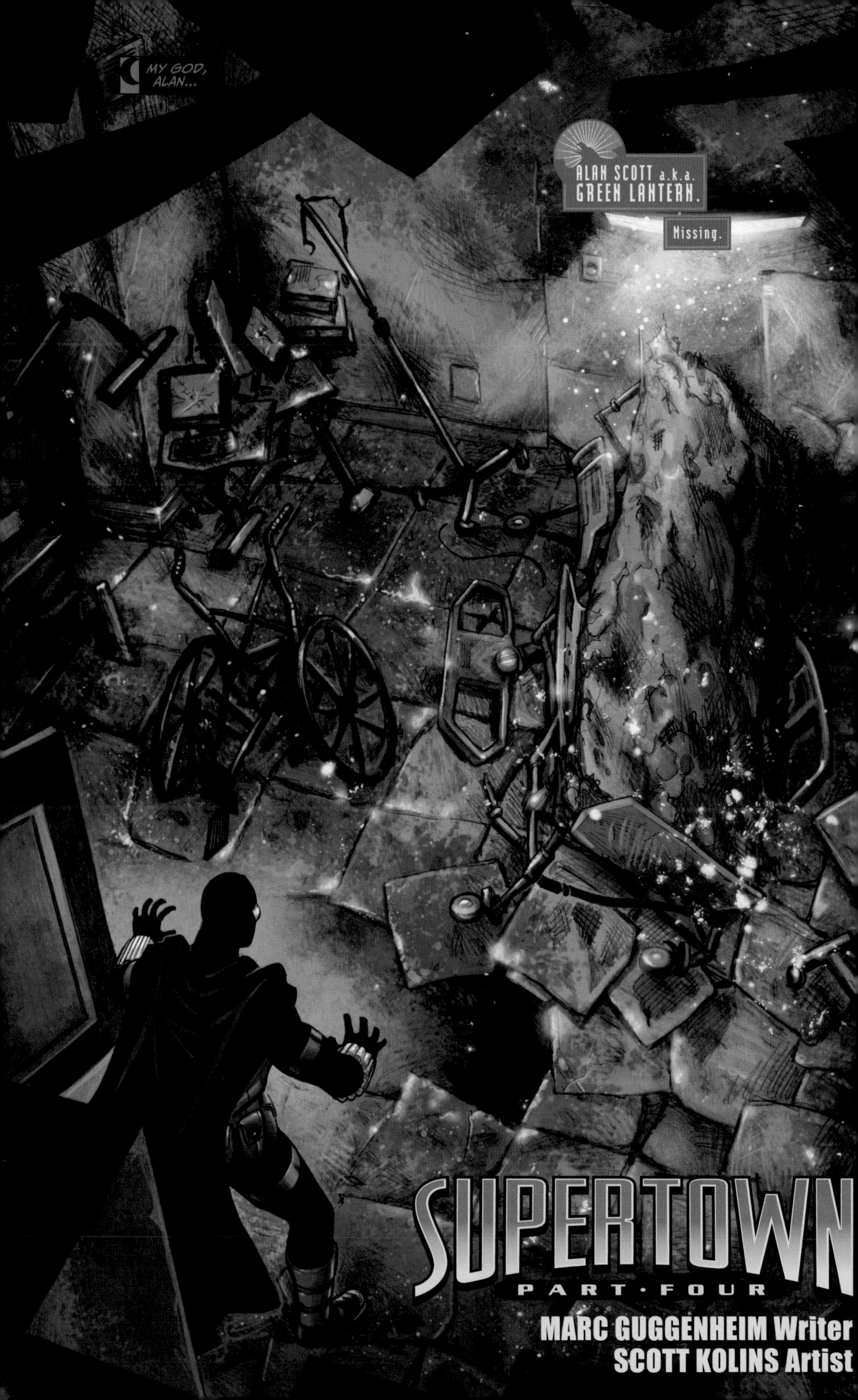

MY GOD, ALAN...
ALAN SCOTT a.k.a. GREEN LANTERN.
Missing.
SUPERTOWN
PART·FOUR
MARC GUGGENHEIM Writer
SCOTT KOLINS Artist

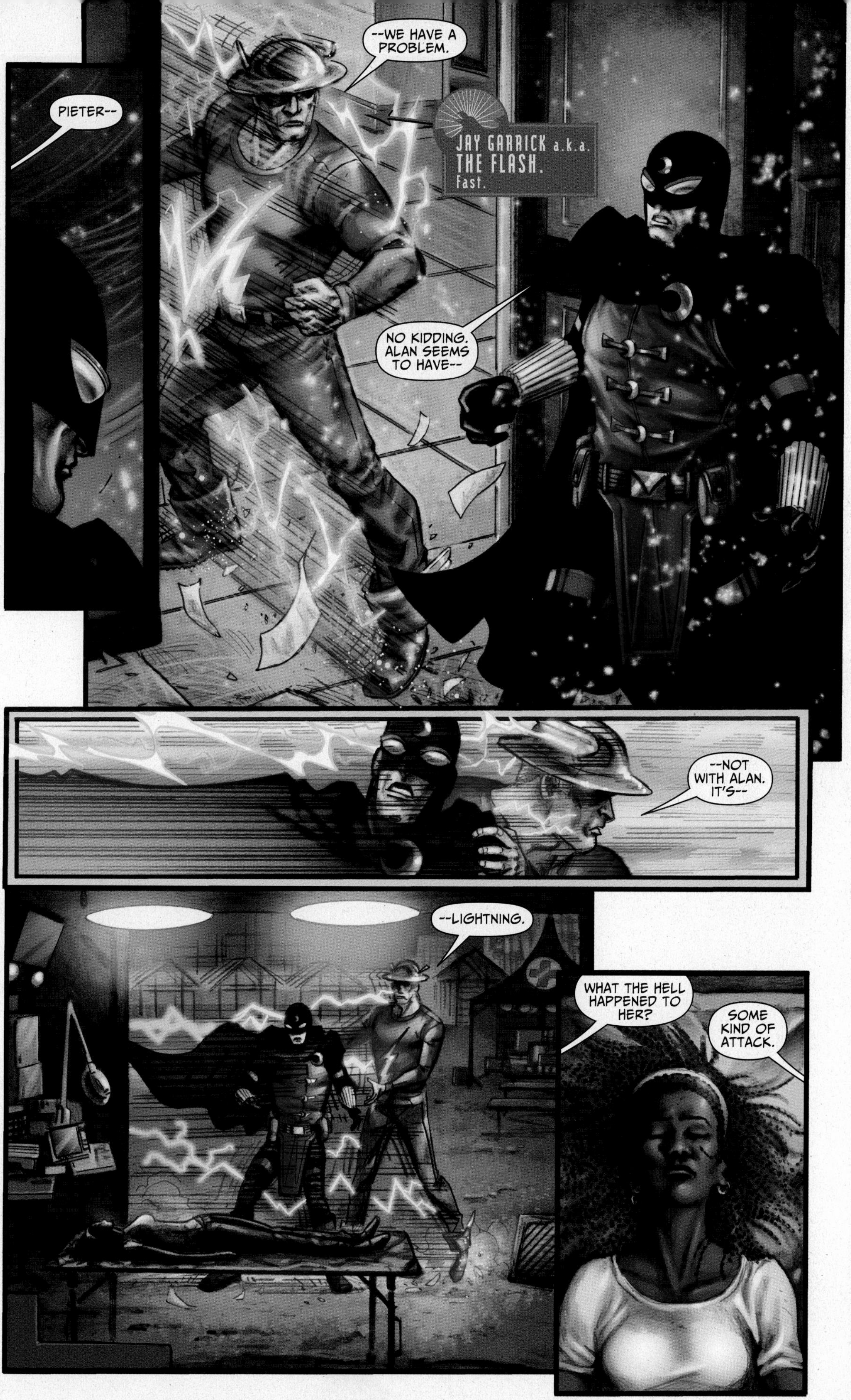
PIETER--
--WE HAVE A PROBLEM.
JAY GARRICK a.k.a. THE FLASH. Fast.
NO KIDDING. ALAN SEEMS TO HAVE--
--NOT WITH ALAN. IT'S--
--LIGHTNING.
WHAT THE HELL HAPPENED TO HER?
SOME KIND OF ATTACK.

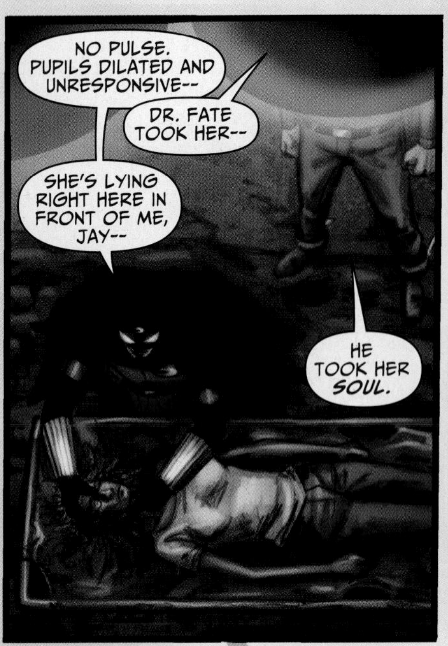
NO PULSE. PUPILS DILATED AND UNRESPONSIVE--
DR. FATE TOOK HER--
SHE'S LYING RIGHT HERE IN FRONT OF ME, JAY--
HE TOOK HER *SOUL.*

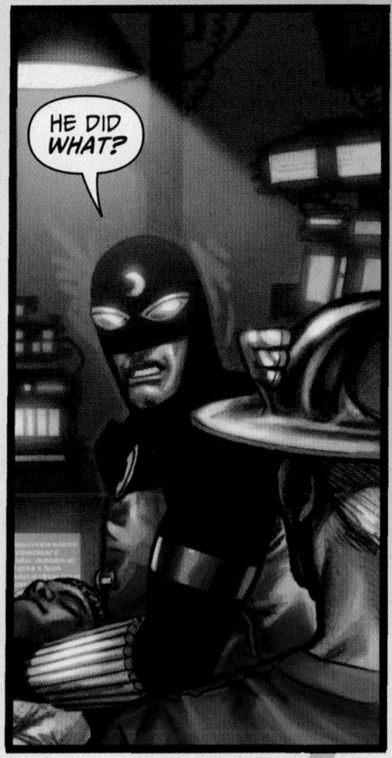
HE DID *WHAT?*

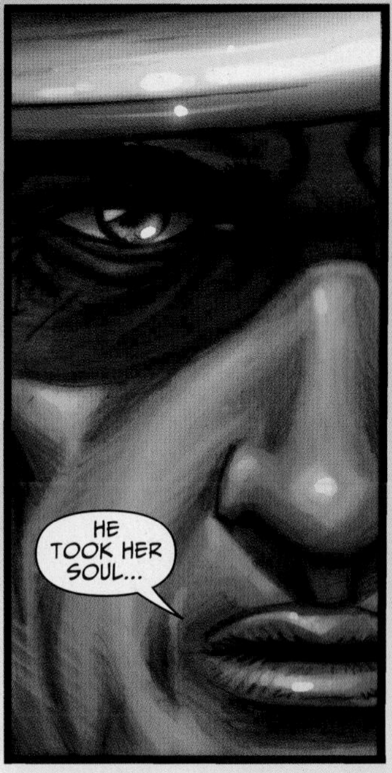
HE TOOK HER SOUL...

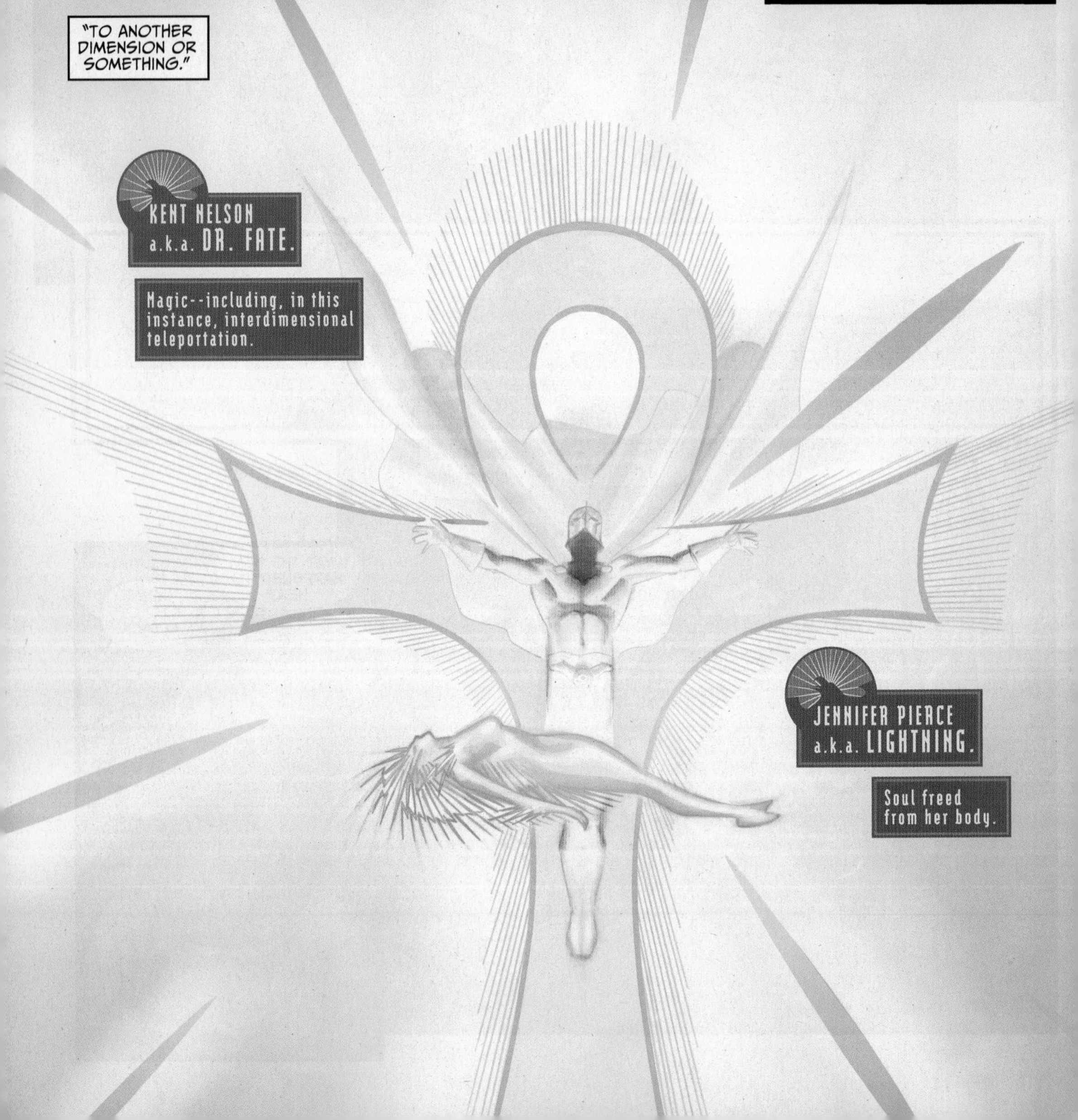
"TO ANOTHER DIMENSION OR SOMETHING."
KENT NELSON a.k.a. DR. FATE.
Magic--including, in this instance, interdimensional teleportation.
JENNIFER PIERCE a.k.a. LIGHTNING.
Soul freed from her body.

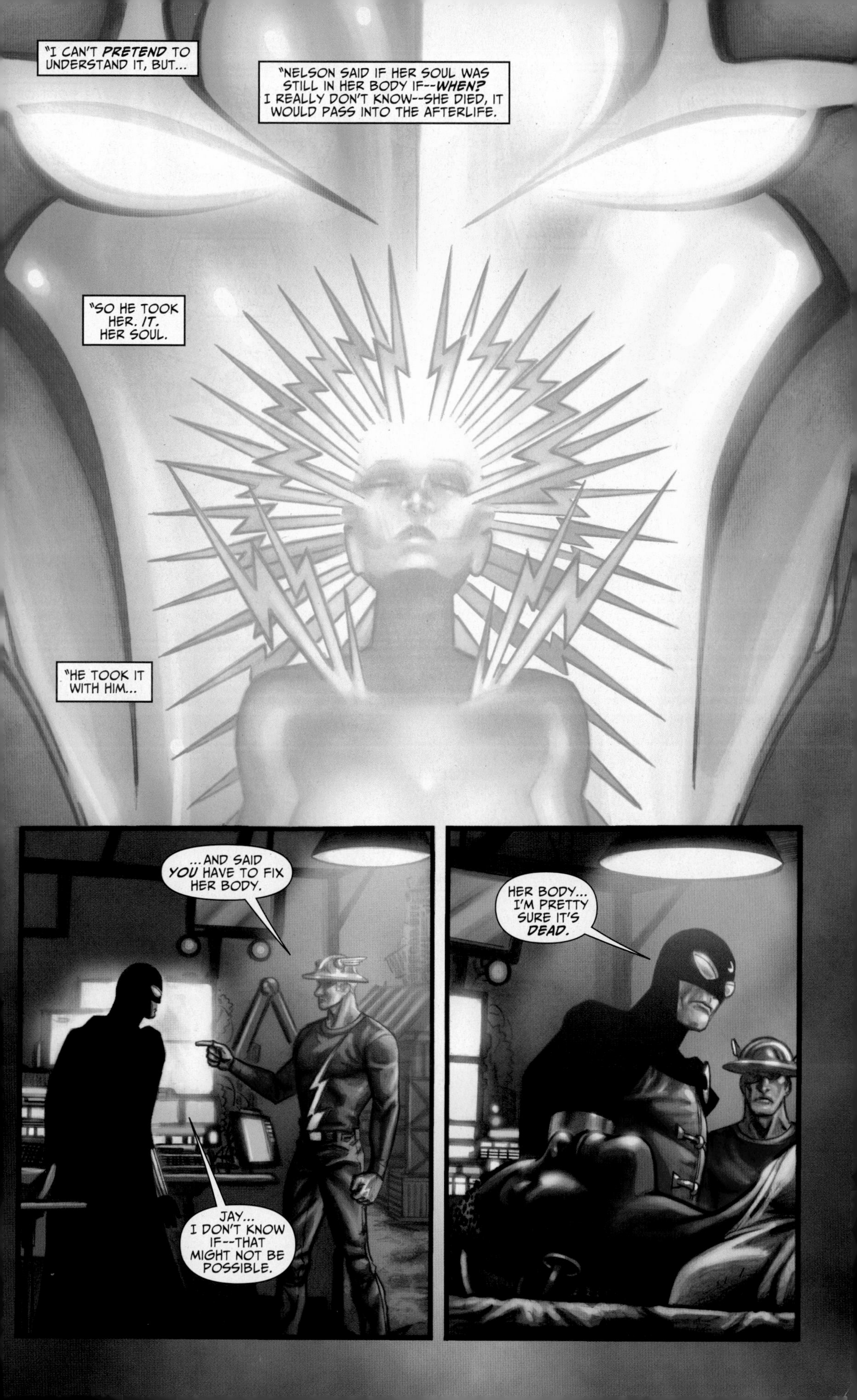
"I CAN'T PRETEND TO UNDERSTAND IT, BUT...
"NELSON SAID IF HER SOUL WAS STILL IN HER BODY IF--WHEN? I REALLY DON'T KNOW--SHE DIED, IT WOULD PASS INTO THE AFTERLIFE.
"SO HE TOOK HER. IT. HER SOUL.
"HE TOOK IT WITH HIM...
...AND SAID YOU HAVE TO FIX HER BODY.
JAY... I DON'T KNOW IF--THAT MIGHT NOT BE POSSIBLE.
HER BODY... I'M PRETTY SURE IT'S DEAD.

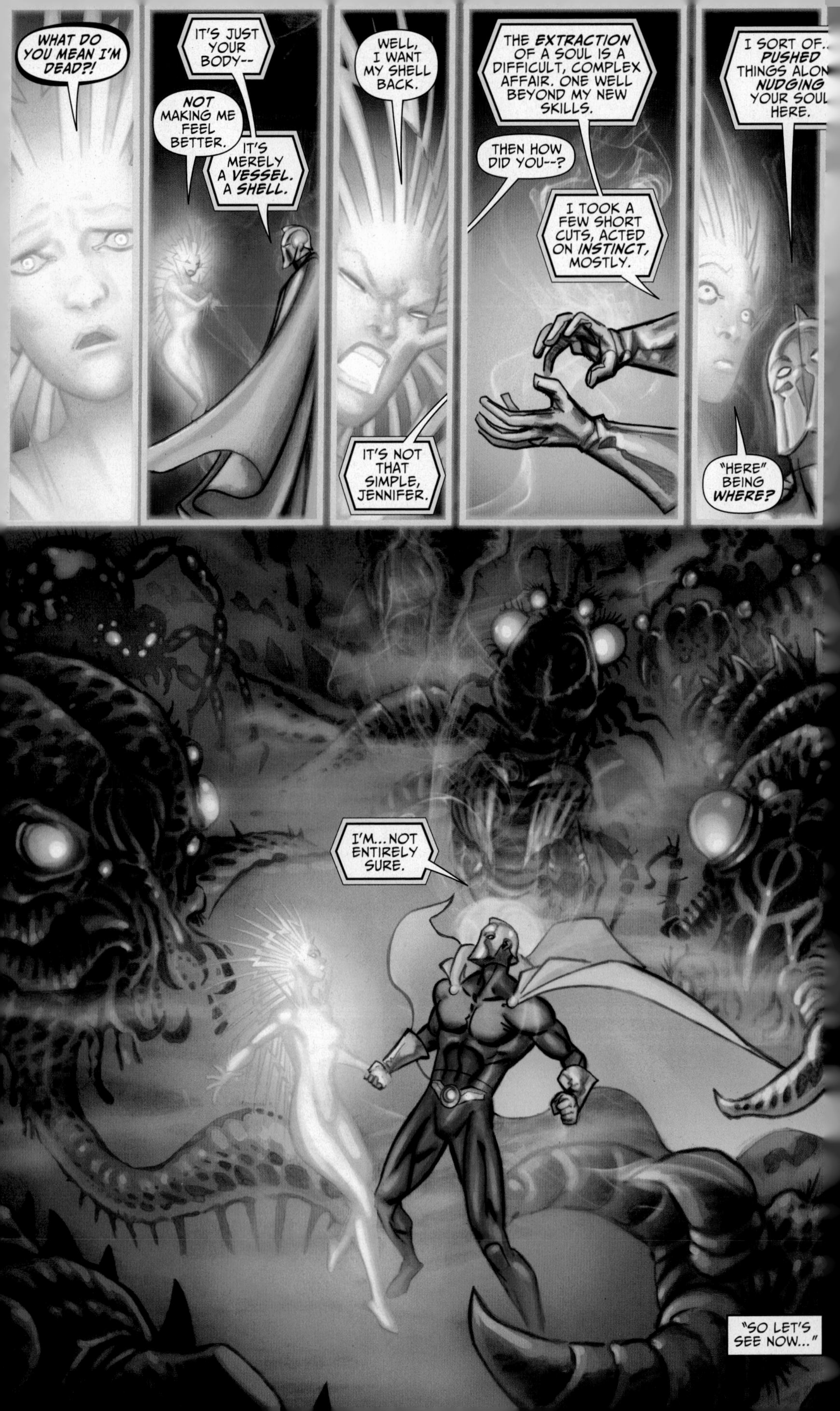
WHAT DO YOU MEAN I'M DEAD?!
IT'S JUST YOUR BODY--
NOT MAKING ME FEEL BETTER.
IT'S MERELY A VESSEL. A SHELL.
WELL, I WANT MY SHELL BACK.
IT'S NOT THAT SIMPLE, JENNIFER.
THE EXTRACTION OF A SOUL IS A DIFFICULT, COMPLEX AFFAIR. ONE WELL BEYOND MY NEW SKILLS.
THEN HOW DID YOU--?
I TOOK A FEW SHORT CUTS, ACTED ON INSTINCT, MOSTLY.
I SORT OF... PUSHED THINGS ALON NUDGING YOUR SOUL HERE.
"HERE" BEING WHERE?
I'M...NOT ENTIRELY SURE.
"SO LET'S SEE NOW..."

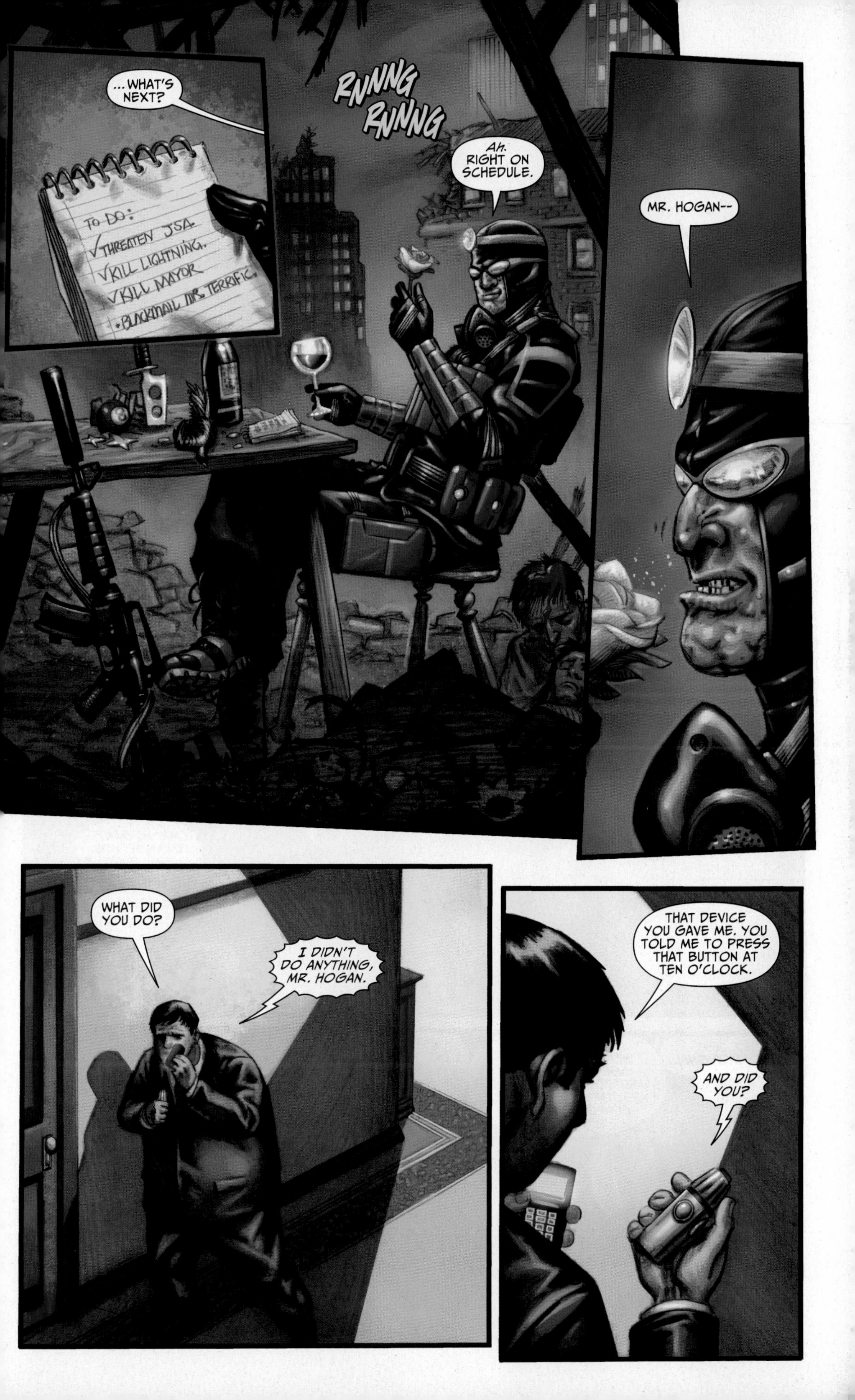

...WHAT'S NEXT?
TO DO:
✓THREATEN JSA
✓KILL LIGHTNING.
✓KILL MAYOR
•BLACKMAIL MR. TERRIFIC
RNNNG RNNNG
Ah. RIGHT ON SCHEDULE.
MR. HOGAN--
WHAT DID YOU DO?
I DIDN'T DO ANYTHING, MR. HOGAN.
THAT DEVICE YOU GAVE ME. YOU TOLD ME TO PRESS THAT BUTTON AT TEN O'CLOCK.
AND DID YOU?

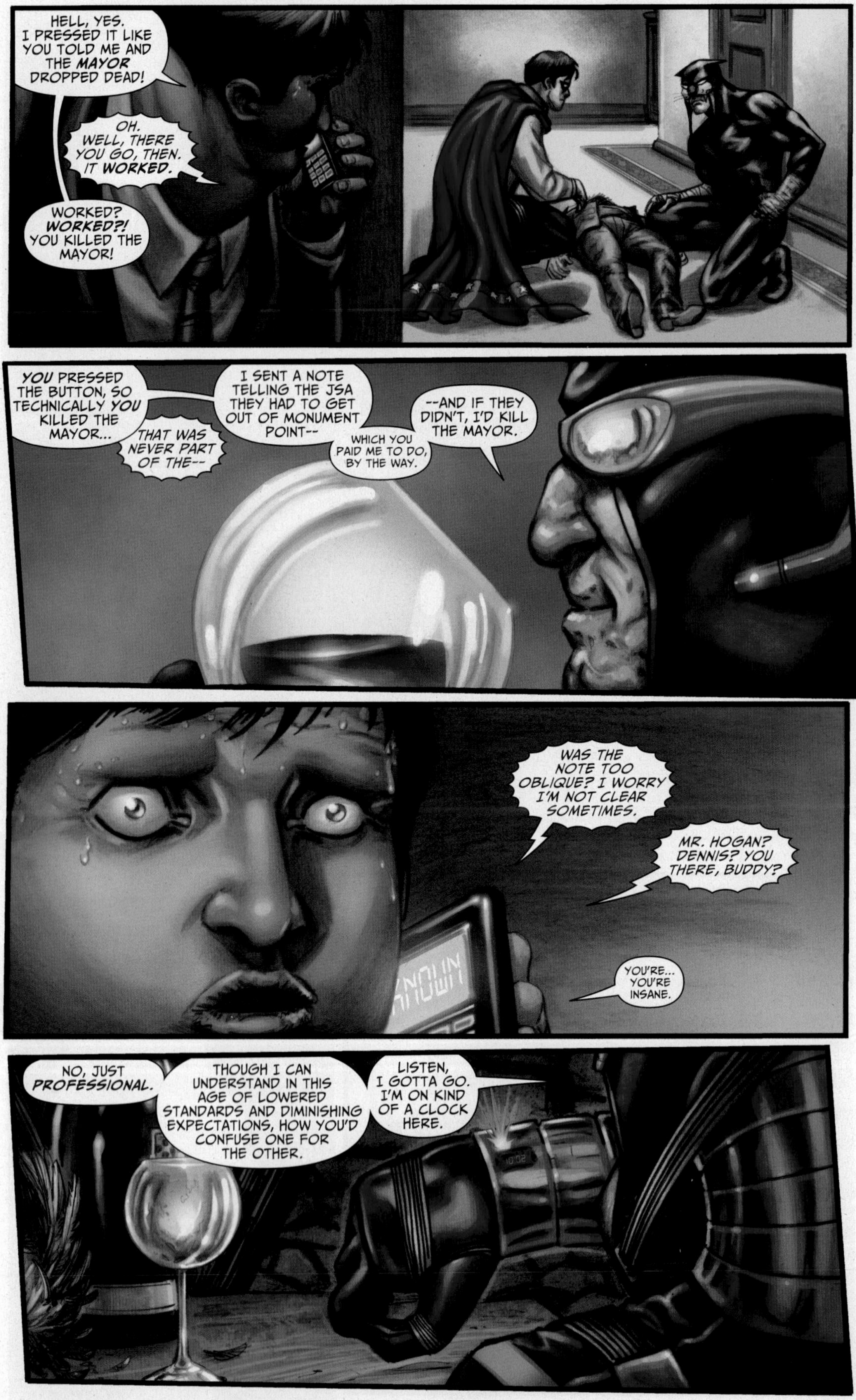
HELL, YES. I PRESSED IT LIKE YOU TOLD ME AND THE MAYOR DROPPED DEAD!
OH. WELL, THERE YOU GO, THEN. IT WORKED.
WORKED? WORKED?! YOU KILLED THE MAYOR!
YOU PRESSED THE BUTTON, SO TECHNICALLY YOU KILLED THE MAYOR...
THAT WAS NEVER PART OF THE--
I SENT A NOTE TELLING THE JSA THEY HAD TO GET OUT OF MONUMENT POINT--
WHICH YOU PAID ME TO DO, BY THE WAY.
--AND IF THEY DIDN'T, I'D KILL THE MAYOR.
WAS THE NOTE TOO OBLIQUE? I WORRY I'M NOT CLEAR SOMETIMES.
MR. HOGAN? DENNIS? YOU THERE, BUDDY?
YOU'RE... YOU'RE INSANE.
NO, JUST PROFESSIONAL.
THOUGH I CAN UNDERSTAND IN THIS AGE OF LOWERED STANDARDS AND DIMINISHING EXPECTATIONS, HOW YOU'D CONFUSE ONE FOR THE OTHER.
LISTEN, I GOTTA GO. I'M ON KIND OF A CLOCK HERE.

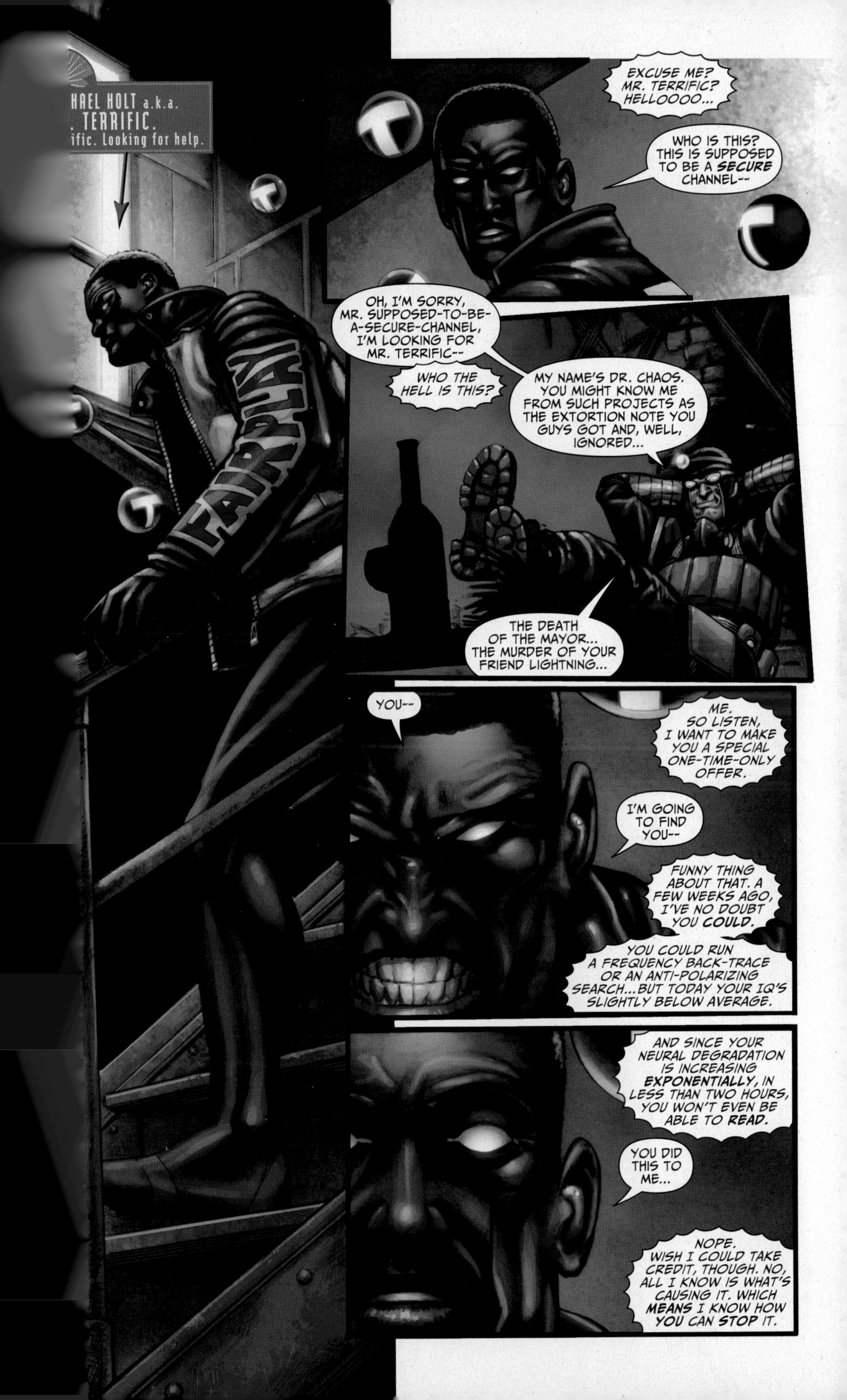
HAEL HOLT a.k.a.
. TERRIFIC.
ific. Looking for help.
EXCUSE ME? MR. TERRIFIC? HELLOOOO...
WHO IS THIS? THIS IS SUPPOSED TO BE A SECURE CHANNEL--
OH, I'M SORRY, MR. SUPPOSED-TO-BE-A-SECURE-CHANNEL, I'M LOOKING FOR MR. TERRIFIC--
WHO THE HELL IS THIS?
MY NAME'S DR. CHAOS. YOU MIGHT KNOW ME FROM SUCH PROJECTS AS THE EXTORTION NOTE YOU GUYS GOT AND, WELL, IGNORED...
THE DEATH OF THE MAYOR... THE MURDER OF YOUR FRIEND LIGHTNING...
FAIRPLAY
YOU--
ME. SO LISTEN, I WANT TO MAKE YOU A SPECIAL ONE-TIME-ONLY OFFER.
I'M GOING TO FIND YOU--
FUNNY THING ABOUT THAT. A FEW WEEKS AGO, I'VE NO DOUBT YOU COULD.
YOU COULD RUN A FREQUENCY BACK-TRACE OR AN ANTI-POLARIZING SEARCH...BUT TODAY YOUR IQ'S SLIGHTLY BELOW AVERAGE.
AND SINCE YOUR NEURAL DEGRADATION IS INCREASING EXPONENTIALLY, IN LESS THAN TWO HOURS, YOU WON'T EVEN BE ABLE TO READ.
YOU DID THIS TO ME...
NOPE. WISH I COULD TAKE CREDIT, THOUGH. NO, ALL I KNOW IS WHAT'S CAUSING IT. WHICH MEANS I KNOW HOW YOU CAN STOP IT.

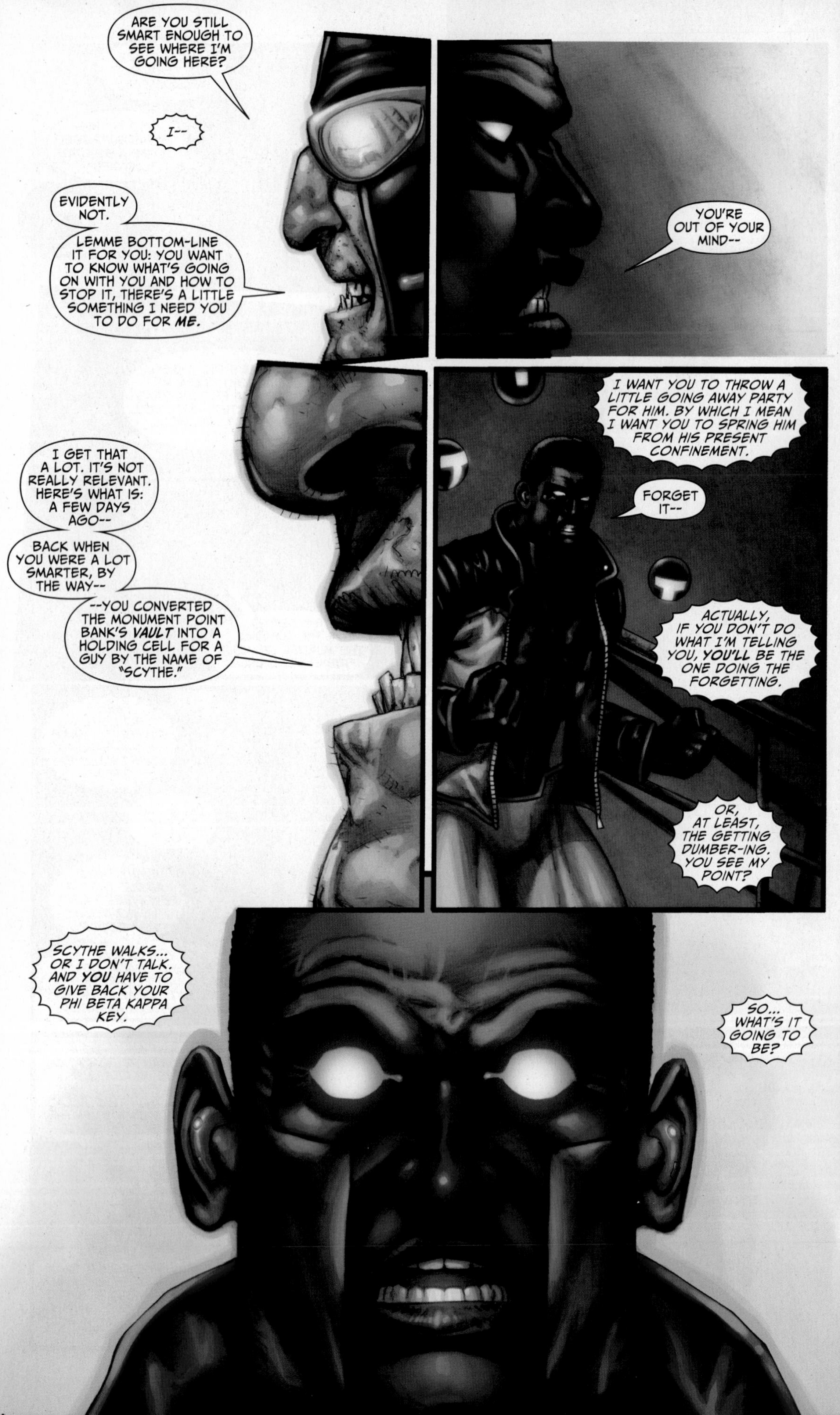
ARE YOU STILL SMART ENOUGH TO SEE WHERE I'M GOING HERE?
I--
EVIDENTLY NOT.
LEMME BOTTOM-LINE IT FOR YOU: YOU WANT TO KNOW WHAT'S GOING ON WITH YOU AND HOW TO STOP IT, THERE'S A LITTLE SOMETHING I NEED YOU TO DO FOR ME.
YOU'RE OUT OF YOUR MIND--
I GET THAT A LOT. IT'S NOT REALLY RELEVANT. HERE'S WHAT IS: A FEW DAYS AGO--
BACK WHEN YOU WERE A LOT SMARTER, BY THE WAY--
--YOU CONVERTED THE MONUMENT POINT BANK'S VAULT INTO A HOLDING CELL FOR A GUY BY THE NAME OF "SCYTHE."
I WANT YOU TO THROW A LITTLE GOING AWAY PARTY FOR HIM. BY WHICH I MEAN I WANT YOU TO SPRING HIM FROM HIS PRESENT CONFINEMENT.
FORGET IT--
ACTUALLY, IF YOU DON'T DO WHAT I'M TELLING YOU, YOU'LL BE THE ONE DOING THE FORGETTING.
OR, AT LEAST, THE GETTING DUMBER-ING. YOU SEE MY POINT?
SCYTHE WALKS... OR I DON'T TALK. AND YOU HAVE TO GIVE BACK YOUR PHI BETA KAPPA KEY.
SO... WHAT'S IT GOING TO BE?

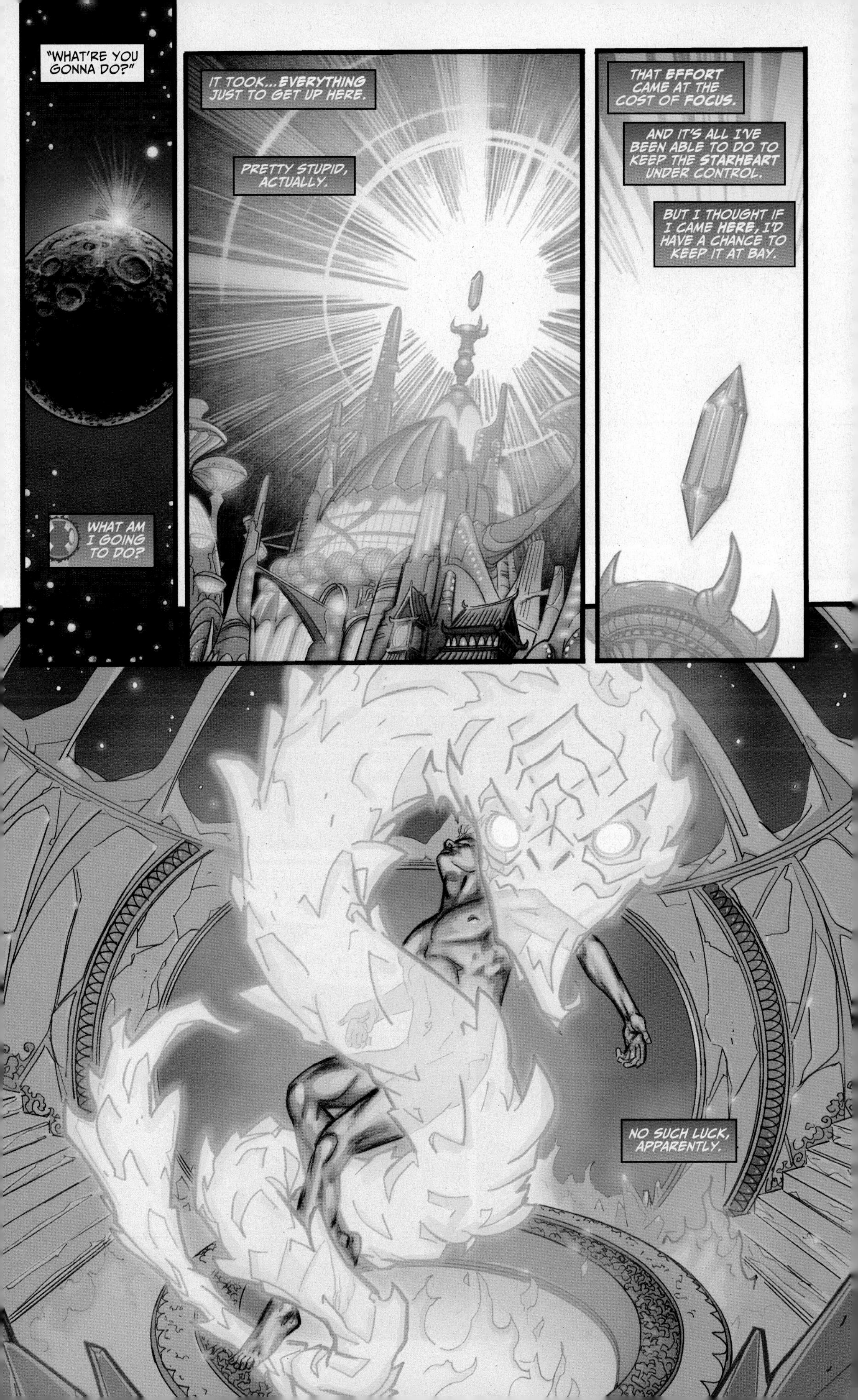
"WHAT'RE YOU GONNA DO?"
WHAT AM I GOING TO DO?
IT TOOK...EVERYTHING JUST TO GET UP HERE.
PRETTY STUPID, ACTUALLY.
THAT EFFORT CAME AT THE COST OF FOCUS.
AND IT'S ALL I'VE BEEN ABLE TO DO TO KEEP THE STARHEART UNDER CONTROL.
BUT I THOUGHT IF I CAME HERE, I'D HAVE A CHANCE TO KEEP IT AT BAY.
NO SUCH LUCK, APPARENTLY.

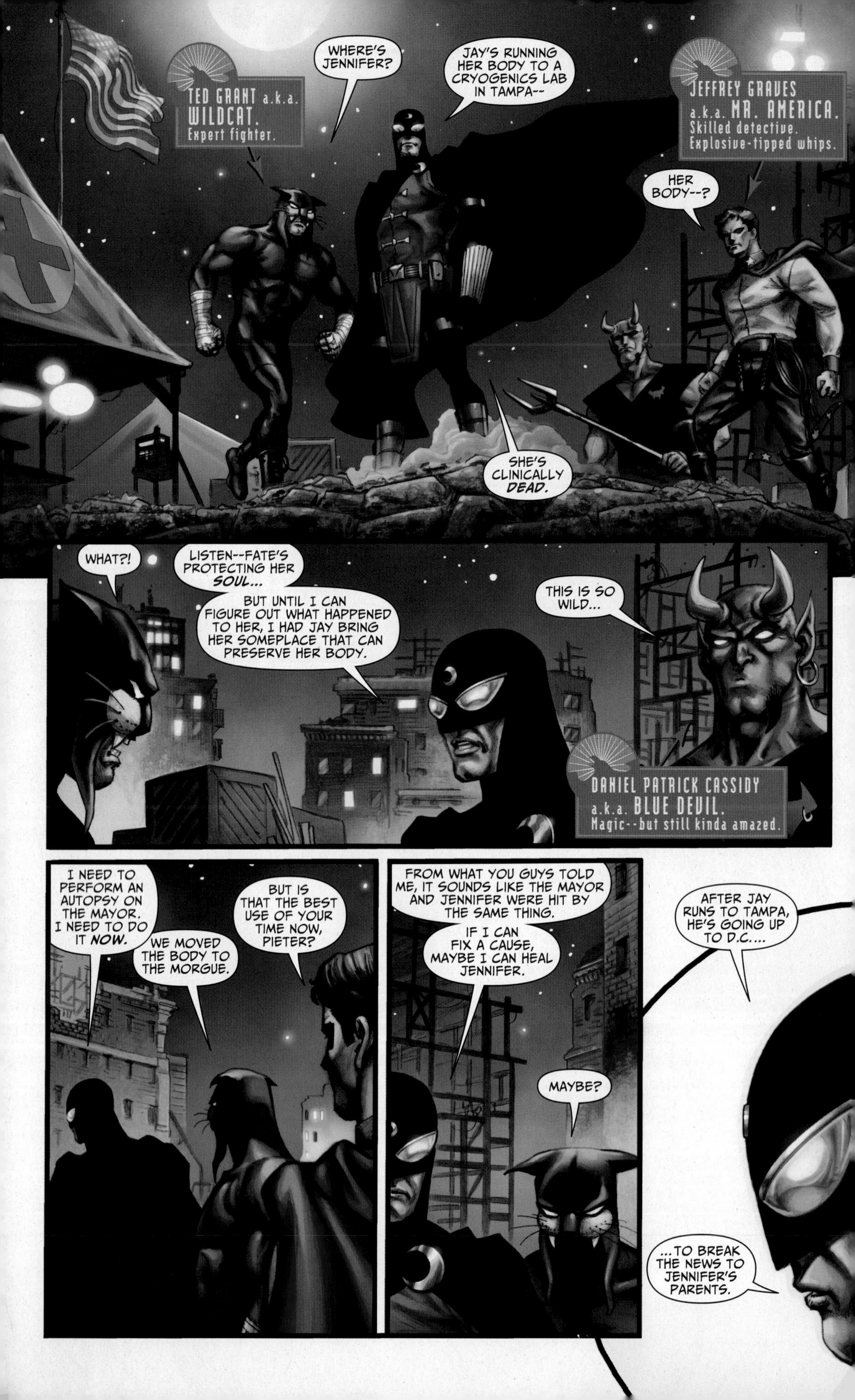
TED GRANT a.k.a. WILDCAT. Expert fighter.
WHERE'S JENNIFER?
JAY'S RUNNING HER BODY TO A CRYOGENICS LAB IN TAMPA--
JEFFREY GRAVES a.k.a. MR. AMERICA. Skilled detective. Explosive-tipped whips.
HER BODY--?
SHE'S CLINICALLY DEAD.
WHAT?!
LISTEN--FATE'S PROTECTING HER SOUL...
BUT UNTIL I CAN FIGURE OUT WHAT HAPPENED TO HER, I HAD JAY BRING HER SOMEPLACE THAT CAN PRESERVE HER BODY.
THIS IS SO WILD...
DANIEL PATRICK CASSIDY a.k.a. BLUE DEVIL. Magic--but still kinda amazed.
I NEED TO PERFORM AN AUTOPSY ON THE MAYOR. I NEED TO DO IT NOW.
WE MOVED THE BODY TO THE MORGUE.
BUT IS THAT THE BEST USE OF YOUR TIME NOW, PIETER?
FROM WHAT YOU GUYS TOLD ME, IT SOUNDS LIKE THE MAYOR AND JENNIFER WERE HIT BY THE SAME THING.
IF I CAN FIX A CAUSE, MAYBE I CAN HEAL JENNIFER.
MAYBE?
AFTER JAY RUNS TO TAMPA, HE'S GOING UP TO D.C....
...TO BREAK THE NEWS TO JENNIFER'S PARENTS.

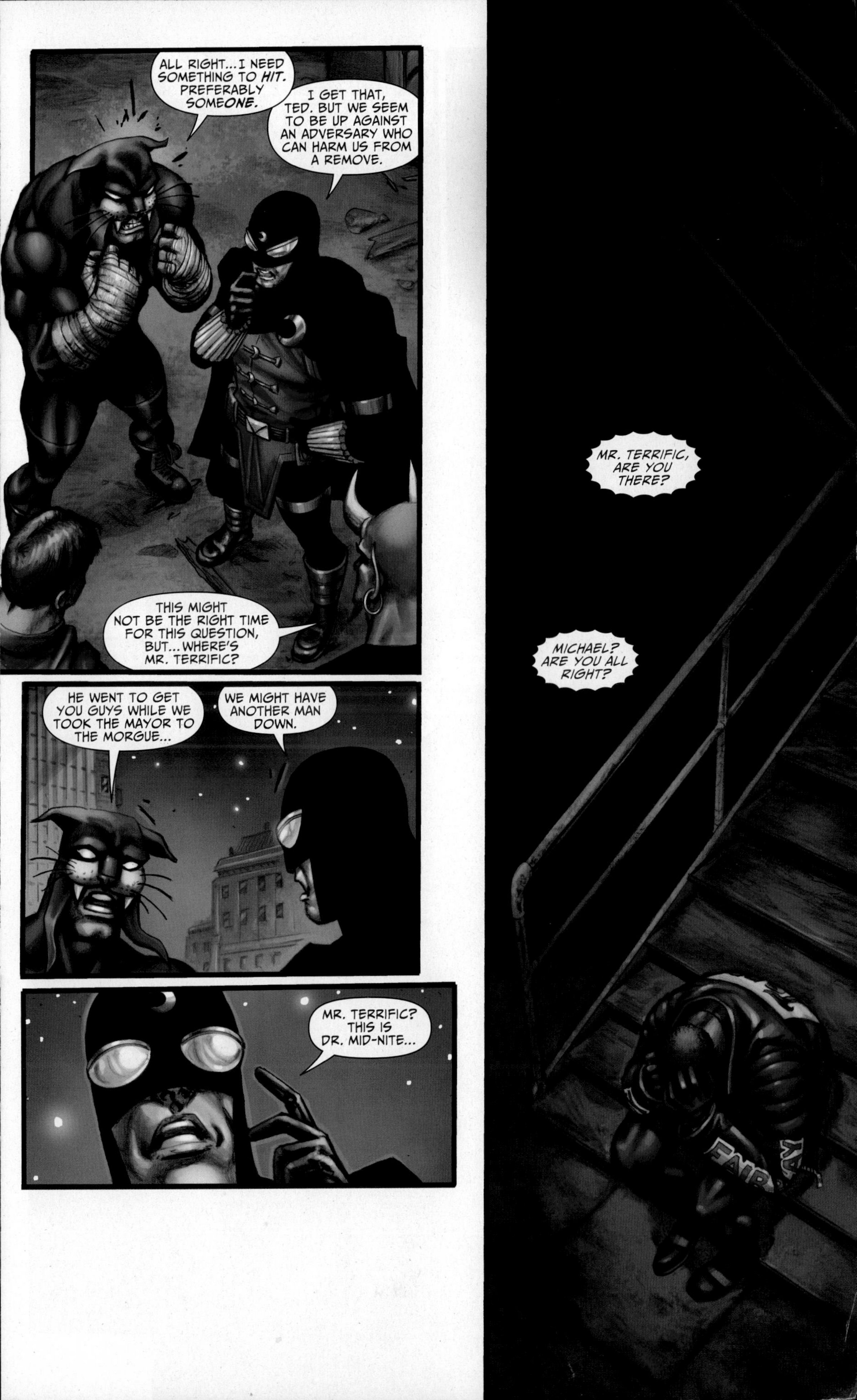
ALL RIGHT... I NEED SOMETHING TO HIT. PREFERABLY SOMEONE.
I GET THAT, TED. BUT WE SEEM TO BE UP AGAINST AN ADVERSARY WHO CAN HARM US FROM A REMOVE.
THIS MIGHT NOT BE THE RIGHT TIME FOR THIS QUESTION, BUT... WHERE'S MR. TERRIFIC?
HE WENT TO GET YOU GUYS WHILE WE TOOK THE MAYOR TO THE MORGUE...
WE MIGHT HAVE ANOTHER MAN DOWN.
MR. TERRIFIC? THIS IS DR. MID-NITE...
MR. TERRIFIC, ARE YOU THERE?
MICHAEL? ARE YOU ALL RIGHT?
FAIR

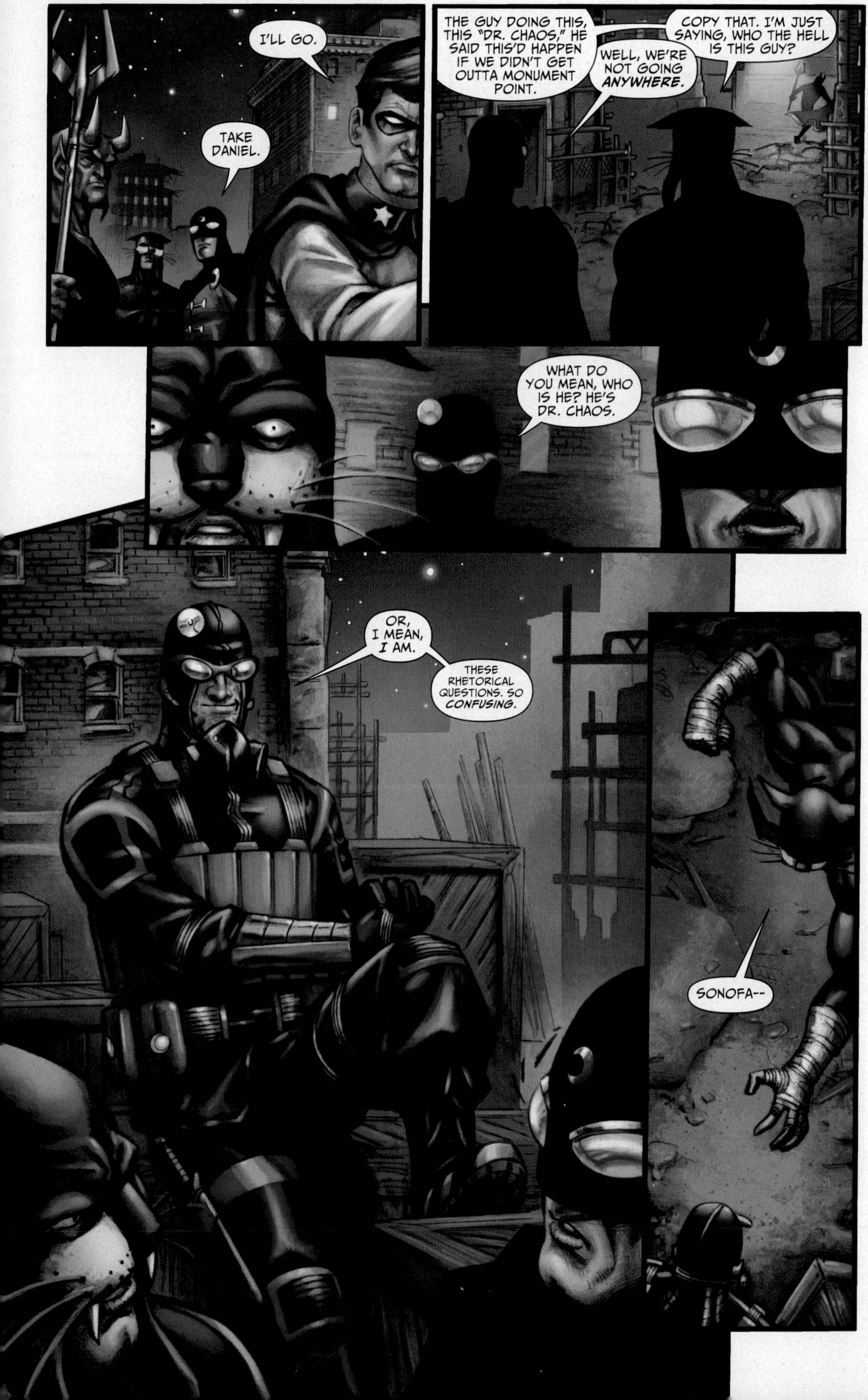
I'LL GO.
TAKE DANIEL.
THE GUY DOING THIS, THIS "DR. CHAOS," HE SAID THIS'D HAPPEN IF WE DIDN'T GET OUTTA MONUMENT POINT.
COPY THAT. I'M JUST SAYING, WHO THE HELL IS THIS GUY?
WELL, WE'RE NOT GOING *ANYWHERE.*
WHAT DO YOU MEAN, WHO IS HE? HE'S DR. CHAOS.
OR, I MEAN, *I* AM.
THESE RHETORICAL QUESTIONS. SO *CONFUSING.*
SONOFA--

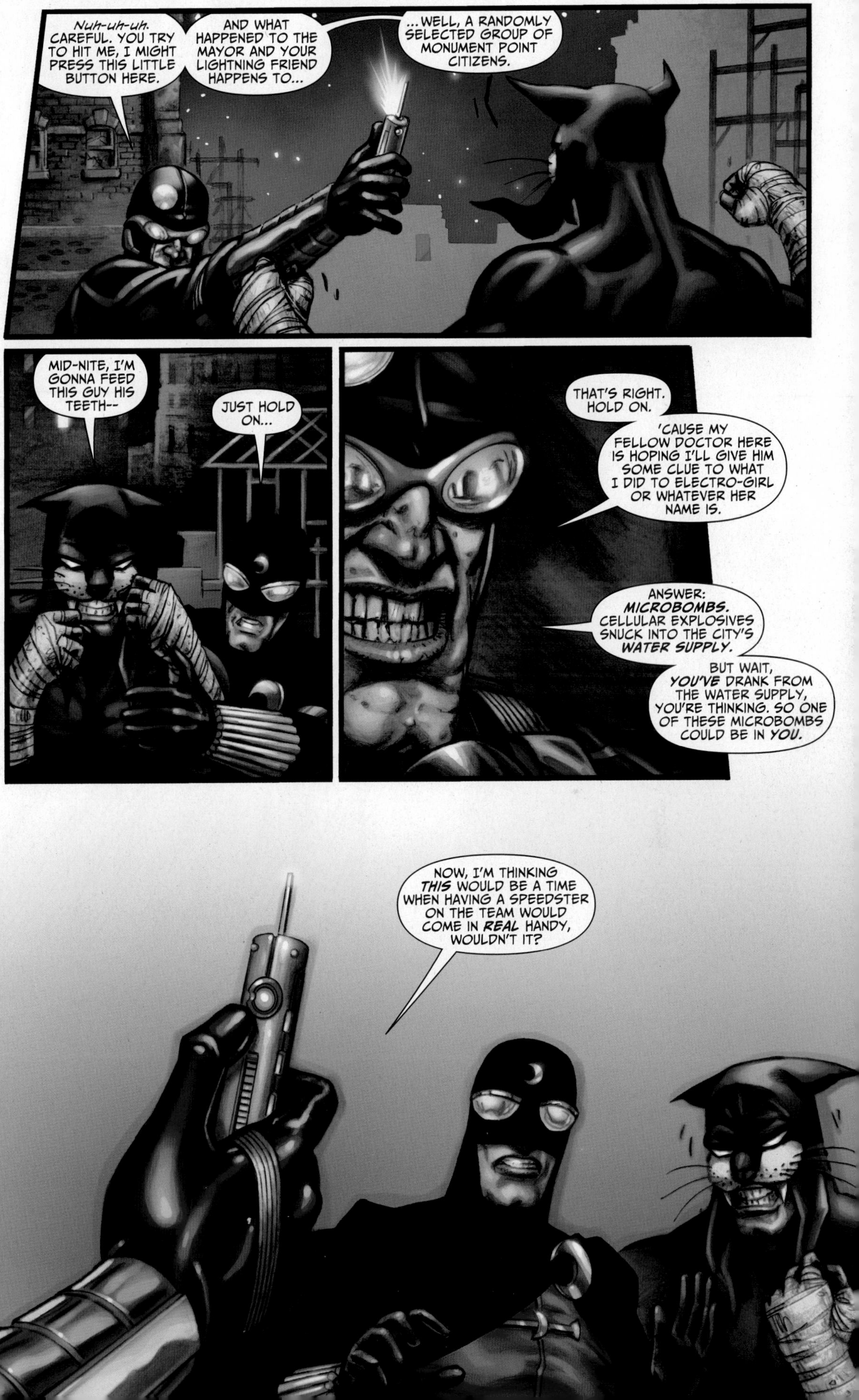
Nuh-uh-uh. CAREFUL. YOU TRY TO HIT ME, I MIGHT PRESS THIS LITTLE BUTTON HERE.
AND WHAT HAPPENED TO THE MAYOR AND YOUR LIGHTNING FRIEND HAPPENS TO...
...WELL, A RANDOMLY SELECTED GROUP OF MONUMENT POINT CITIZENS.
MID-NITE, I'M GONNA FEED THIS GUY HIS TEETH--
JUST HOLD ON...
THAT'S RIGHT. HOLD ON.
'CAUSE MY FELLOW DOCTOR HERE IS HOPING I'LL GIVE HIM SOME CLUE TO WHAT I DID TO ELECTRO-GIRL OR WHATEVER HER NAME IS.
ANSWER: ***MICROBOMBS.*** CELLULAR EXPLOSIVES SNUCK INTO THE CITY'S ***WATER SUPPLY.***
BUT WAIT, ***YOU'VE*** DRANK FROM THE WATER SUPPLY, YOU'RE THINKING. SO ONE OF THESE MICROBOMBS COULD BE IN ***YOU.***
NOW, I'M THINKING ***THIS*** WOULD BE A TIME WHEN HAVING A SPEEDSTER ON THE TEAM WOULD COME IN ***REAL*** HANDY, WOULDN'T IT?

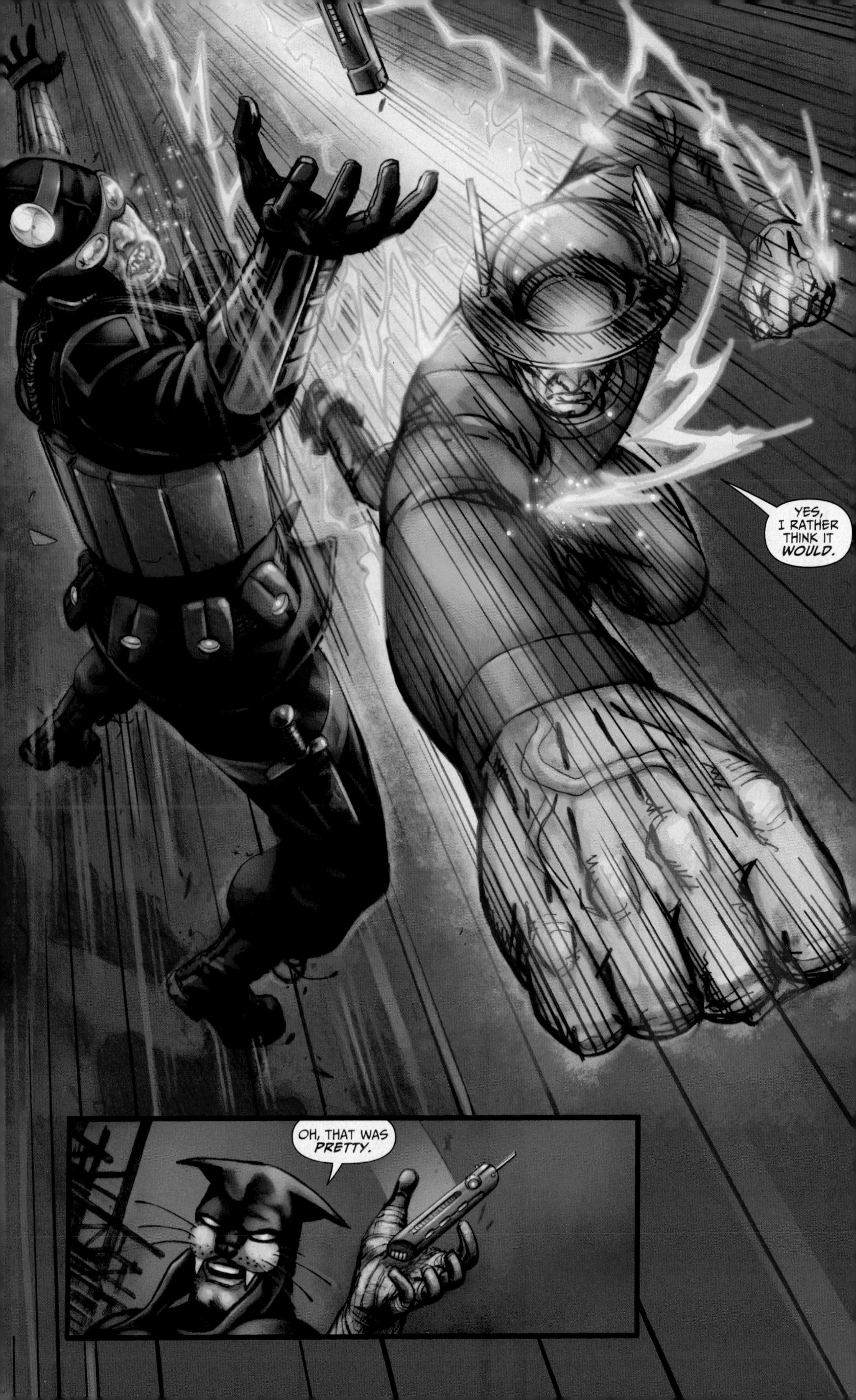
YES, I RATHER THINK IT WOULD.
OH, THAT WAS PRETTY.

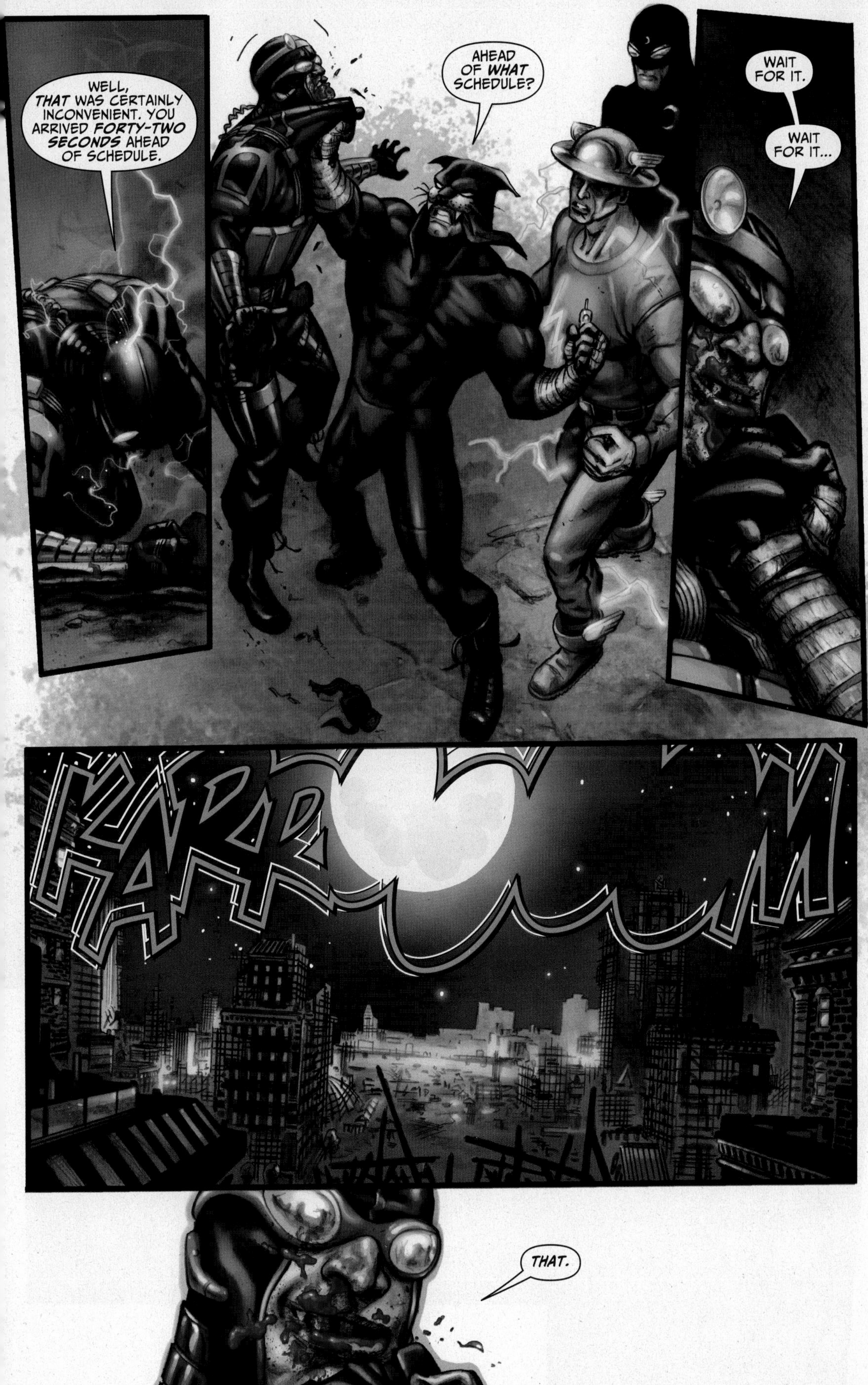

WELL, THAT WAS CERTAINLY INCONVENIENT. YOU ARRIVED FORTY-TWO SECONDS AHEAD OF SCHEDULE.
AHEAD OF WHAT SCHEDULE?
WAIT FOR IT.
WAIT FOR IT...
KAPOOOM
THAT.

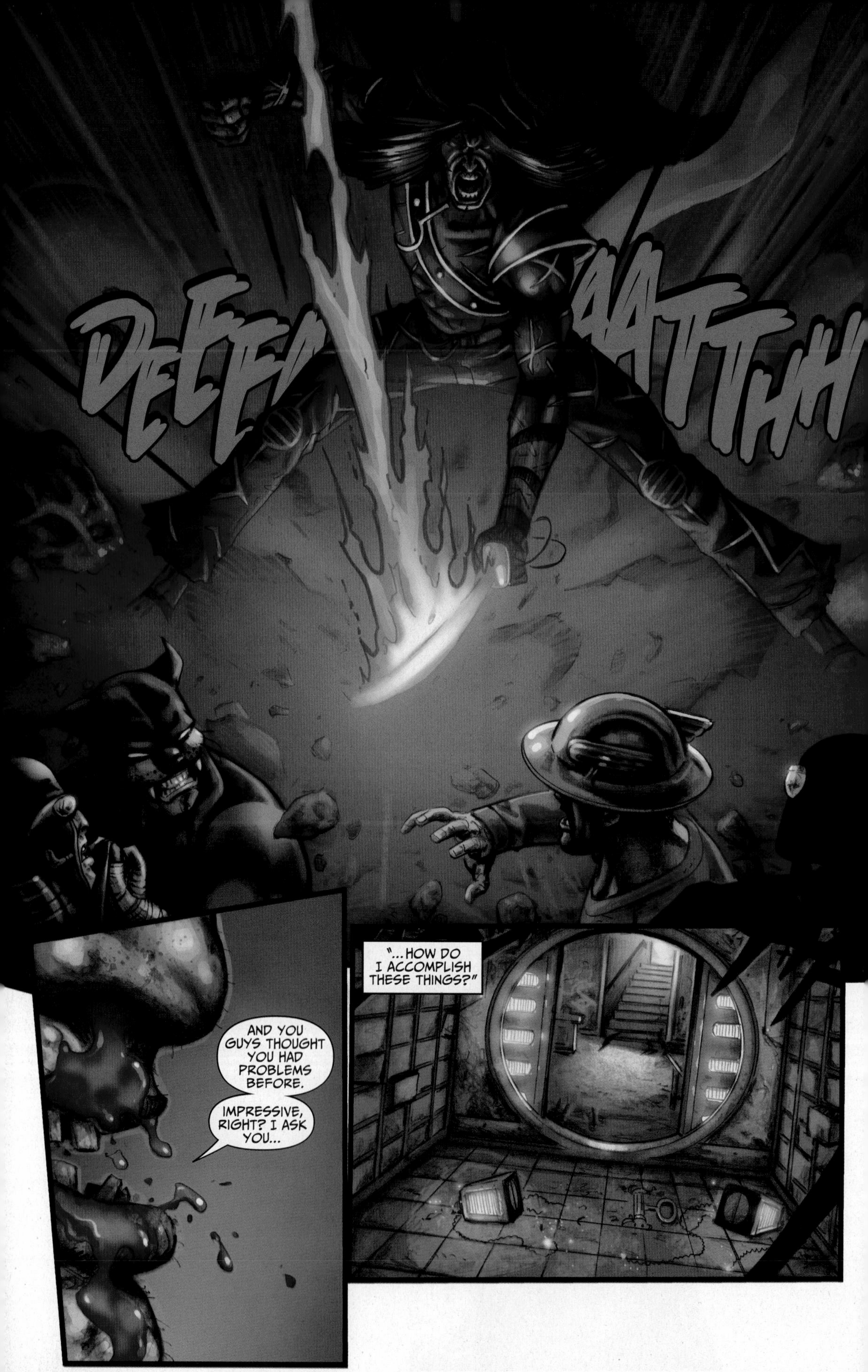
DEEEA
AAATTTHH
AND YOU GUYS THOUGHT YOU HAD PROBLEMS BEFORE.
IMPRESSIVE, RIGHT? I ASK YOU...
"...HOW DO I ACCOMPLISH THESE THINGS?"

SUPERTOWN Part Five

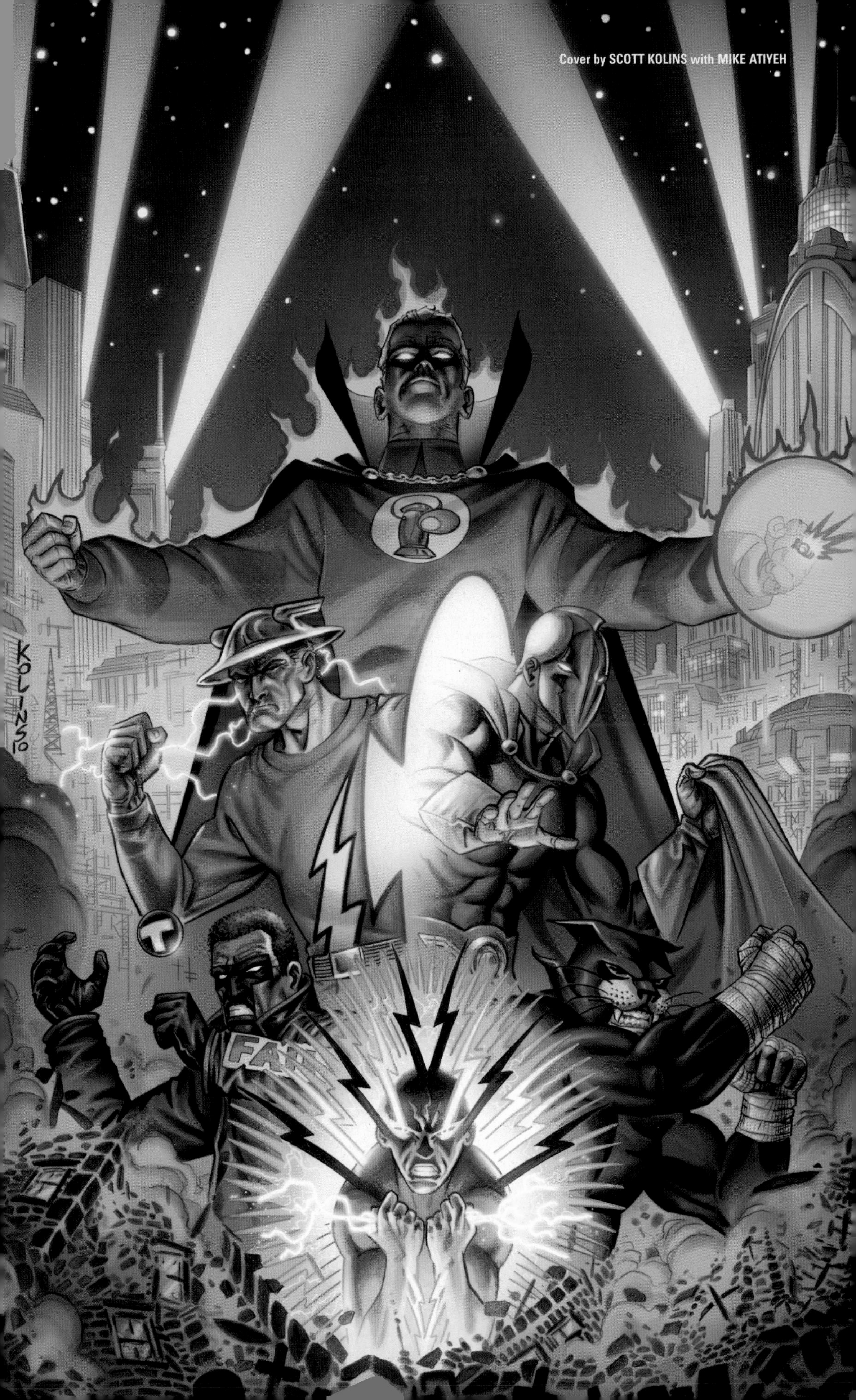

Cover by SCOTT KOLINS with MIKE ATIYEH

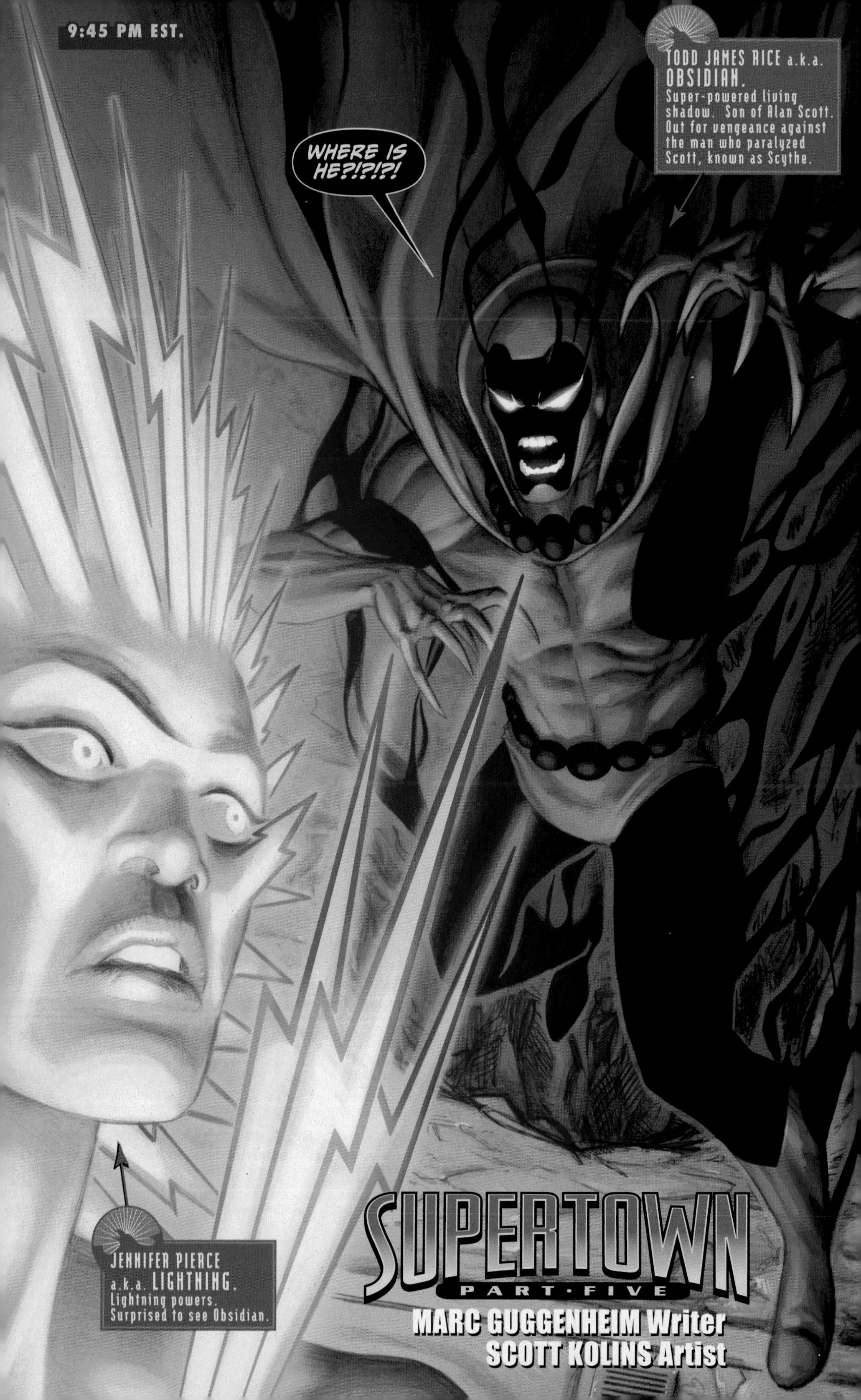
9:45 PM EST.
TODD JAMES RICE a.k.a. OBSIDIAN. Super-powered living shadow. Son of Alan Scott. Out for vengeance against the man who paralyzed Scott, known as Scythe.
WHERE IS HE?!?!?!
JENNIFER PIERCE a.k.a. LIGHTNING. Lightning powers. Surprised to see Obsidian.
SUPERTOWN
PART·FIVE
MARC GUGGENHEIM Writer
SCOTT KOLINS Artist

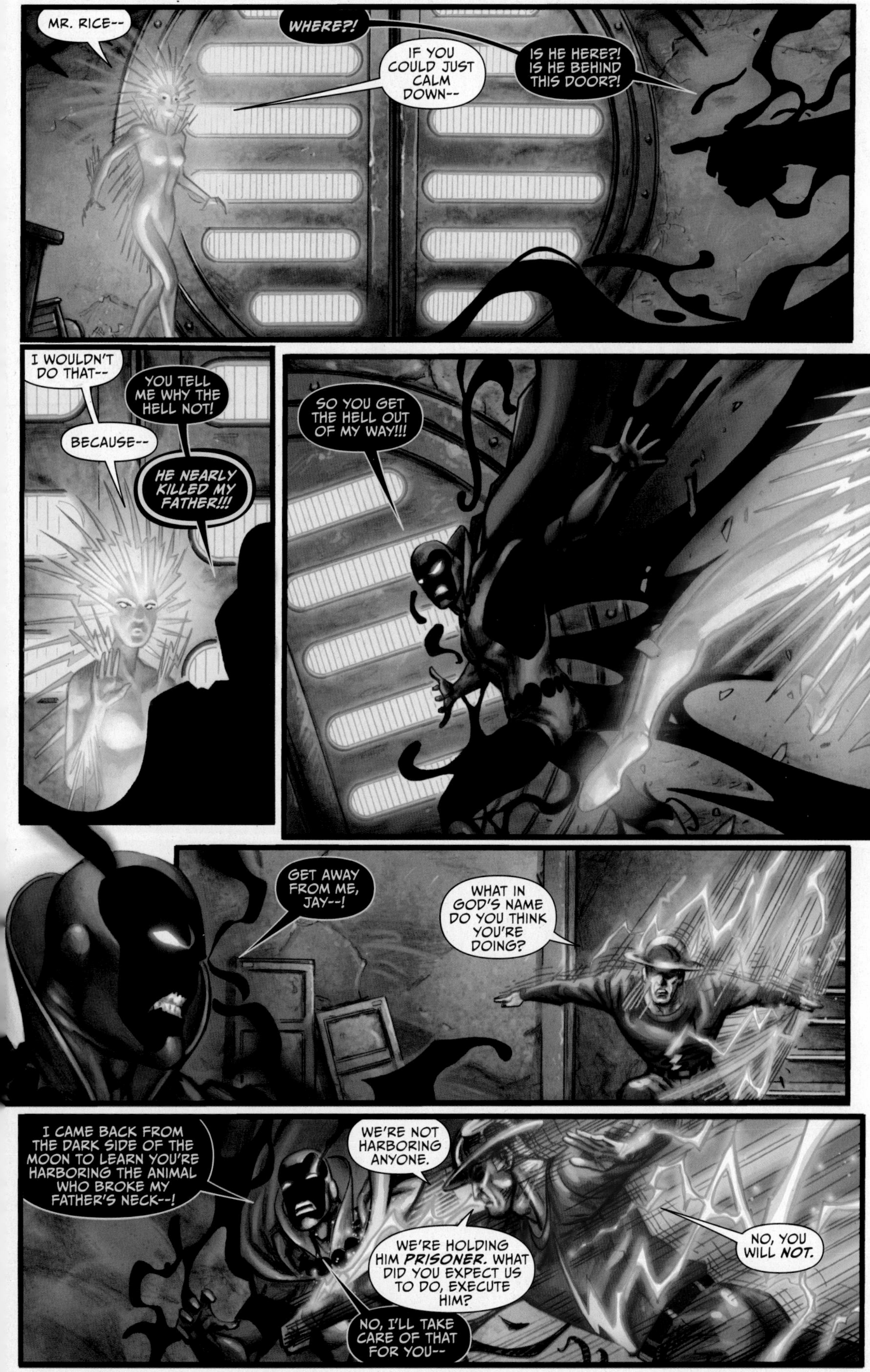
MR. RICE--
WHERE?!
IF YOU COULD JUST CALM DOWN--
IS HE HERE?! IS HE BEHIND THIS DOOR?!
I WOULDN'T DO THAT--
YOU TELL ME WHY THE HELL NOT!
BECAUSE--
HE NEARLY KILLED MY FATHER!!!
SO YOU GET THE HELL OUT OF MY WAY!!!
GET AWAY FROM ME, JAY--!
WHAT IN GOD'S NAME DO YOU THINK YOU'RE DOING?
I CAME BACK FROM THE DARK SIDE OF THE MOON TO LEARN YOU'RE HARBORING THE ANIMAL WHO BROKE MY FATHER'S NECK--!
WE'RE NOT HARBORING ANYONE.
WE'RE HOLDING HIM PRISONER. WHAT DID YOU EXPECT US TO DO, EXECUTE HIM?
NO, I'LL TAKE CARE OF THAT FOR YOU--
NO, YOU WILL NOT.

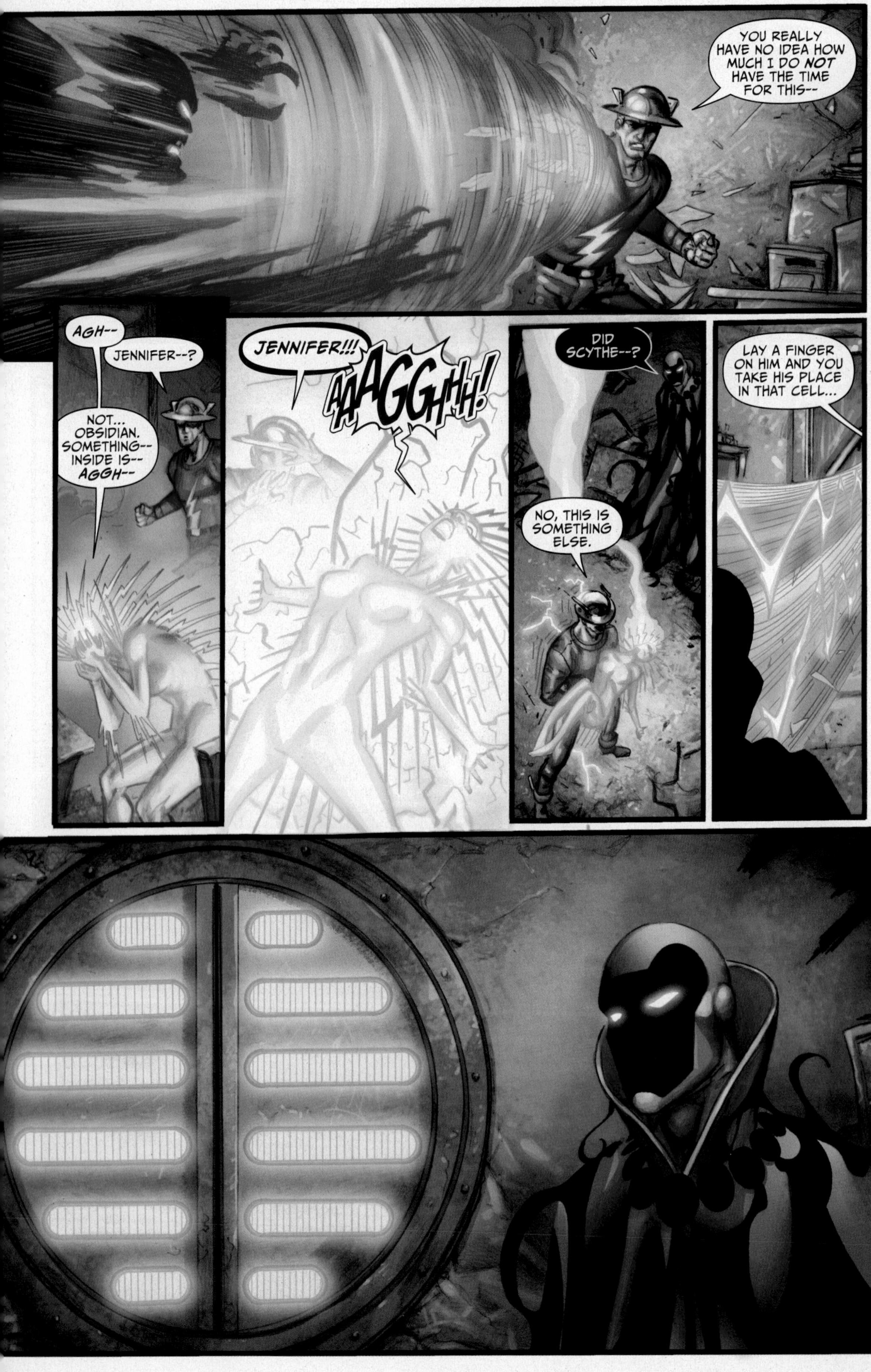
YOU REALLY HAVE NO IDEA HOW MUCH I DO NOT HAVE THE TIME FOR THIS--
AGH--
JENNIFER--?
NOT... OBSIDIAN. SOMETHING-- INSIDE IS-- AGGH--
JENNIFER!!!
AAAGGHHH!
DID SCYTHE--?
NO, THIS IS SOMETHING ELSE.
LAY A FINGER ON HIM AND YOU TAKE HIS PLACE IN THAT CELL...

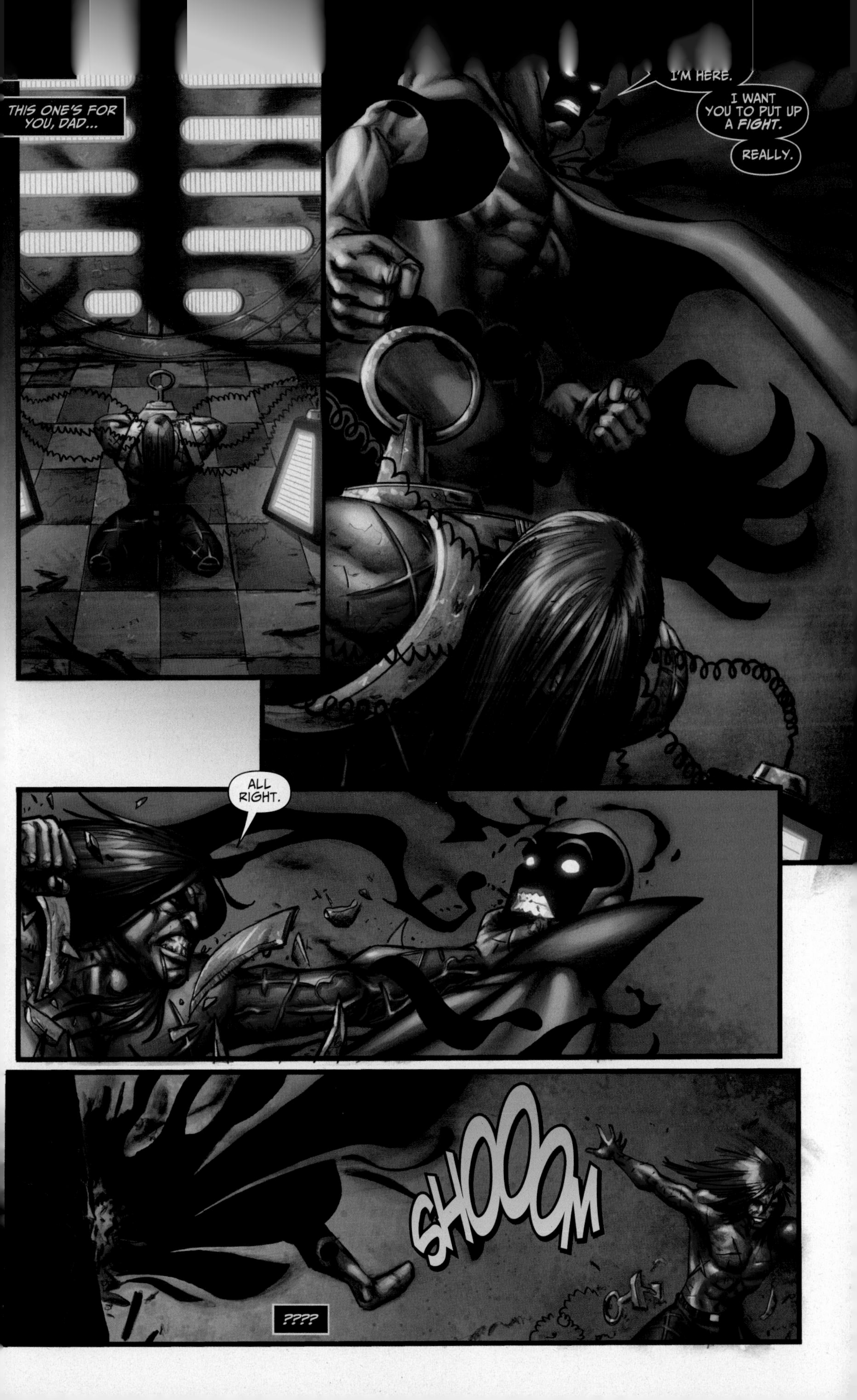
THIS ONE'S FOR YOU, DAD...
I'M HERE.
I WANT YOU TO PUT UP A FIGHT.
REALLY.
ALL RIGHT.
SHOOOM
????

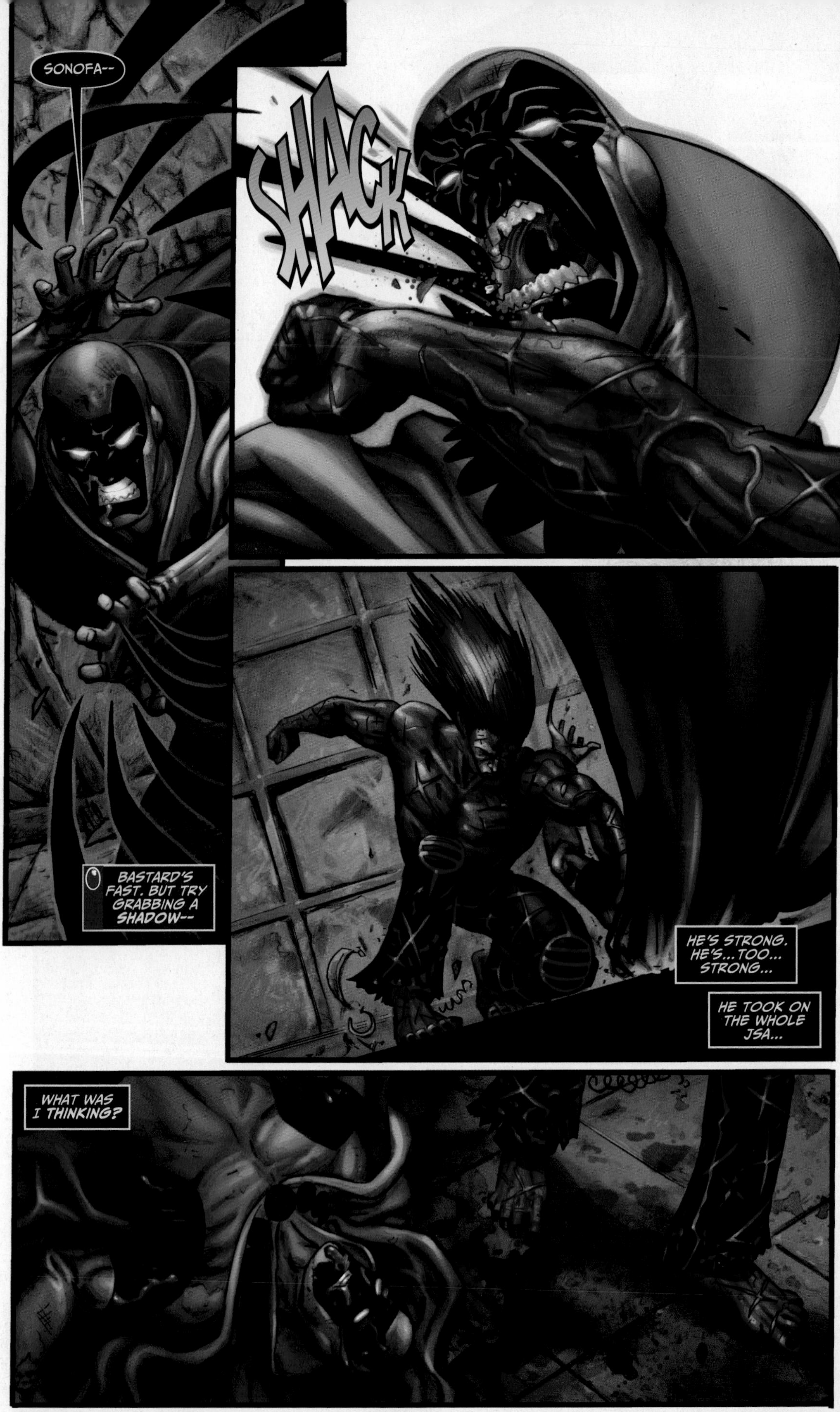
SONOFA--
SHACK
BASTARD'S FAST. BUT TRY GRABBING A SHADOW--
HE'S STRONG. HE'S...TOO... STRONG...
HE TOOK ON THE WHOLE JSA...
WHAT WAS I THINKING?

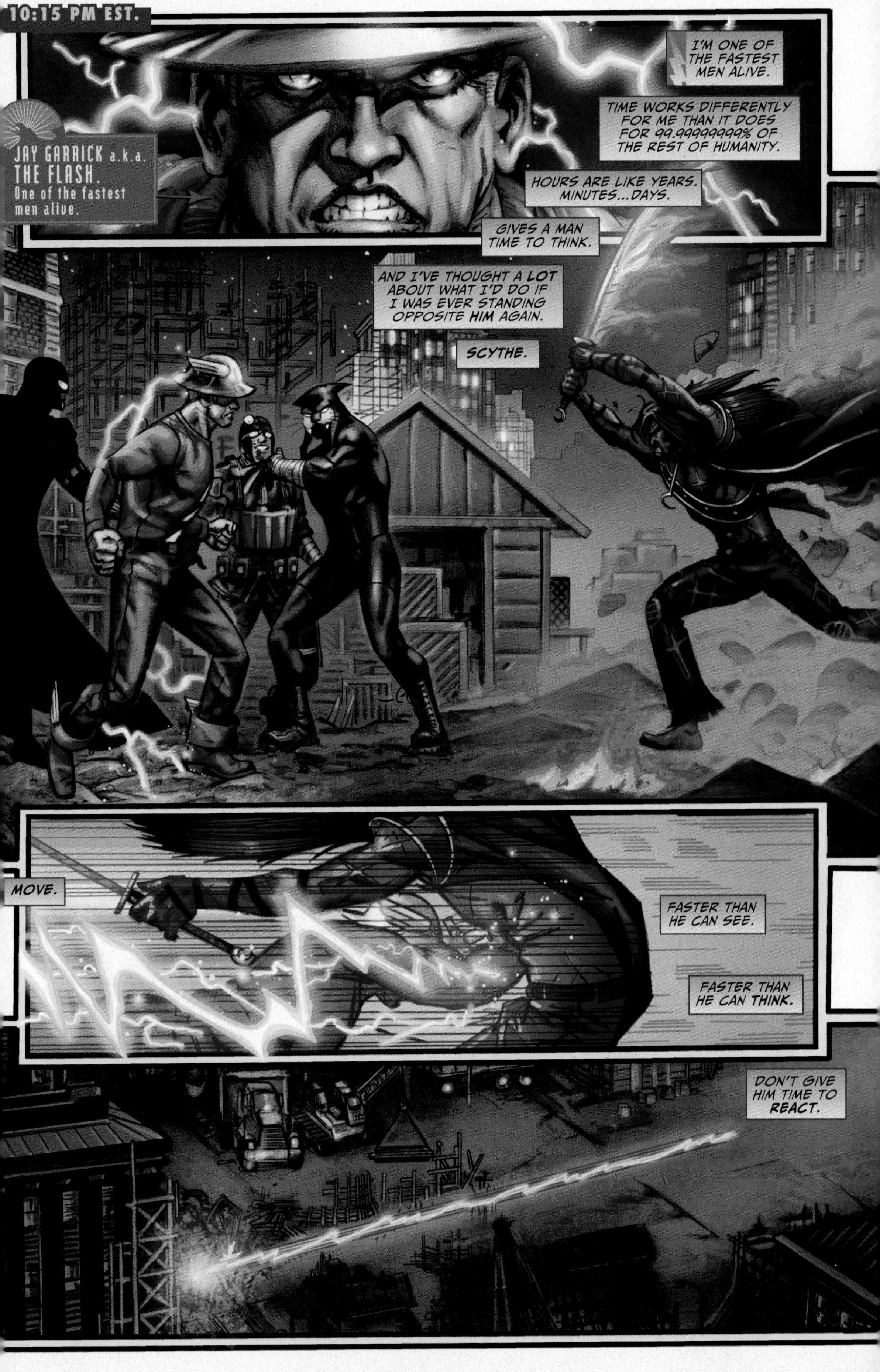
10:15 PM EST.
JAY GARRICK a.k.a. THE FLASH. One of the fastest men alive.
I'M ONE OF THE FASTEST MEN ALIVE.
TIME WORKS DIFFERENTLY FOR ME THAN IT DOES FOR 99.99999999% OF THE REST OF HUMANITY.
HOURS ARE LIKE YEARS. MINUTES...DAYS.
GIVES A MAN TIME TO THINK.
AND I'VE THOUGHT A LOT ABOUT WHAT I'D DO IF I WAS EVER STANDING OPPOSITE HIM AGAIN.
SCYTHE.
MOVE.
FASTER THAN HE CAN SEE.
FASTER THAN HE CAN THINK.
DON'T GIVE HIM TIME TO REACT.

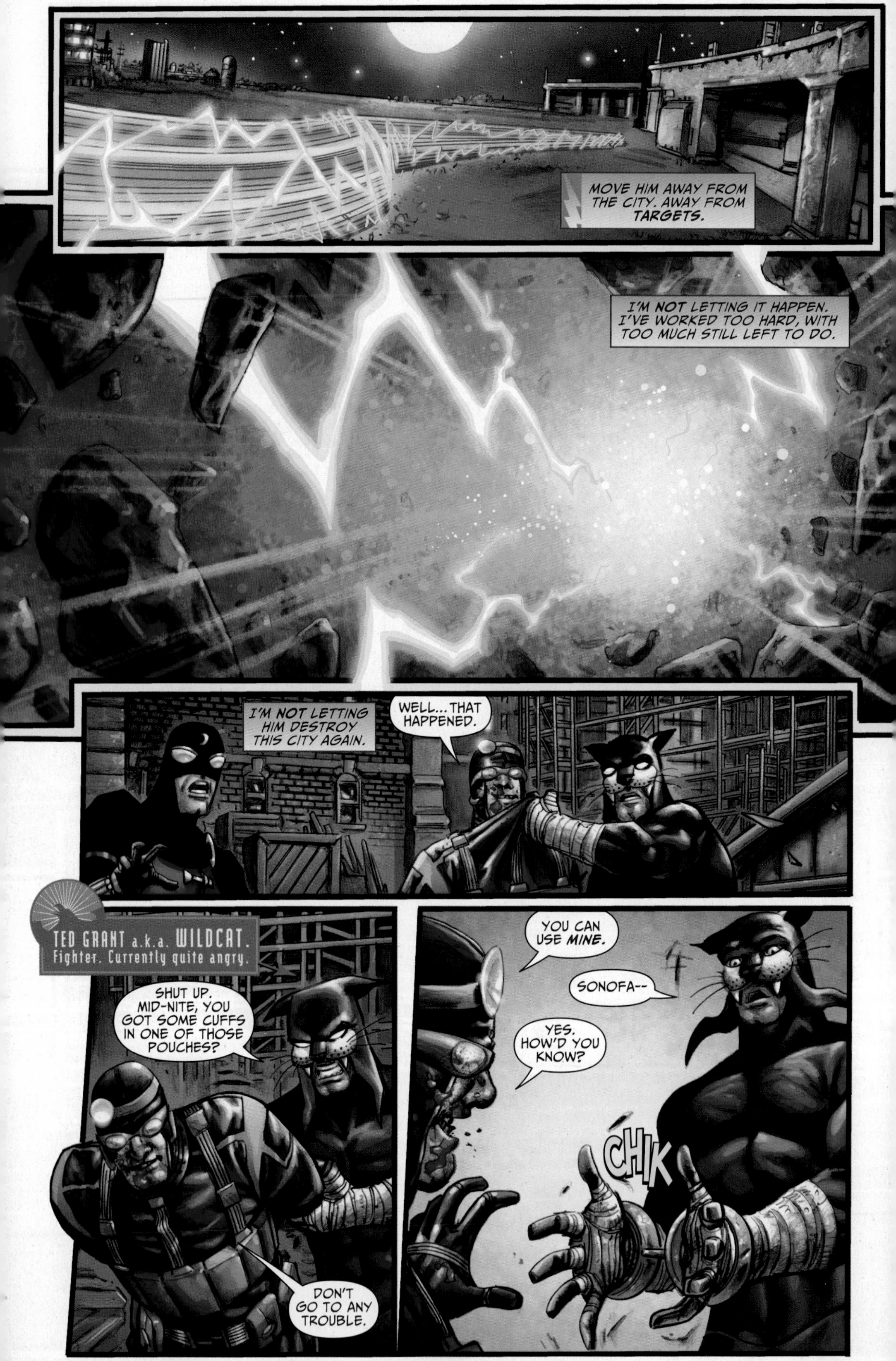
MOVE HIM AWAY FROM THE CITY. AWAY FROM **TARGETS.**
I'M **NOT** LETTING IT HAPPEN. I'VE WORKED TOO HARD, WITH TOO MUCH STILL LEFT TO DO.
I'M **NOT** LETTING HIM DESTROY THIS CITY AGAIN.
WELL... THAT HAPPENED.
TED GRANT a.k.a. WILDCAT.
Fighter. Currently quite angry.
SHUT UP. MID-NITE, YOU GOT SOME CUFFS IN ONE OF THOSE POUCHES?
DON'T GO TO ANY TROUBLE.
YOU CAN USE **MINE.**
SONOFA--
YES. HOW'D YOU KNOW?
CHIK

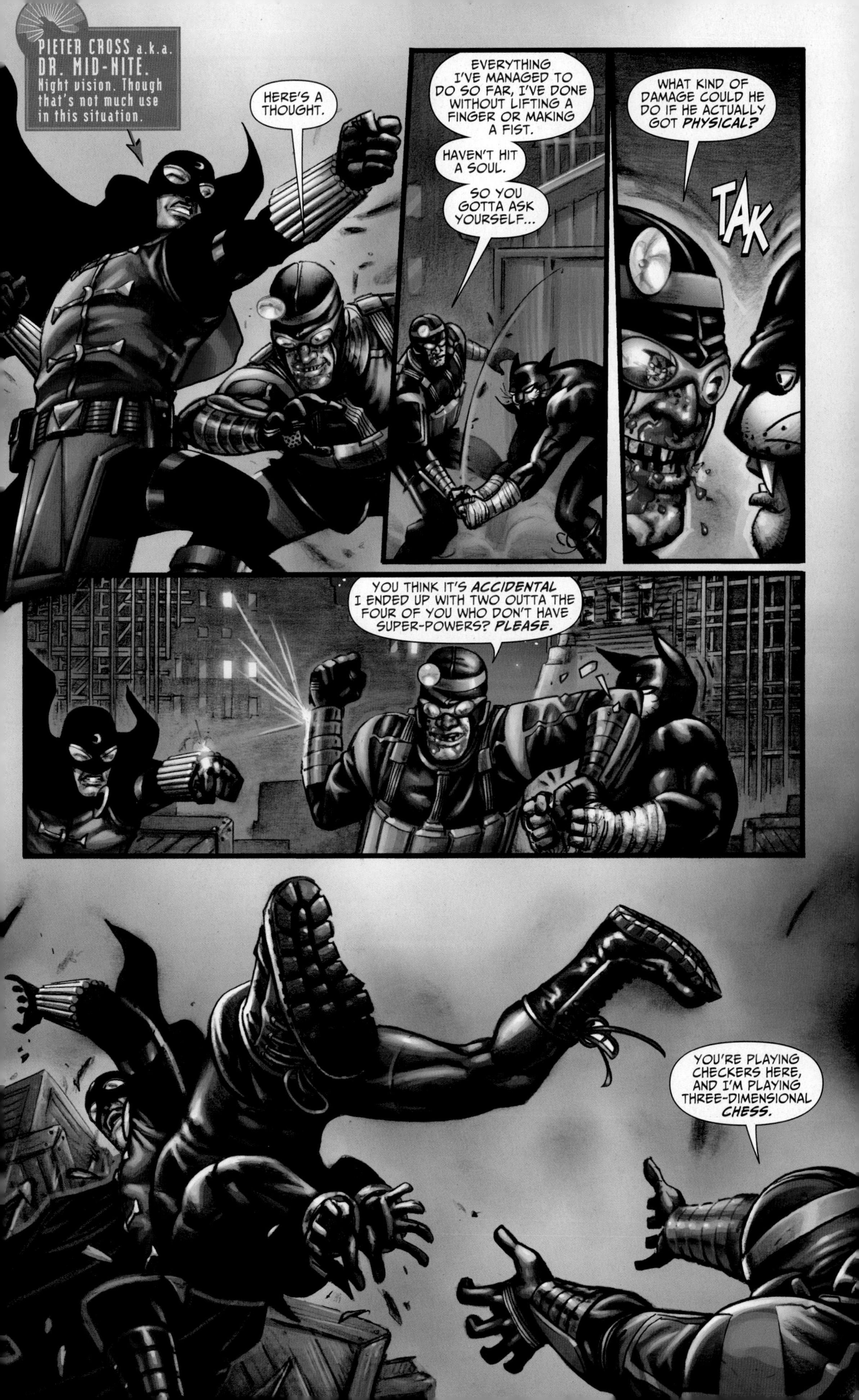
PIETER CROSS a.k.a. DR. MID-NITE. Night vision. Though that's not much use in this situation.
HERE'S A THOUGHT.
EVERYTHING I'VE MANAGED TO DO SO FAR, I'VE DONE WITHOUT LIFTING A FINGER OR MAKING A FIST.
HAVEN'T HIT A SOUL.
SO YOU GOTTA ASK YOURSELF...
WHAT KIND OF DAMAGE COULD HE DO IF HE ACTUALLY GOT PHYSICAL?
TAK
YOU THINK IT'S ACCIDENTAL I ENDED UP WITH TWO OUTTA THE FOUR OF YOU WHO DON'T HAVE SUPER-POWERS? PLEASE.
YOU'RE PLAYING CHECKERS HERE, AND I'M PLAYING THREE-DIMENSIONAL CHESS.

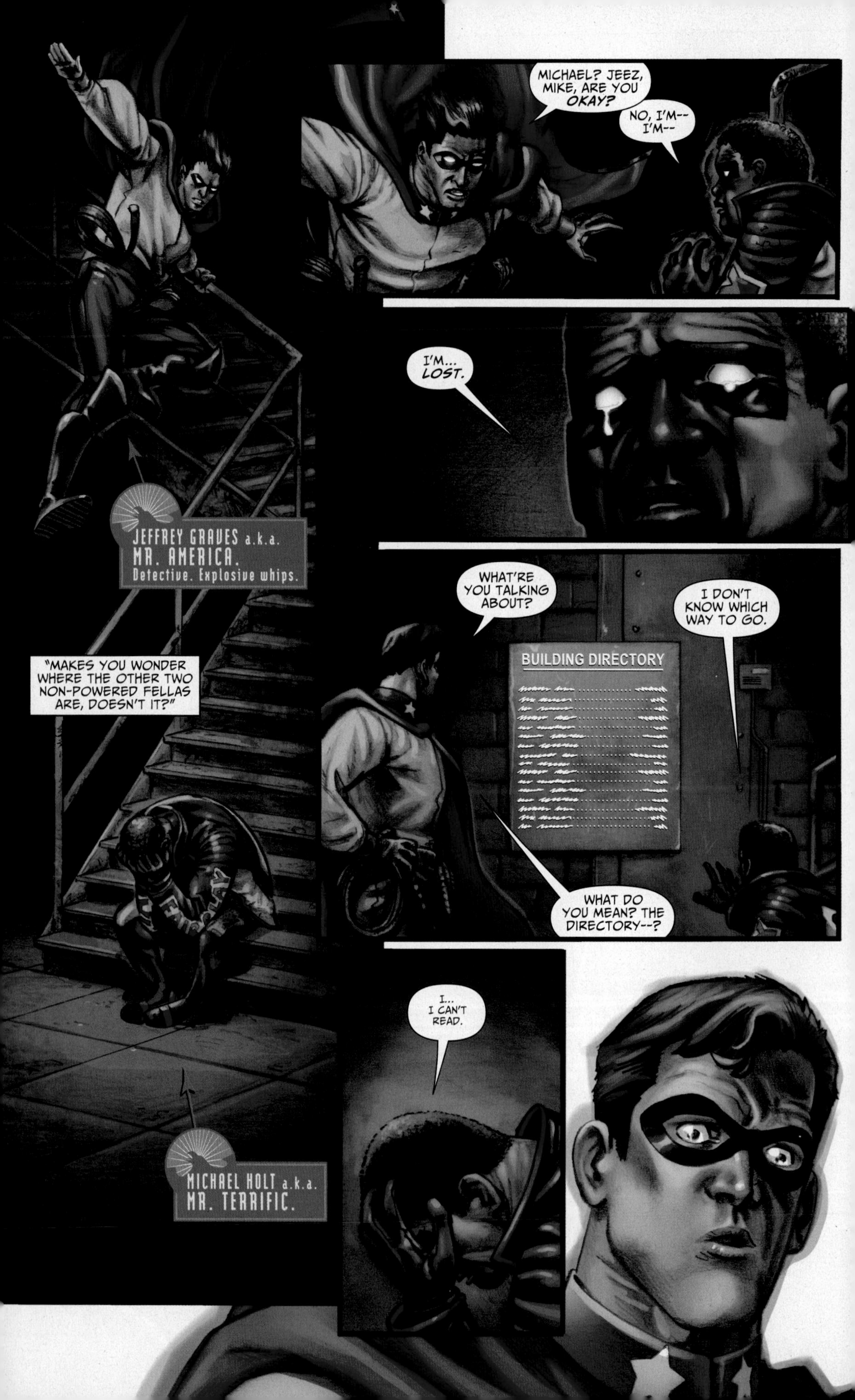
JEFFREY GRAVES a.k.a.
MR. AMERICA.
Detective. Explosive whips.
"MAKES YOU WONDER WHERE THE OTHER TWO NON-POWERED FELLAS ARE, DOESN'T IT?"
MICHAEL HOLT a.k.a.
MR. TERRIFIC.
MICHAEL? JEEZ, MIKE, ARE YOU OKAY?
NO, I'M-- I'M--
I'M... LOST.
WHAT'RE YOU TALKING ABOUT?
I DON'T KNOW WHICH WAY TO GO.
BUILDING DIRECTORY
WHAT DO YOU MEAN? THE DIRECTORY--?
I... I CAN'T READ.

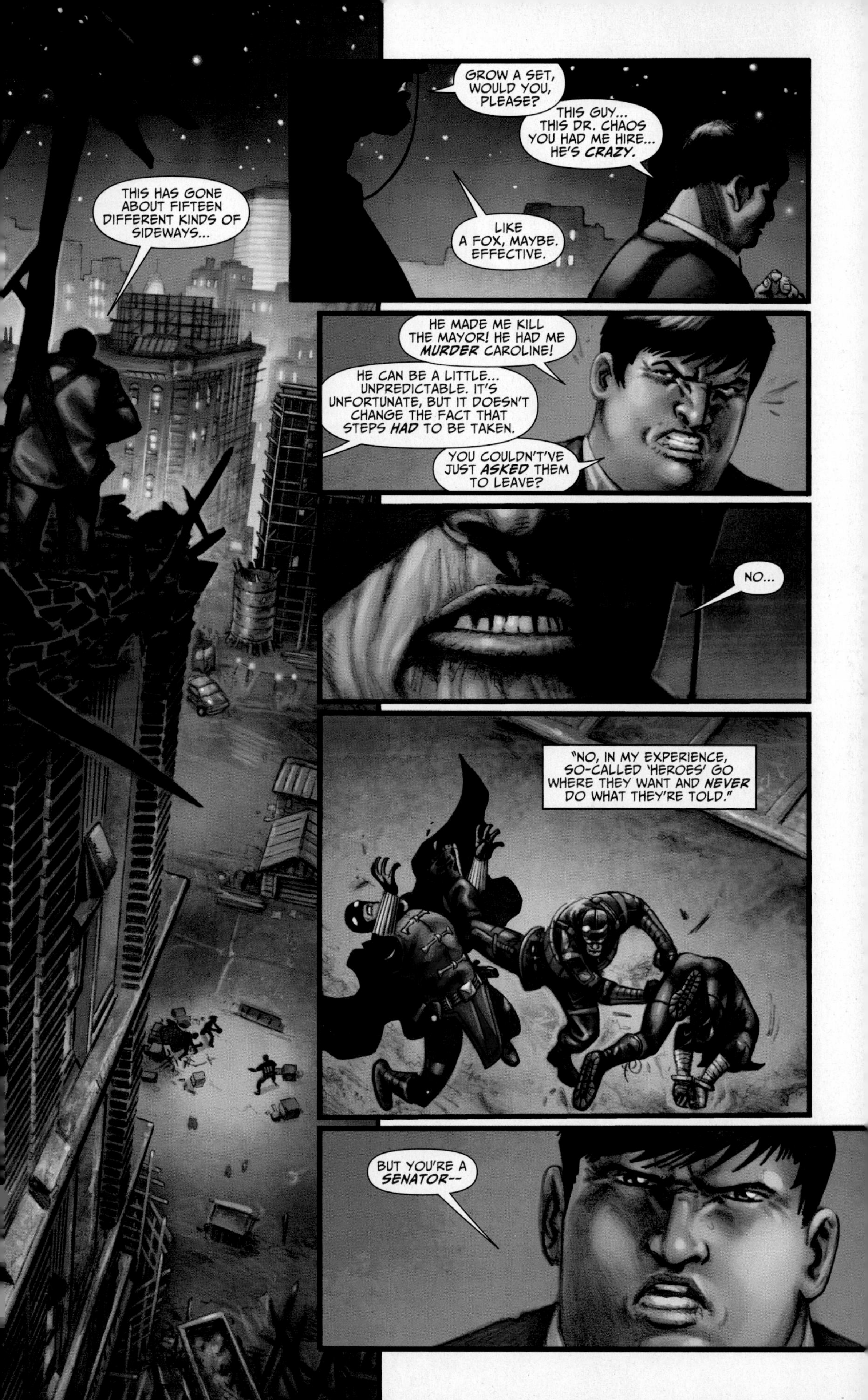
THIS HAS GONE ABOUT FIFTEEN DIFFERENT KINDS OF SIDEWAYS...
GROW A SET, WOULD YOU, PLEASE?
THIS GUY... THIS DR. CHAOS YOU HAD ME HIRE... HE'S CRAZY.
LIKE A FOX, MAYBE. EFFECTIVE.
HE MADE ME KILL THE MAYOR! HE HAD ME MURDER CAROLINE!
HE CAN BE A LITTLE... UNPREDICTABLE. IT'S UNFORTUNATE, BUT IT DOESN'T CHANGE THE FACT THAT STEPS HAD TO BE TAKEN.
YOU COULDN'T'VE JUST ASKED THEM TO LEAVE?
NO...
"NO, IN MY EXPERIENCE, SO-CALLED 'HEROES' GO WHERE THEY WANT AND NEVER DO WHAT THEY'RE TOLD."
BUT YOU'RE A SENATOR--

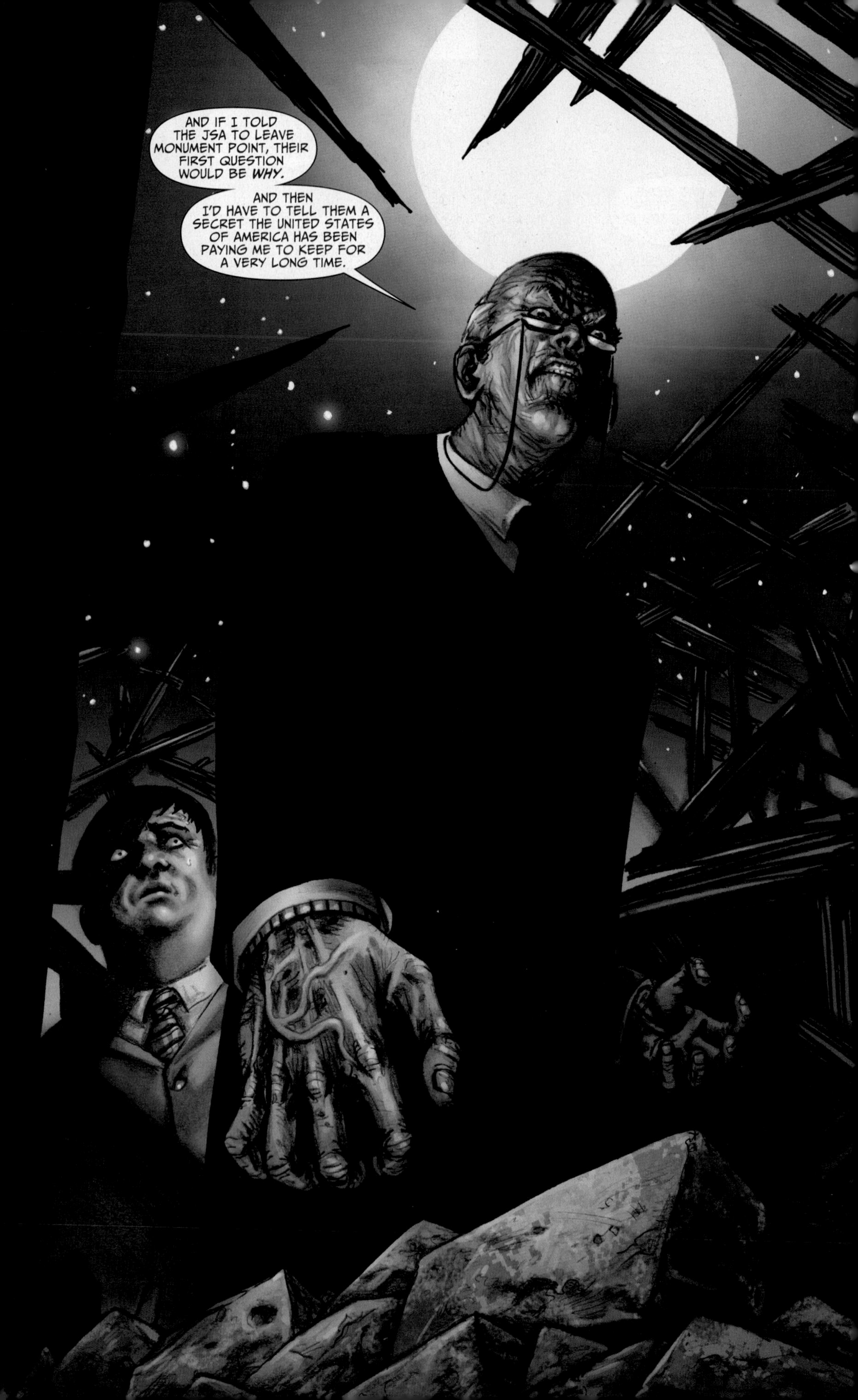
AND IF I TOLD THE JSA TO LEAVE MONUMENT POINT, THEIR FIRST QUESTION WOULD BE *WHY.*
AND THEN I'D HAVE TO TELL THEM A SECRET THE UNITED STATES OF AMERICA HAS BEEN PAYING ME TO KEEP FOR A VERY LONG TIME.

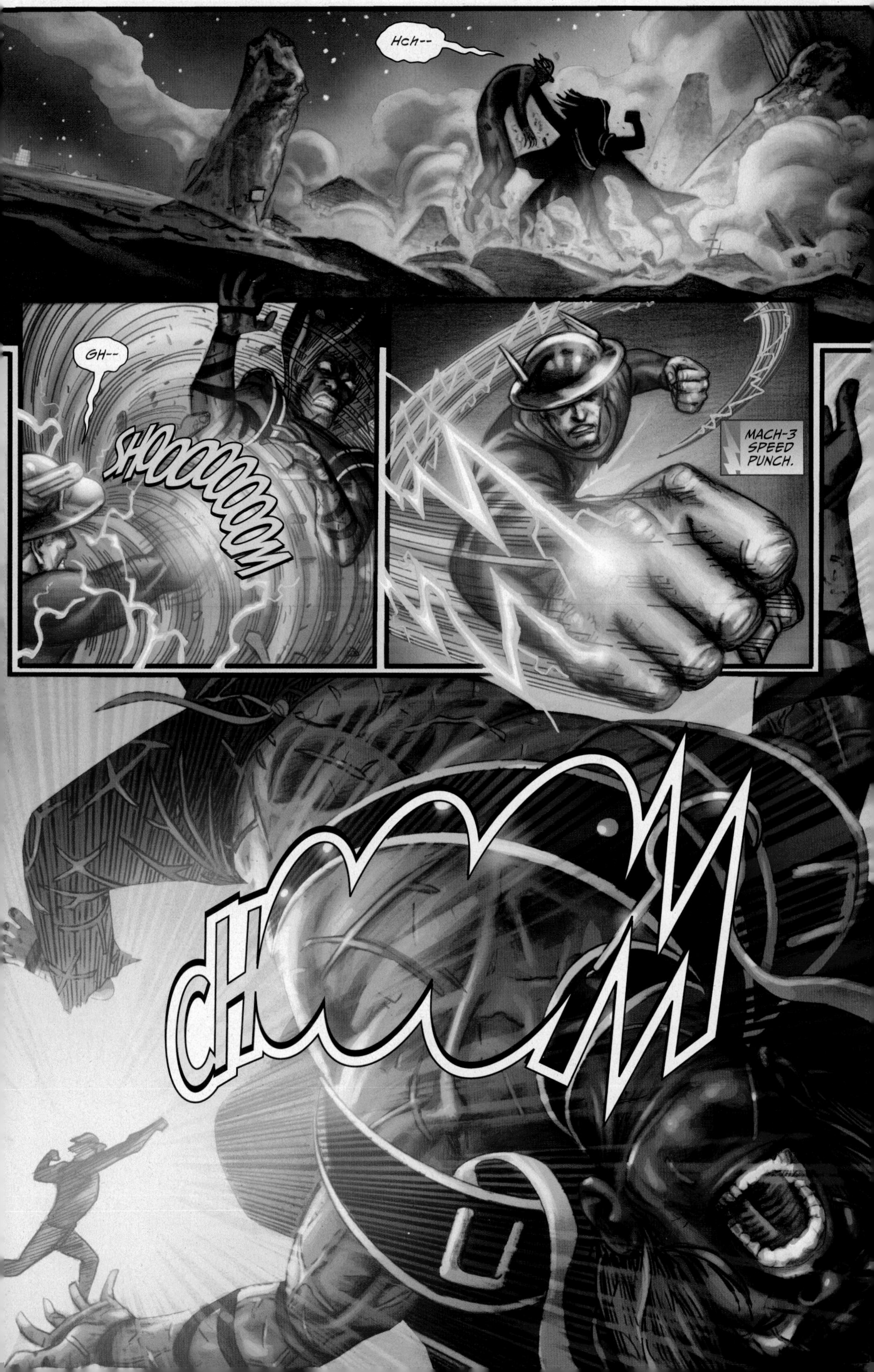
Hch--
GH--
SHOOOOOOOOM
MACH-3 SPEED PUNCH.
CHOOOM

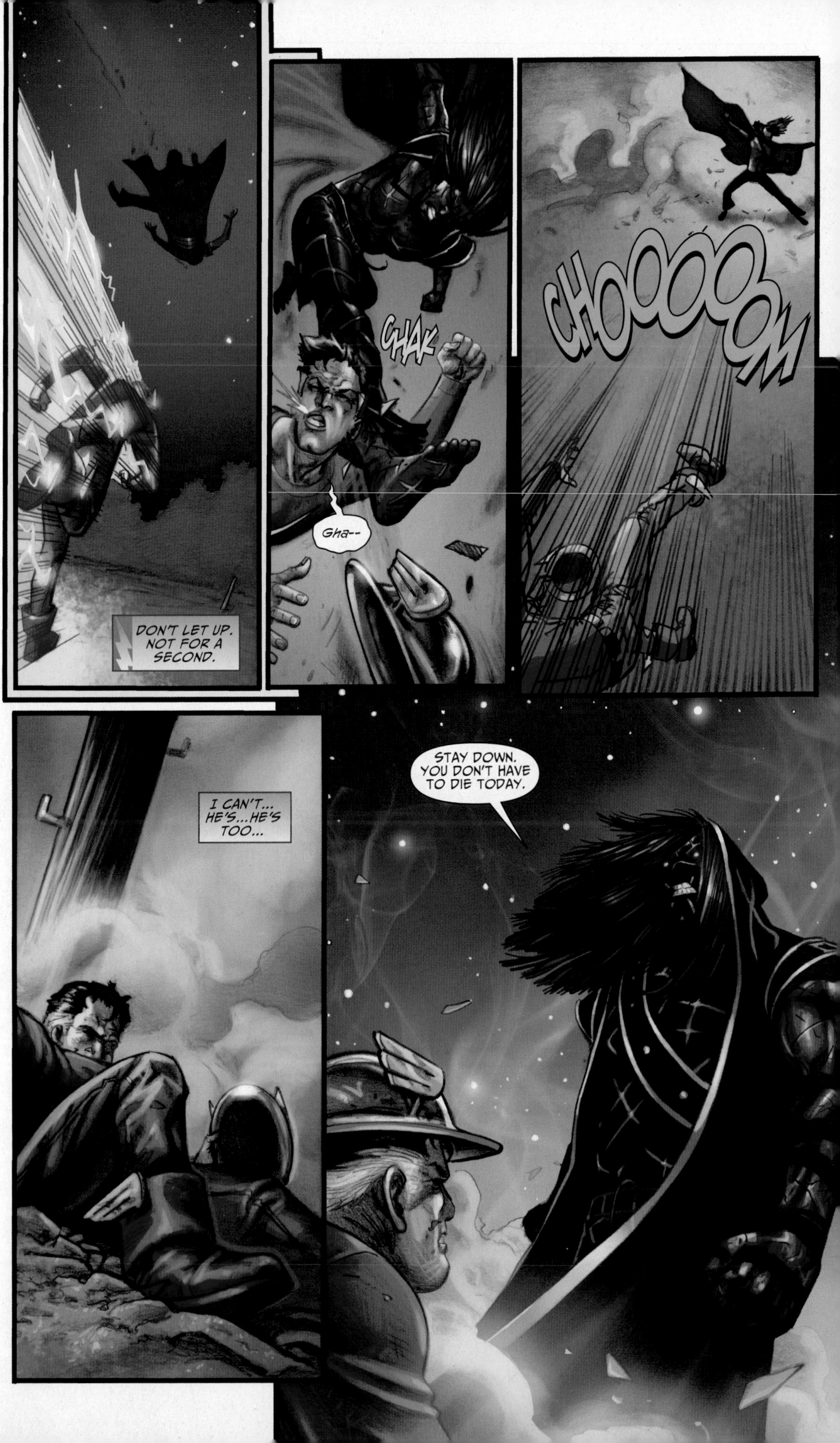
DON'T LET UP. NOT FOR A SECOND.
CHAK
Gha--
CHOOOOOOM
I CAN'T... HE'S...HE'S TOO...
STAY DOWN. YOU DON'T HAVE TO DIE TODAY.

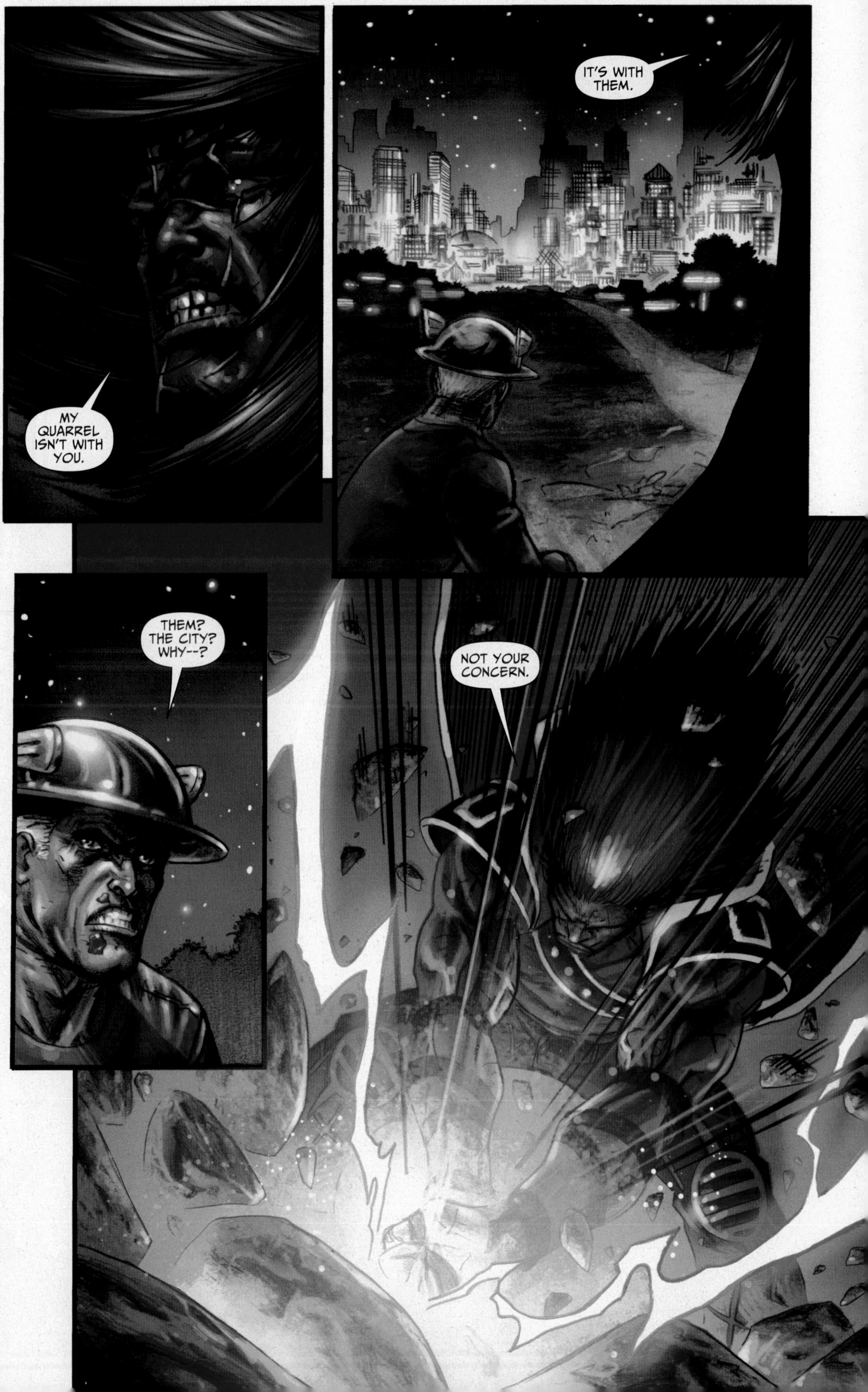
MY QUARREL ISN'T WITH YOU.
IT'S WITH THEM.
THEM? THE CITY? WHY--?
NOT YOUR CONCERN.

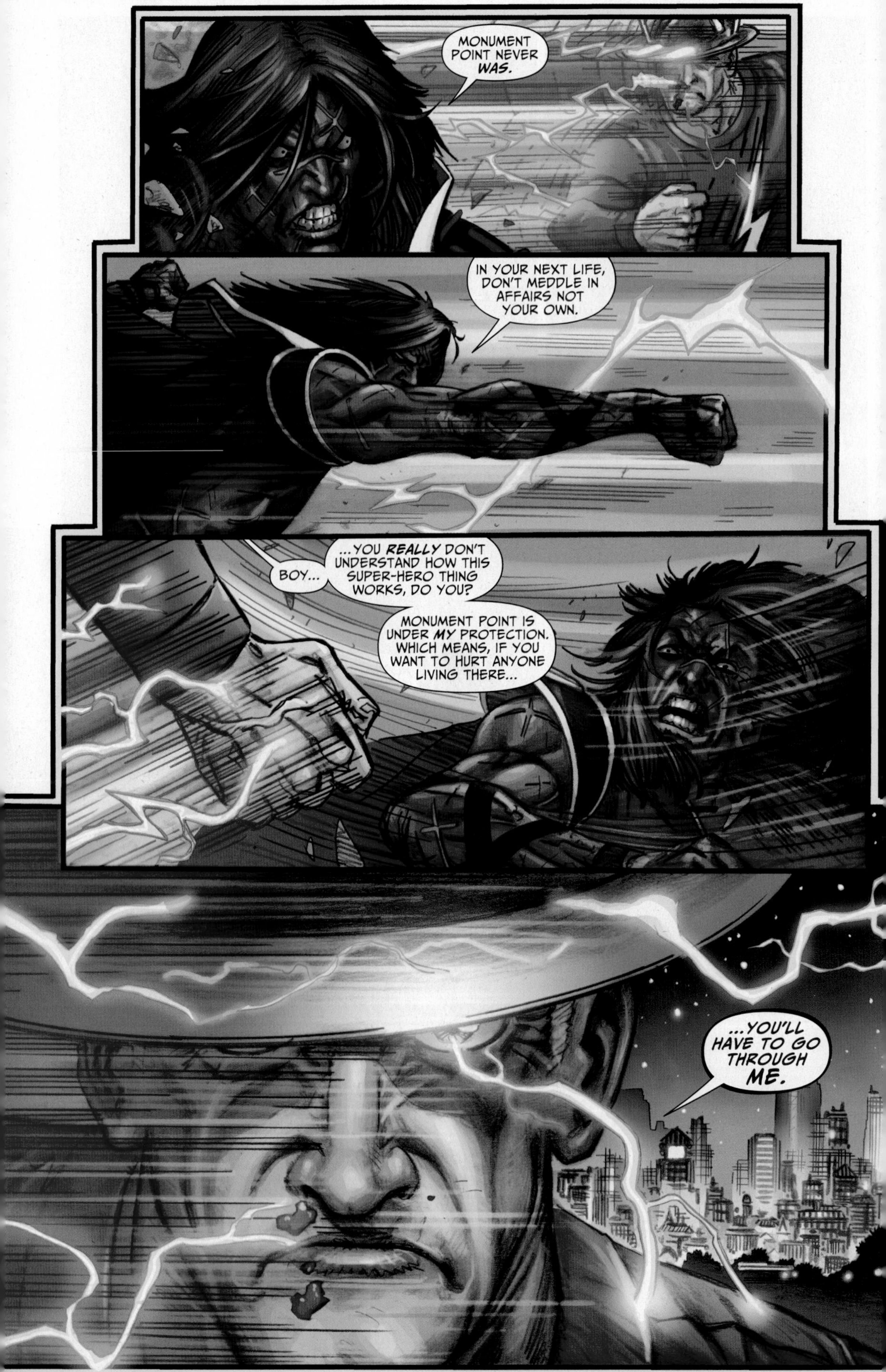
MONUMENT POINT NEVER WAS.
IN YOUR NEXT LIFE, DON'T MEDDLE IN AFFAIRS NOT YOUR OWN.
BOY...
...YOU REALLY DON'T UNDERSTAND HOW THIS SUPER-HERO THING WORKS, DO YOU?
MONUMENT POINT IS UNDER MY PROTECTION. WHICH MEANS, IF YOU WANT TO HURT ANYONE LIVING THERE...
...YOU'LL HAVE TO GO THROUGH ME.

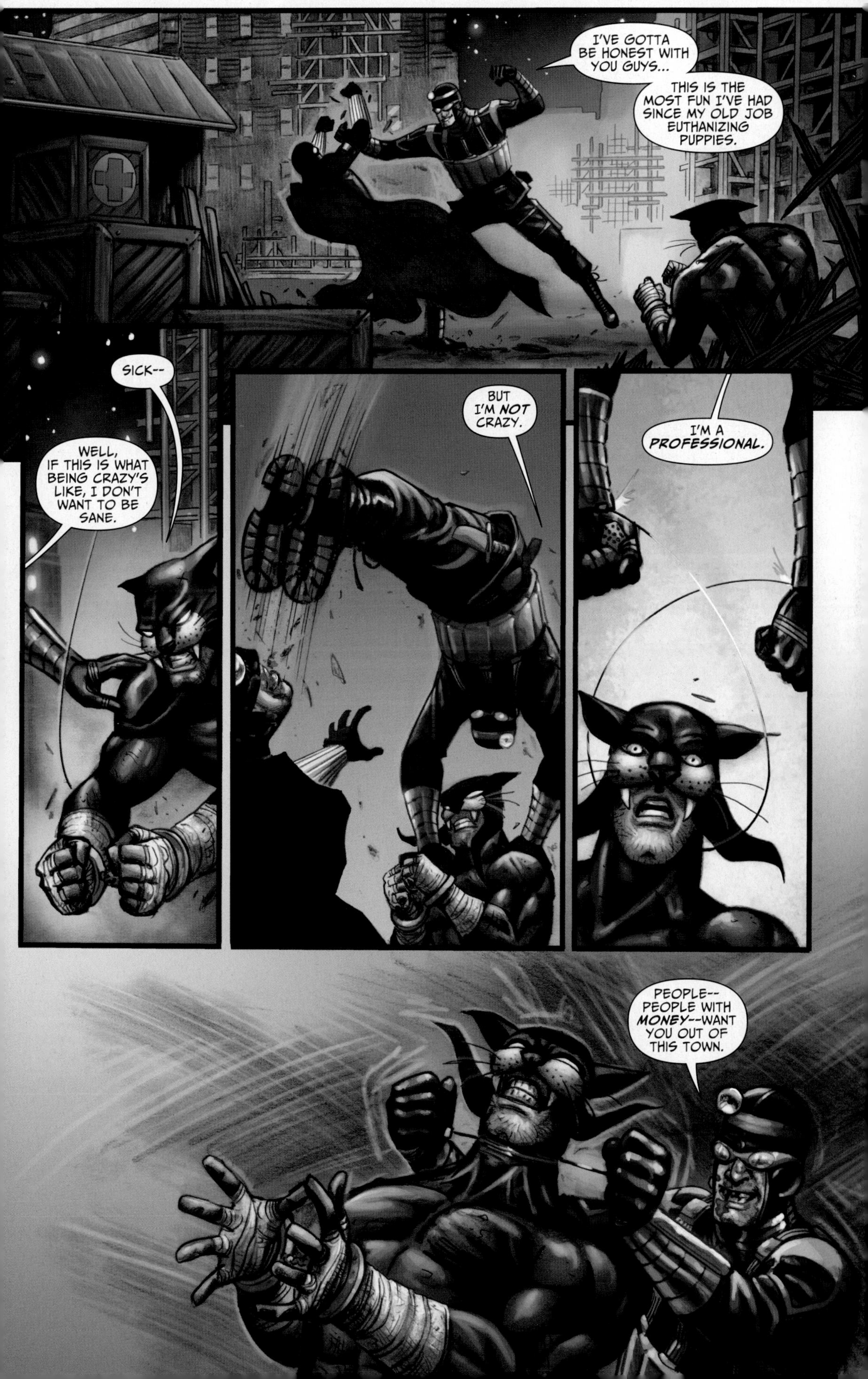
I'VE GOTTA BE HONEST WITH YOU GUYS...
THIS IS THE MOST FUN I'VE HAD SINCE MY OLD JOB EUTHANIZING PUPPIES.
SICK--
WELL, IF THIS IS WHAT BEING CRAZY'S LIKE, I DON'T WANT TO BE SANE.
BUT I'M *NOT* CRAZY.
I'M A *PROFESSIONAL.*
PEOPLE--PEOPLE WITH *MONEY*--WANT YOU OUT OF THIS TOWN.

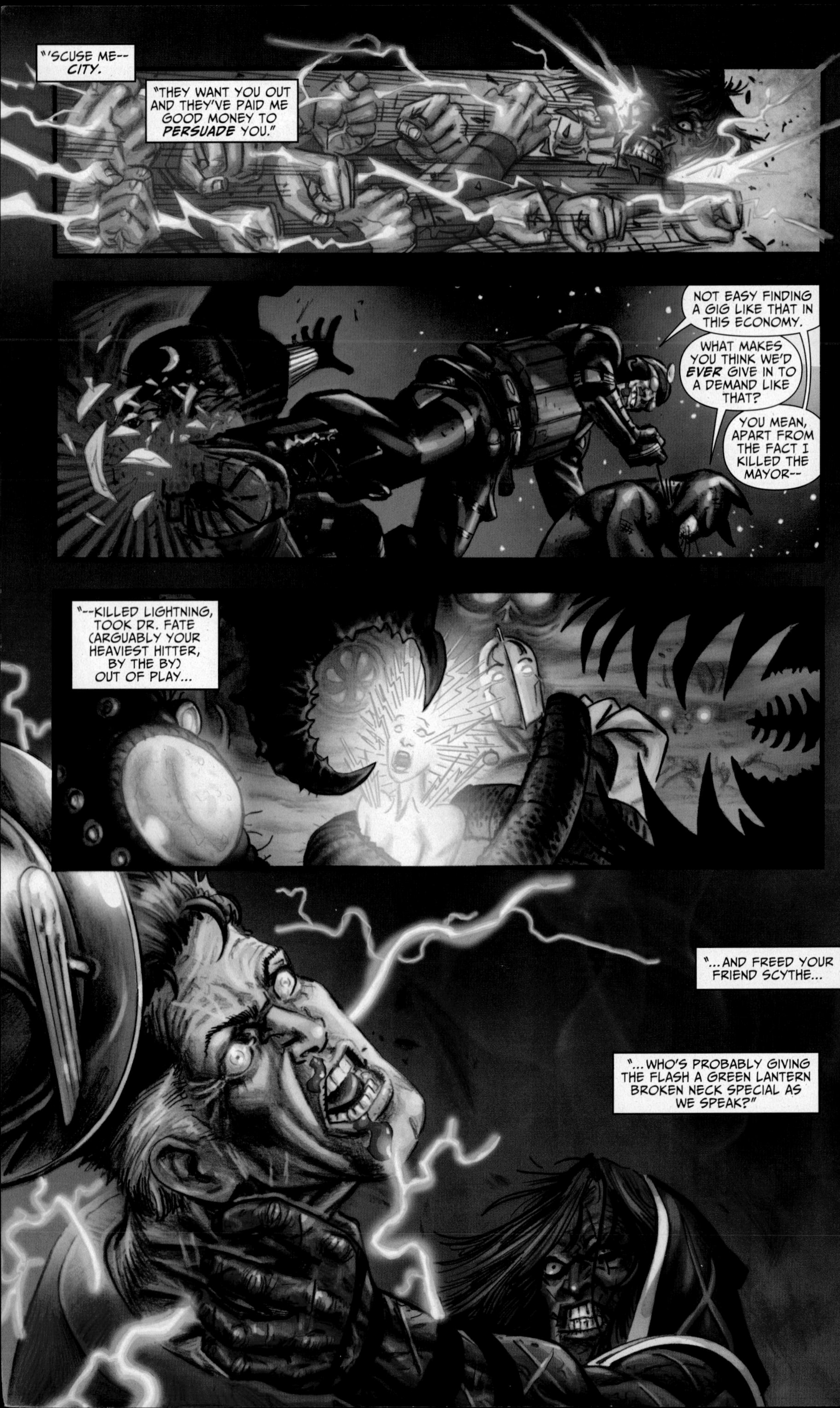
"'SCUSE ME-- CITY.
"THEY WANT YOU OUT AND THEY'VE PAID ME GOOD MONEY TO PERSUADE YOU."
NOT EASY FINDING A GIG LIKE THAT IN THIS ECONOMY.
WHAT MAKES YOU THINK WE'D EVER GIVE IN TO A DEMAND LIKE THAT?
YOU MEAN, APART FROM THE FACT I KILLED THE MAYOR--
"--KILLED LIGHTNING, TOOK DR. FATE (ARGUABLY YOUR HEAVIEST HITTER, BY THE BY) OUT OF PLAY...
"...AND FREED YOUR FRIEND SCYTHE...
"...WHO'S PROBABLY GIVING THE FLASH A GREEN LANTERN BROKEN NECK SPECIAL AS WE SPEAK?"

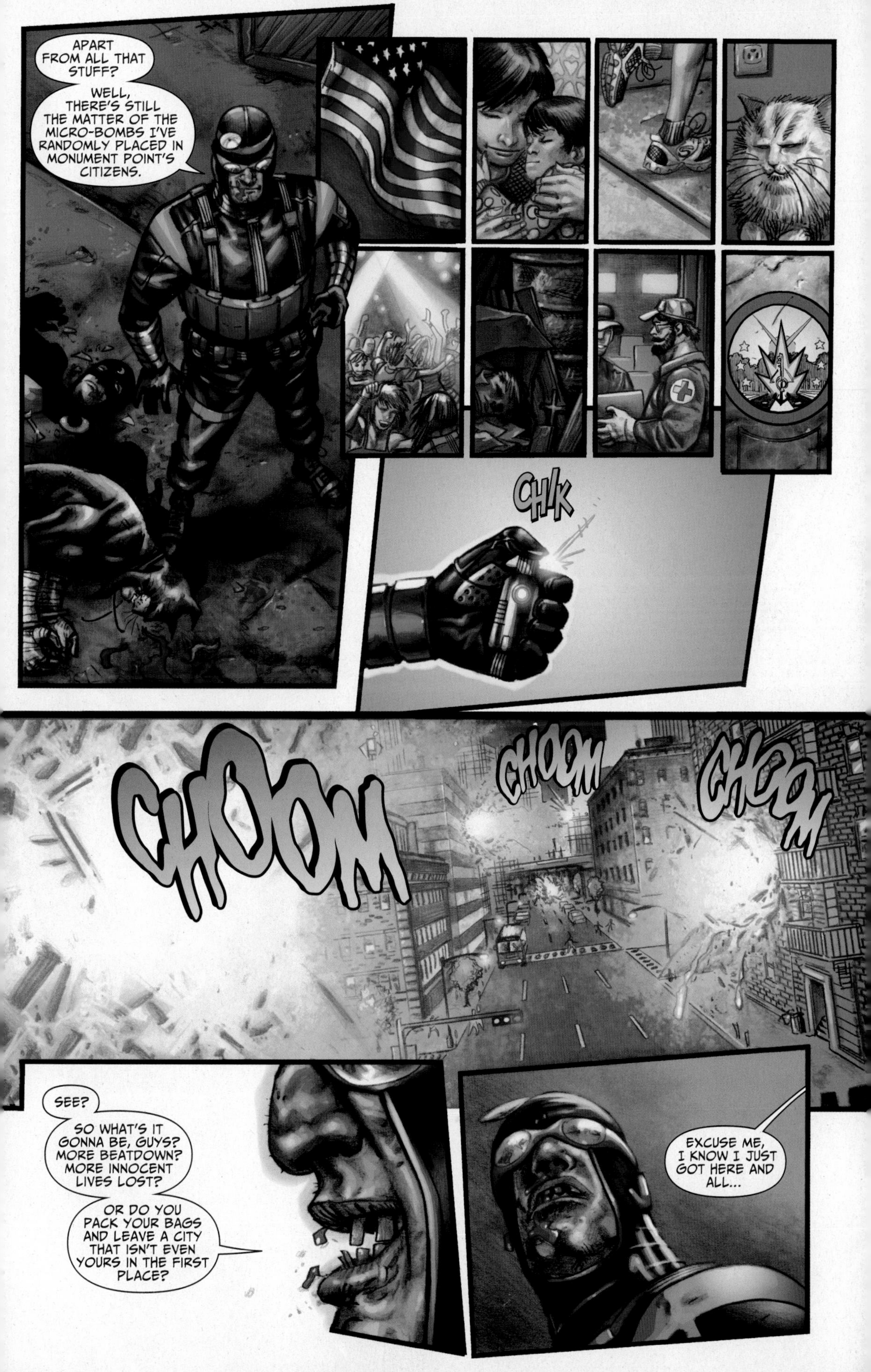
APART FROM ALL THAT STUFF?
WELL, THERE'S STILL THE MATTER OF THE MICRO-BOMBS I'VE RANDOMLY PLACED IN MONUMENT POINT'S CITIZENS.
CHIK
CHOOM
CHOOM
CHOOM
SEE?
SO WHAT'S IT GONNA BE, GUYS? MORE BEATDOWN? MORE INNOCENT LIVES LOST?
OR DO YOU PACK YOUR BAGS AND LEAVE A CITY THAT ISN'T EVEN YOURS IN THE FIRST PLACE?
EXCUSE ME, I KNOW I JUST GOT HERE AND ALL...

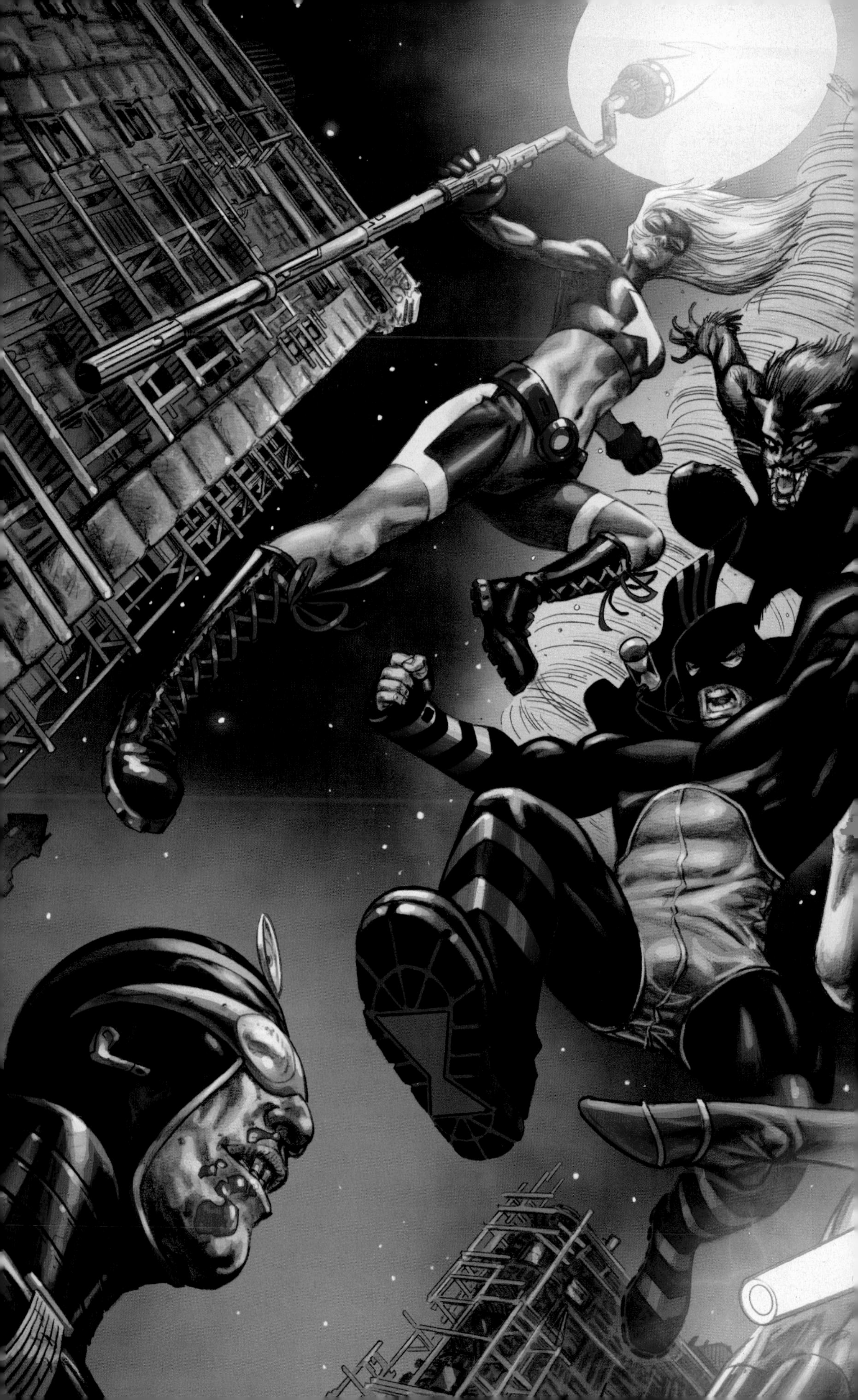

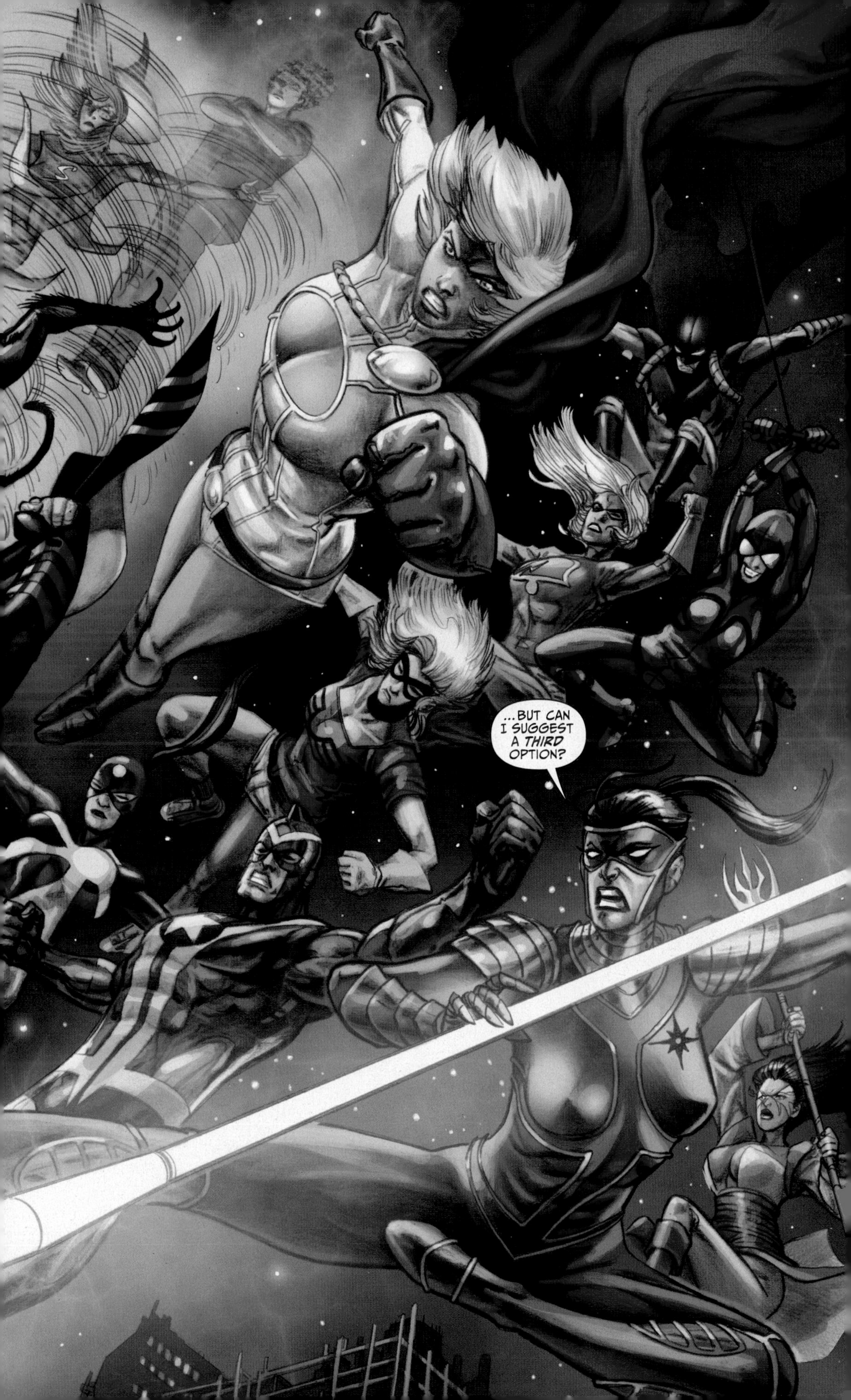
...BUT CAN I SUGGEST A *THIRD* OPTION?

 SUPERTOWN Conclusion

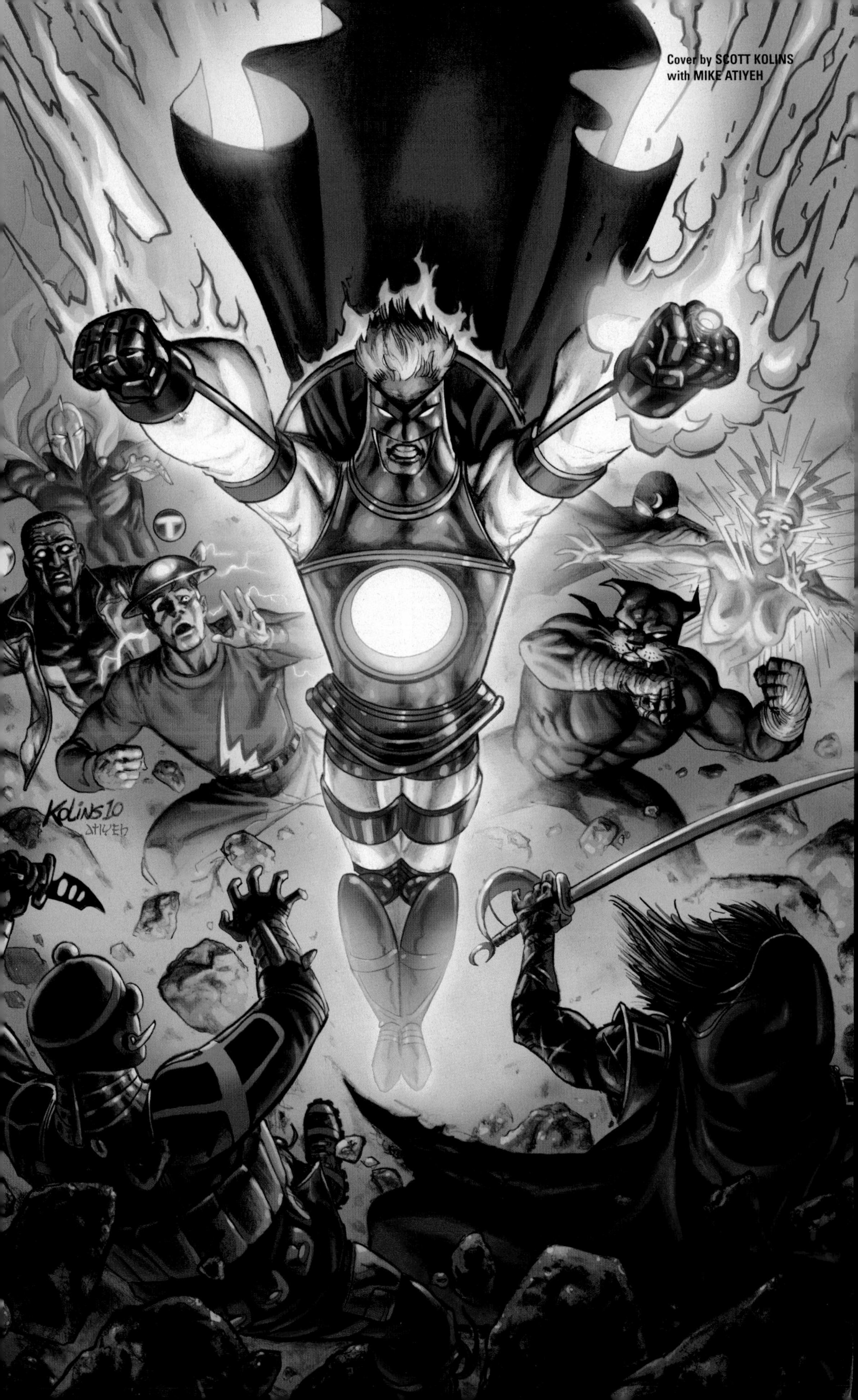
KOLINS 10
ATIYEH

Cover by SCOTT KOLINS
with MIKE ATIYEH

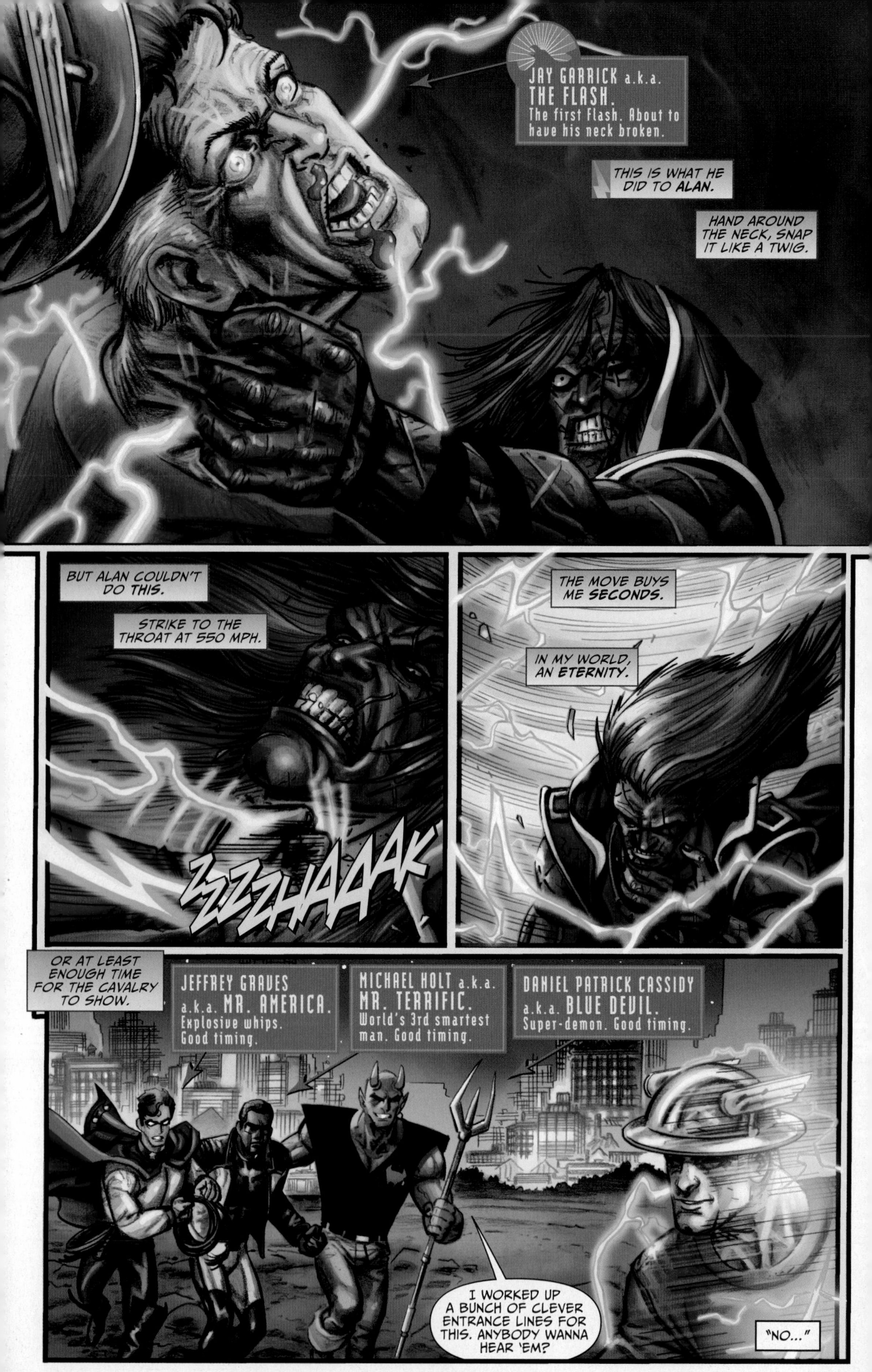
JAY GARRICK a.k.a.
THE FLASH.
The first Flash. About to have his neck broken.
THIS IS WHAT HE DID TO ALAN.
HAND AROUND THE NECK, SNAP IT LIKE A TWIG.
BUT ALAN COULDN'T DO THIS.
STRIKE TO THE THROAT AT 550 MPH.
ZZZZHAAAAK
THE MOVE BUYS ME SECONDS.
IN MY WORLD, AN ETERNITY.
OR AT LEAST ENOUGH TIME FOR THE CAVALRY TO SHOW.
JEFFREY GRAVES a.k.a. MR. AMERICA.
Explosive whips. Good timing.
MICHAEL HOLT a.k.a. MR. TERRIFIC.
World's 3rd smartest man. Good timing.
DANIEL PATRICK CASSIDY a.k.a. BLUE DEVIL.
Super-demon. Good timing.
I WORKED UP A BUNCH OF CLEVER ENTRANCE LINES FOR THIS. ANYBODY WANNA HEAR 'EM?
"NO..."

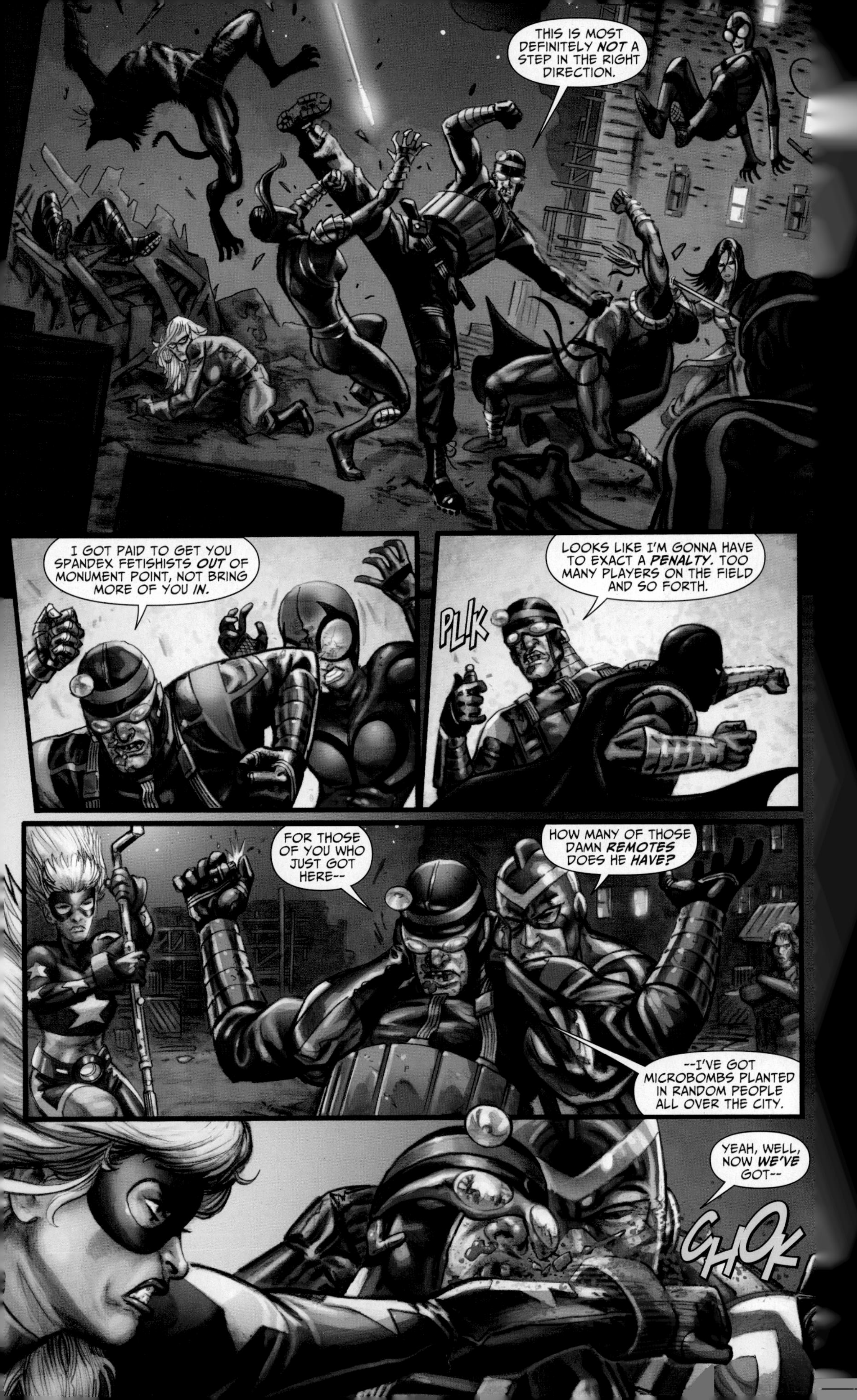
THIS IS MOST DEFINITELY NOT A STEP IN THE RIGHT DIRECTION.
I GOT PAID TO GET YOU SPANDEX FETISHISTS OUT OF MONUMENT POINT, NOT BRING MORE OF YOU IN.
LOOKS LIKE I'M GONNA HAVE TO EXACT A PENALTY. TOO MANY PLAYERS ON THE FIELD AND SO FORTH.
PLIK
FOR THOSE OF YOU WHO JUST GOT HERE--
HOW MANY OF THOSE DAMN REMOTES DOES HE HAVE?
--I'VE GOT MICROBOMBS PLANTED IN RANDOM PEOPLE ALL OVER THE CITY.
YEAH, WELL, NOW WE'VE GOT--
CHOK

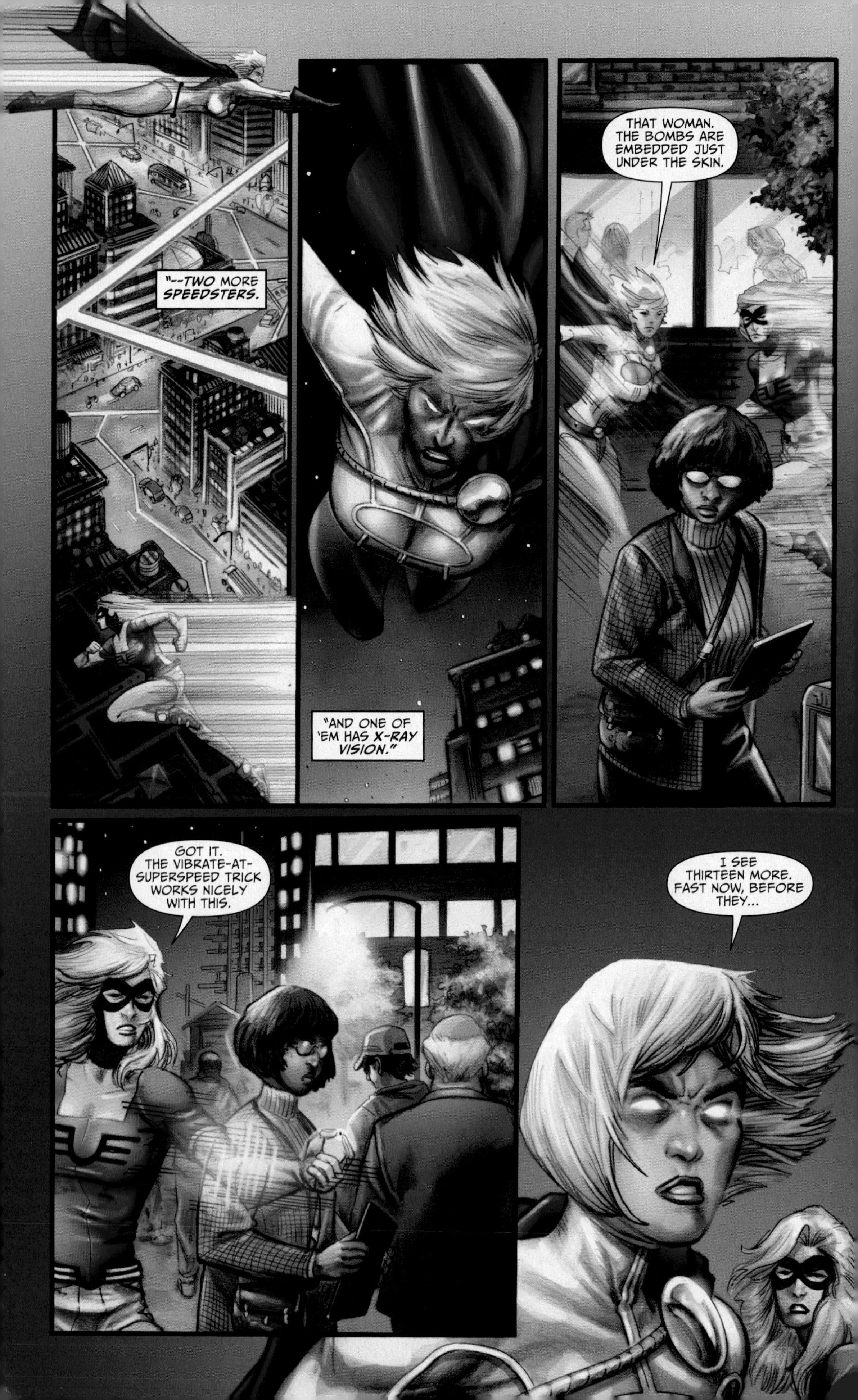
"--TWO MORE SPEEDSTERS.
"AND ONE OF 'EM HAS X-RAY VISION."
THAT WOMAN. THE BOMBS ARE EMBEDDED JUST UNDER THE SKIN.
GOT IT. THE VIBRATE-AT-SUPERSPEED TRICK WORKS NICELY WITH THIS.
I SEE THIRTEEN MORE. FAST NOW, BEFORE THEY...

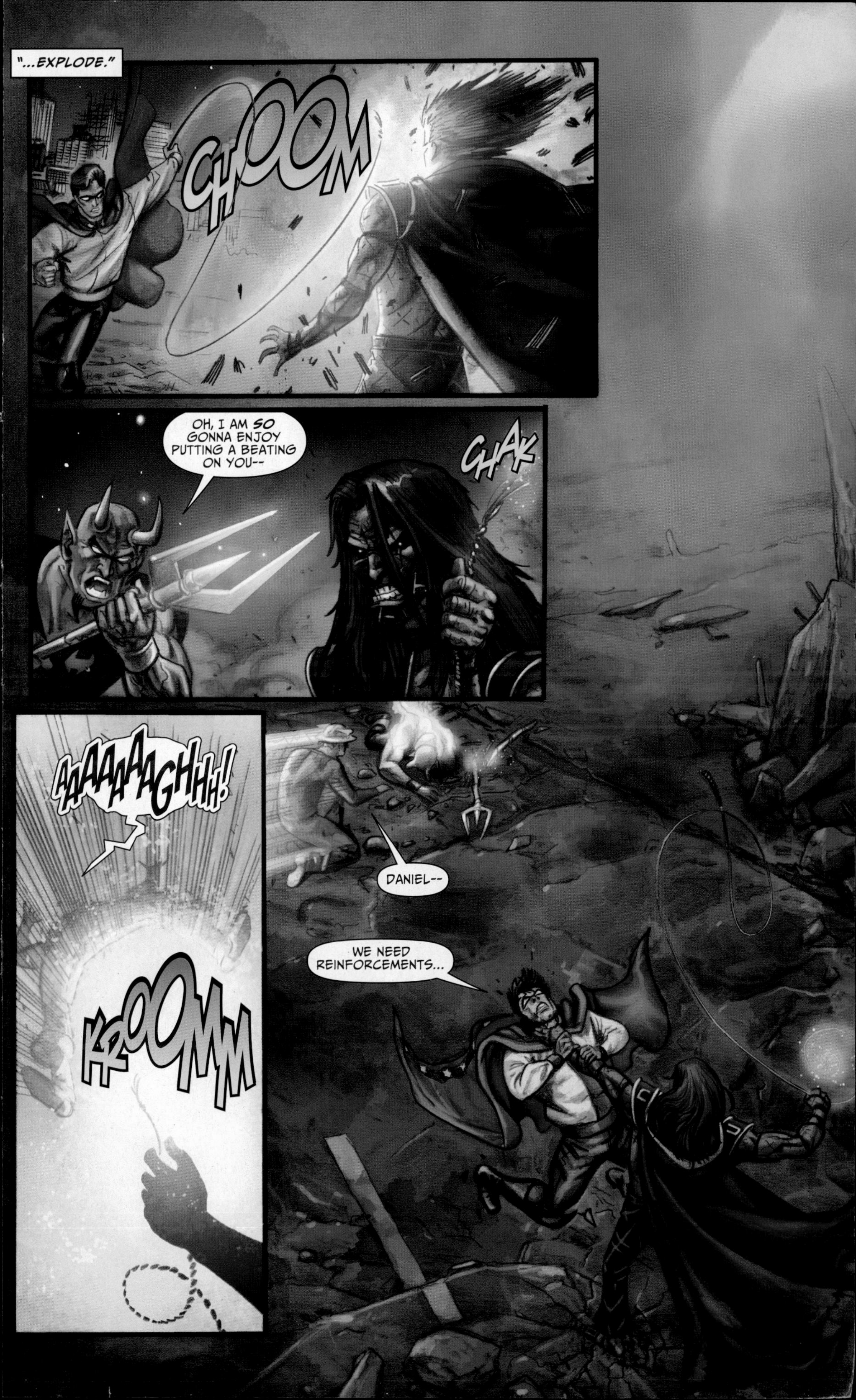
"...EXPLODE."
CHOOOM
OH, I AM SO GONNA ENJOY PUTTING A BEATING ON YOU--
CHAK
AAAAAAAGHHH!
KROOMM
DANIEL--
WE NEED REINFORCEMENTS...

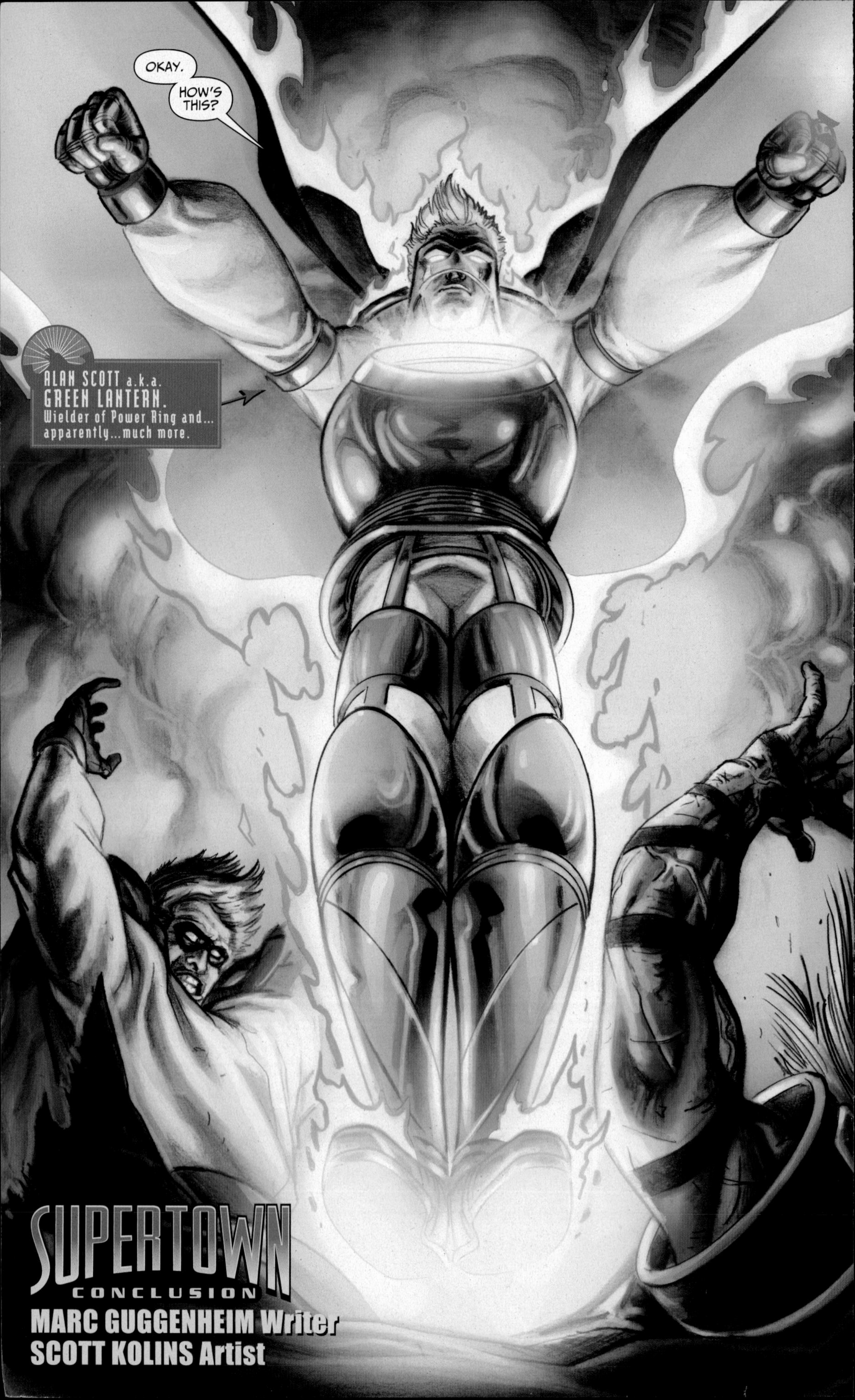
OKAY.
HOW'S THIS?
ALAN SCOTT a.k.a. GREEN LANTERN. Wielder of Power Ring and... apparently...much more.
SUPERTOWN
CONCLUSION
MARC GUGGENHEIM Writer
SCOTT KOLINS Artist

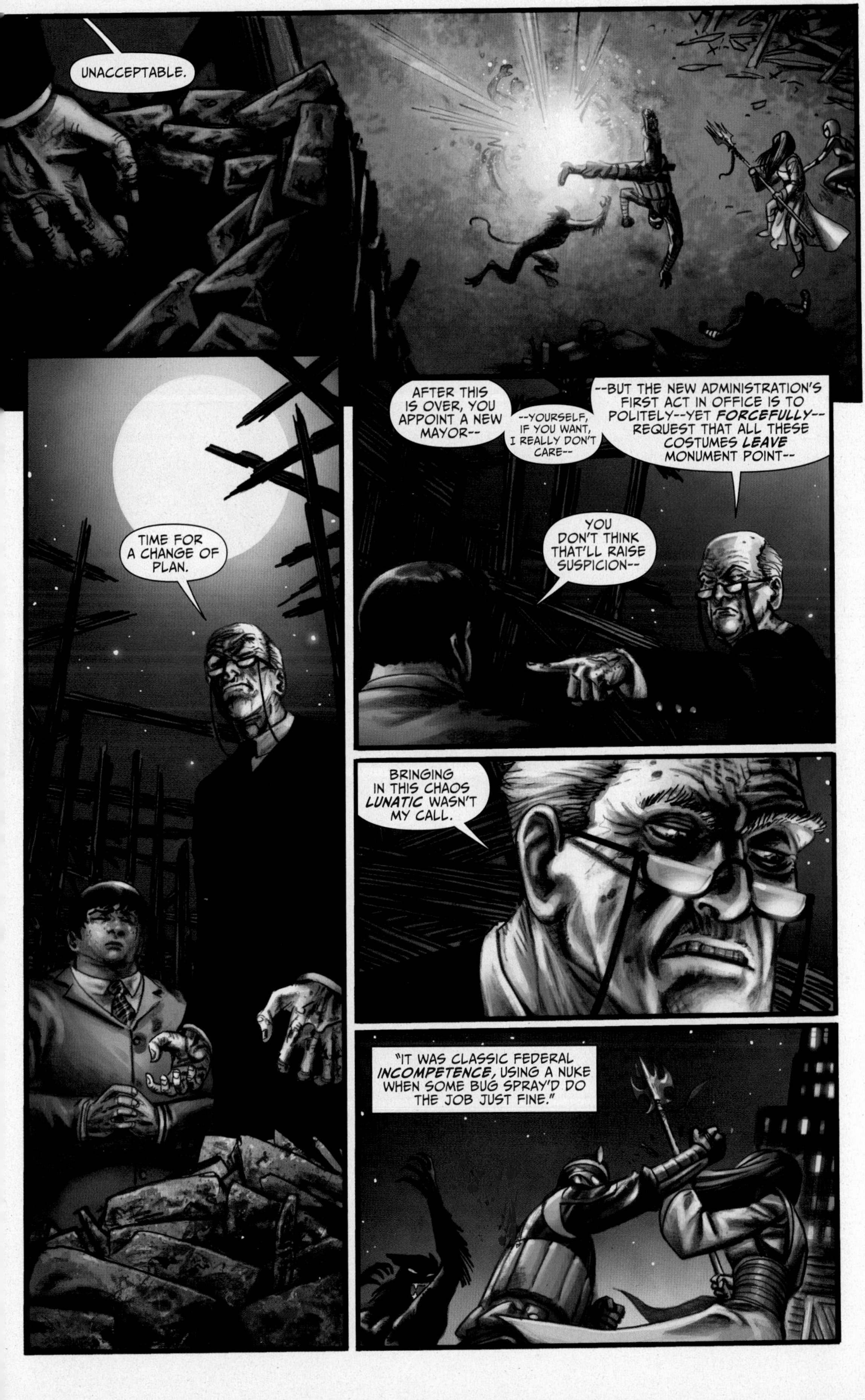
UNACCEPTABLE.
TIME FOR A CHANGE OF PLAN.
AFTER THIS IS OVER, YOU APPOINT A NEW MAYOR--
--YOURSELF, IF YOU WANT, I REALLY DON'T CARE--
--BUT THE NEW ADMINISTRATION'S FIRST ACT IN OFFICE IS TO POLITELY--YET FORCEFULLY--REQUEST THAT ALL THESE COSTUMES LEAVE MONUMENT POINT--
YOU DON'T THINK THAT'LL RAISE SUSPICION--
BRINGING IN THIS CHAOS LUNATIC WASN'T MY CALL.
"IT WAS CLASSIC FEDERAL INCOMPETENCE, USING A NUKE WHEN SOME BUG SPRAY'D DO THE JOB JUST FINE."

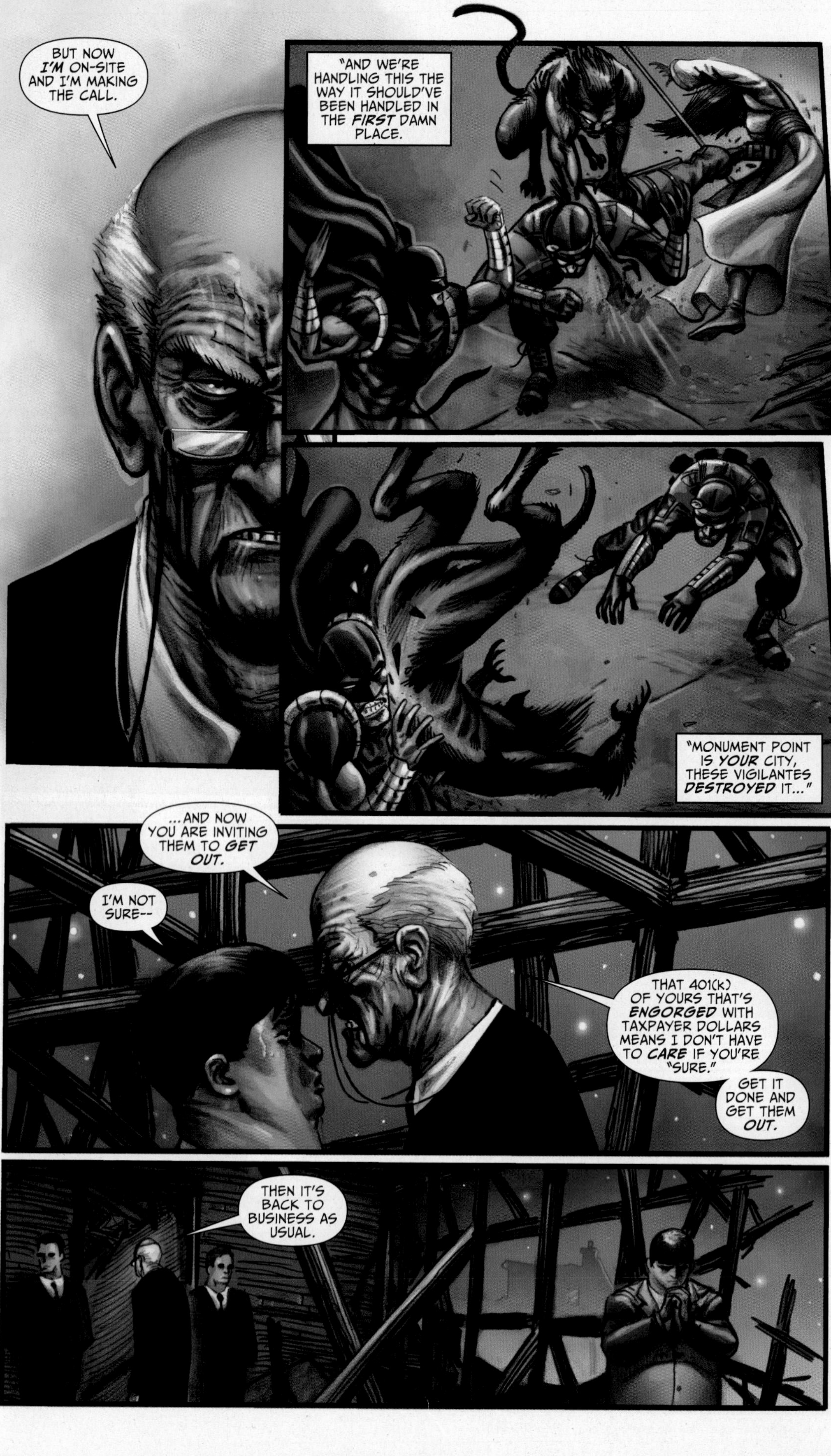
BUT NOW I'M ON-SITE AND I'M MAKING THE CALL.
"AND WE'RE HANDLING THIS THE WAY IT SHOULD'VE BEEN HANDLED IN THE FIRST DAMN PLACE.
"MONUMENT POINT IS YOUR CITY, THESE VIGILANTES DESTROYED IT..."
...AND NOW YOU ARE INVITING THEM TO GET OUT.
I'M NOT SURE--
THAT 401(k) OF YOURS THAT'S ENGORGED WITH TAXPAYER DOLLARS MEANS I DON'T HAVE TO CARE IF YOU'RE "SURE."
GET IT DONE AND GET THEM OUT.
THEN IT'S BACK TO BUSINESS AS USUAL.

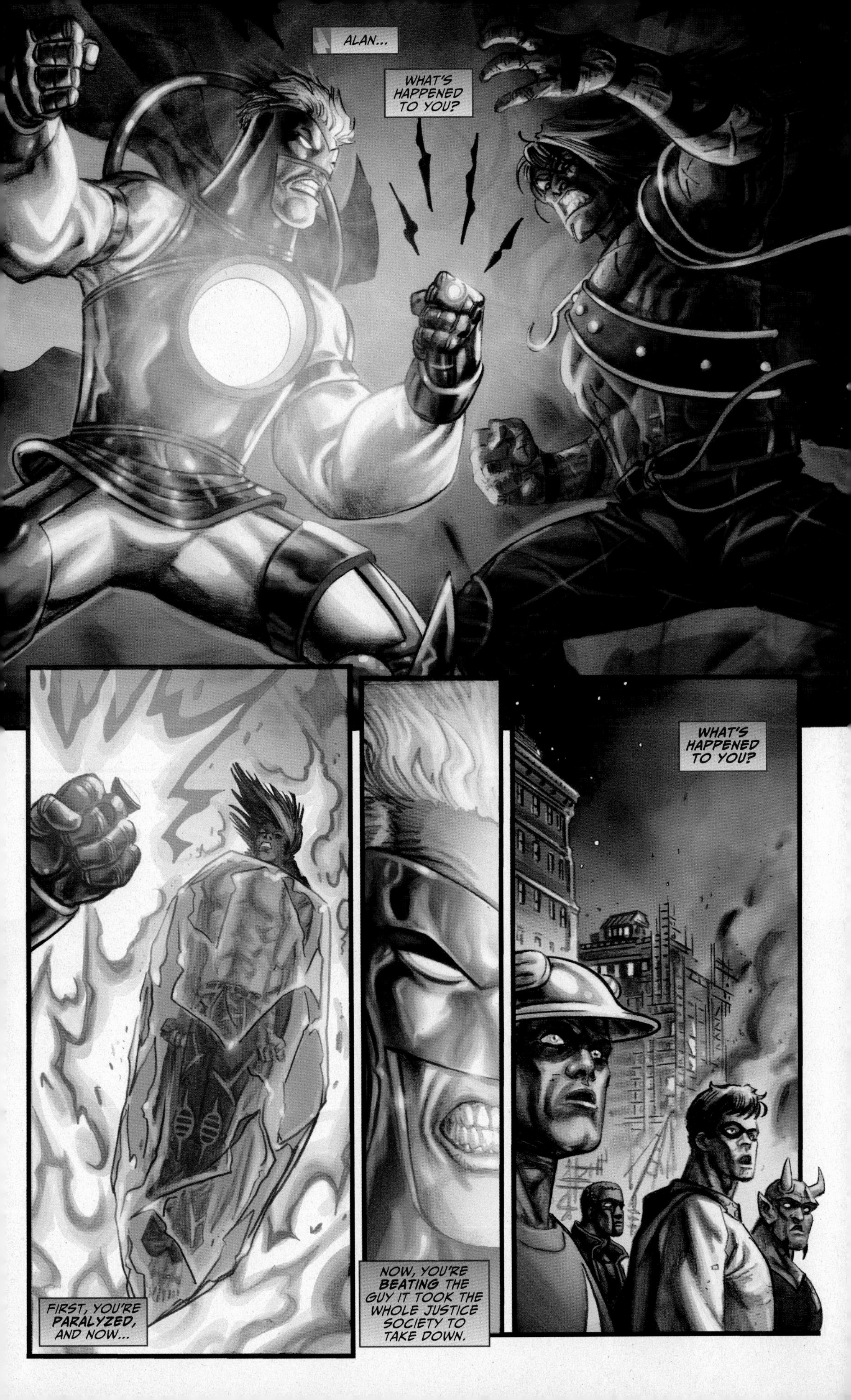
ALAN...
WHAT'S HAPPENED TO YOU?
WHAT'S HAPPENED TO YOU?
FIRST, YOU'RE PARALYZED, AND NOW...
NOW, YOU'RE BEATING THE GUY IT TOOK THE WHOLE JUSTICE SOCIETY TO TAKE DOWN.

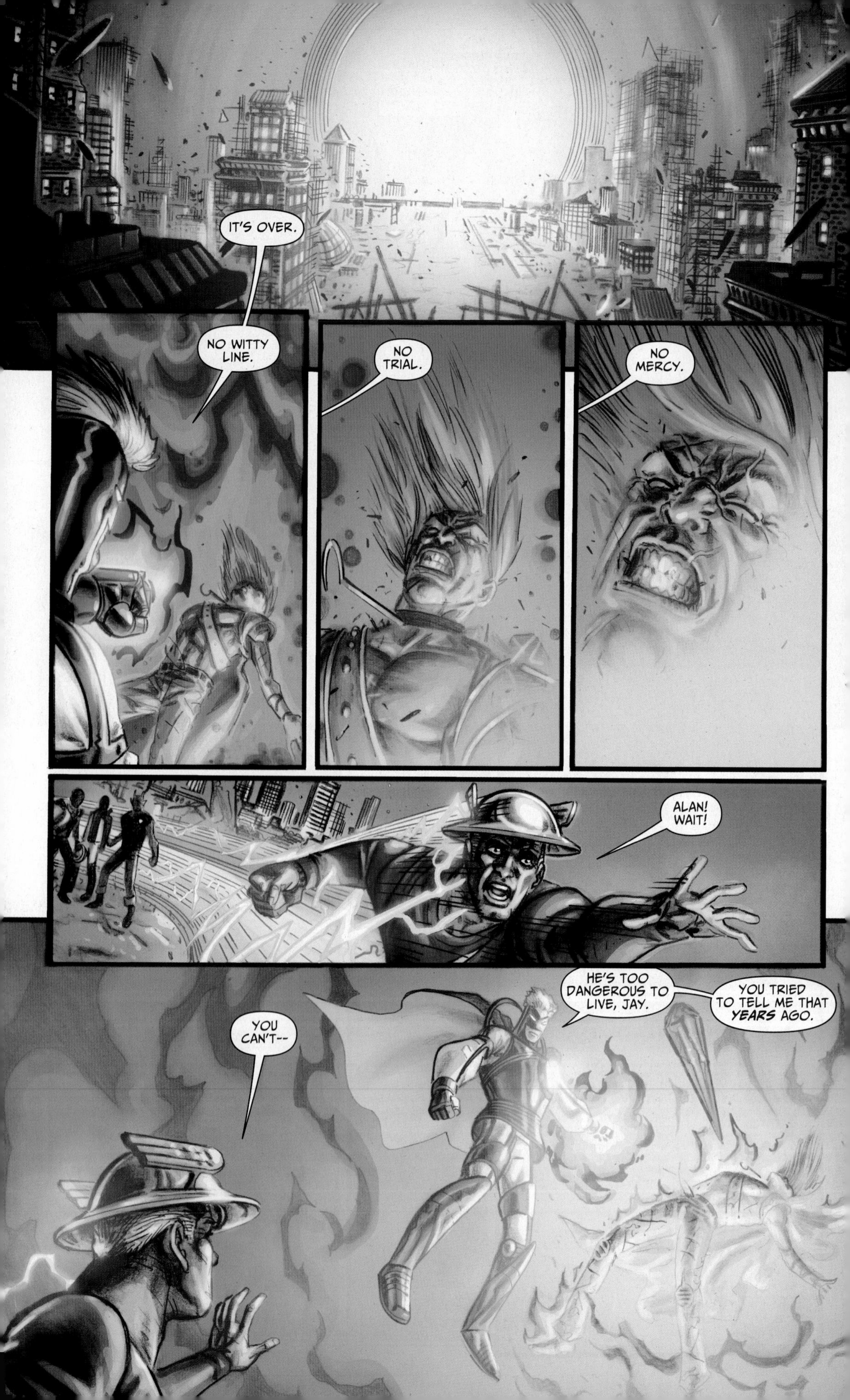
IT'S OVER.
NO WITTY LINE.
NO TRIAL.
NO MERCY.
ALAN! WAIT!
YOU CAN'T--
HE'S TOO DANGEROUS TO LIVE, JAY.
YOU TRIED TO TELL ME THAT YEARS AGO.

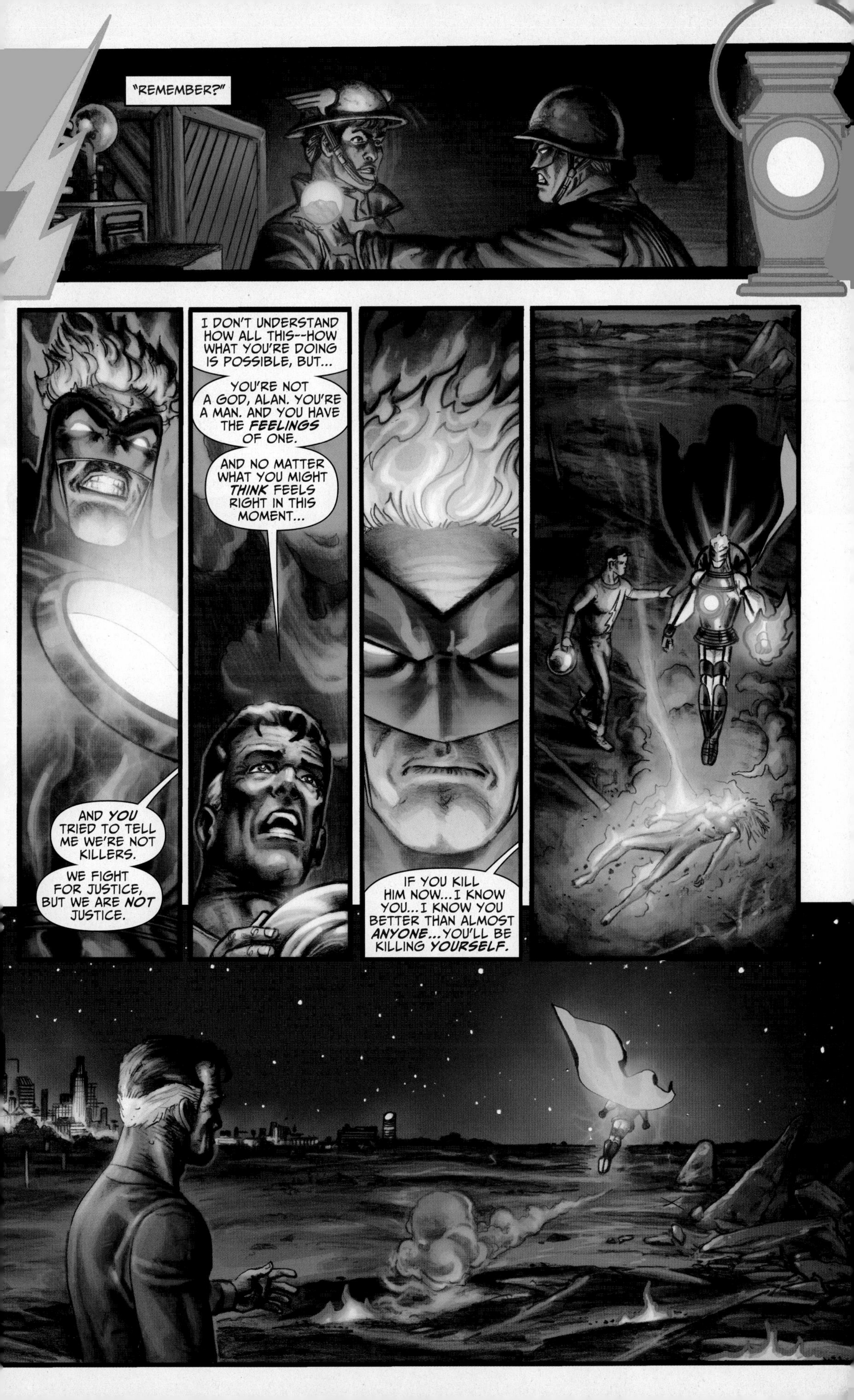
"REMEMBER?"
AND YOU TRIED TO TELL ME WE'RE NOT KILLERS.
WE FIGHT FOR JUSTICE, BUT WE ARE NOT JUSTICE.
I DON'T UNDERSTAND HOW ALL THIS--HOW WHAT YOU'RE DOING IS POSSIBLE, BUT...
YOU'RE NOT A GOD, ALAN. YOU'RE A MAN. AND YOU HAVE THE FEELINGS OF ONE.
AND NO MATTER WHAT YOU MIGHT THINK FEELS RIGHT IN THIS MOMENT...
IF YOU KILL HIM NOW...I KNOW YOU...I KNOW YOU BETTER THAN ALMOST ANYONE...YOU'LL BE KILLING YOURSELF.

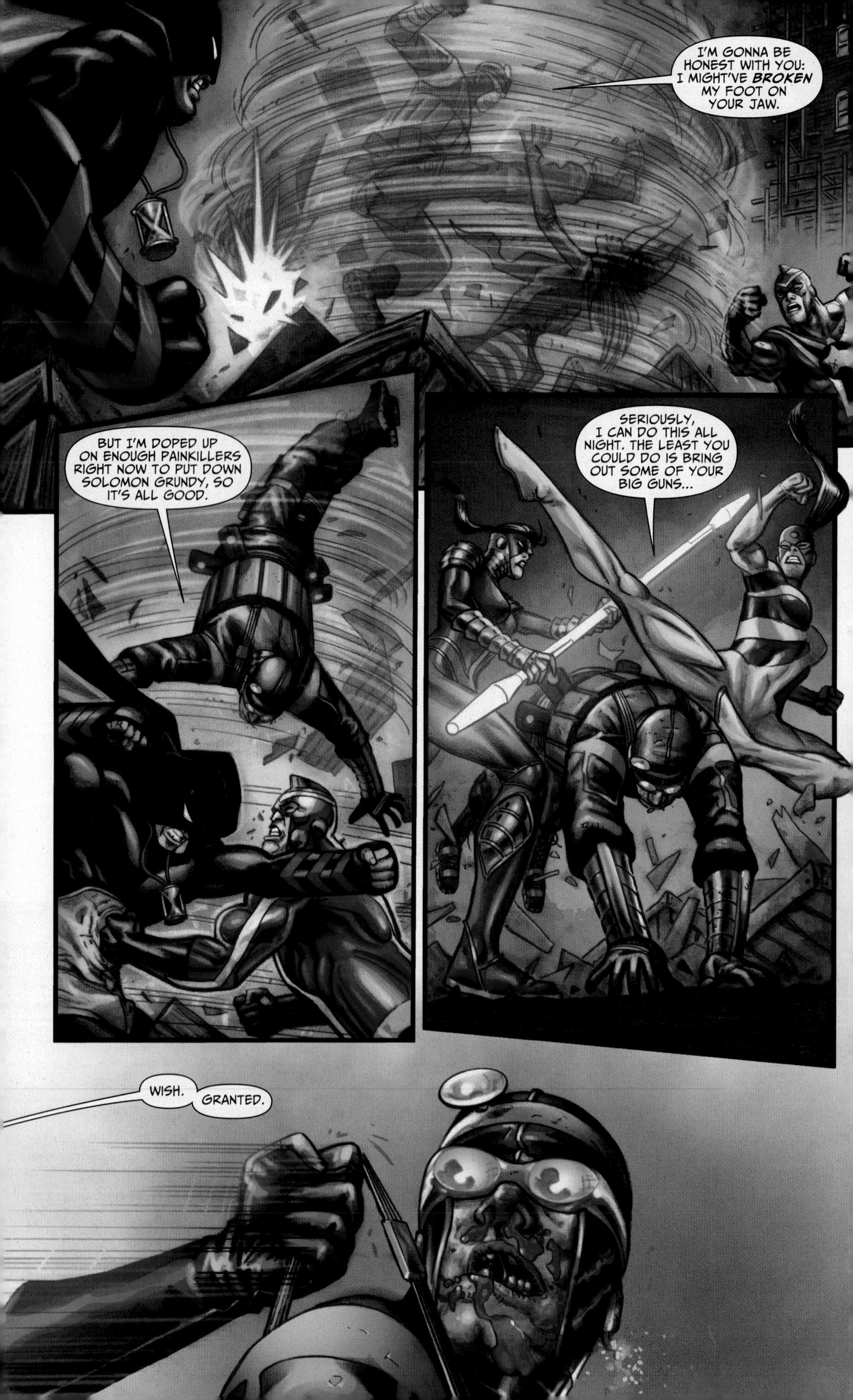
I'M GONNA BE HONEST WITH YOU: I MIGHT'VE **BROKEN** MY FOOT ON YOUR JAW.
BUT I'M DOPED UP ON ENOUGH PAINKILLERS RIGHT NOW TO PUT DOWN SOLOMON GRUNDY, SO IT'S ALL GOOD.
SERIOUSLY, I CAN DO THIS ALL NIGHT. THE LEAST YOU COULD DO IS BRING OUT SOME OF YOUR BIG GUNS...
WISH.
GRANTED.

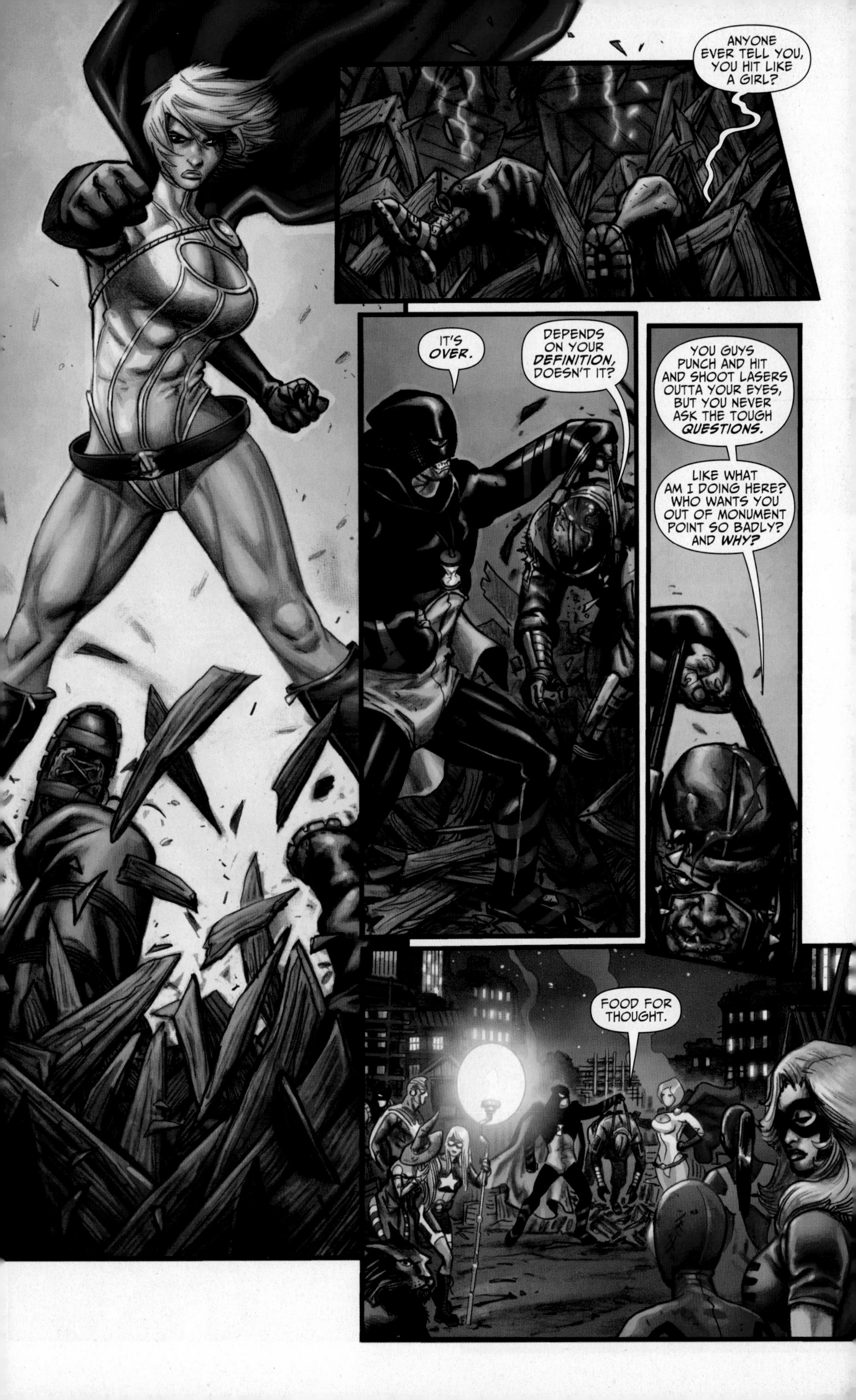
ANYONE EVER TELL YOU, YOU HIT LIKE A GIRL?
IT'S OVER.
DEPENDS ON YOUR DEFINITION, DOESN'T IT?
YOU GUYS PUNCH AND HIT AND SHOOT LASERS OUTTA YOUR EYES, BUT YOU NEVER ASK THE TOUGH QUESTIONS.
LIKE WHAT AM I DOING HERE? WHO WANTS YOU OUT OF MONUMENT POINT SO BADLY? AND WHY?
FOOD FOR THOUGHT.

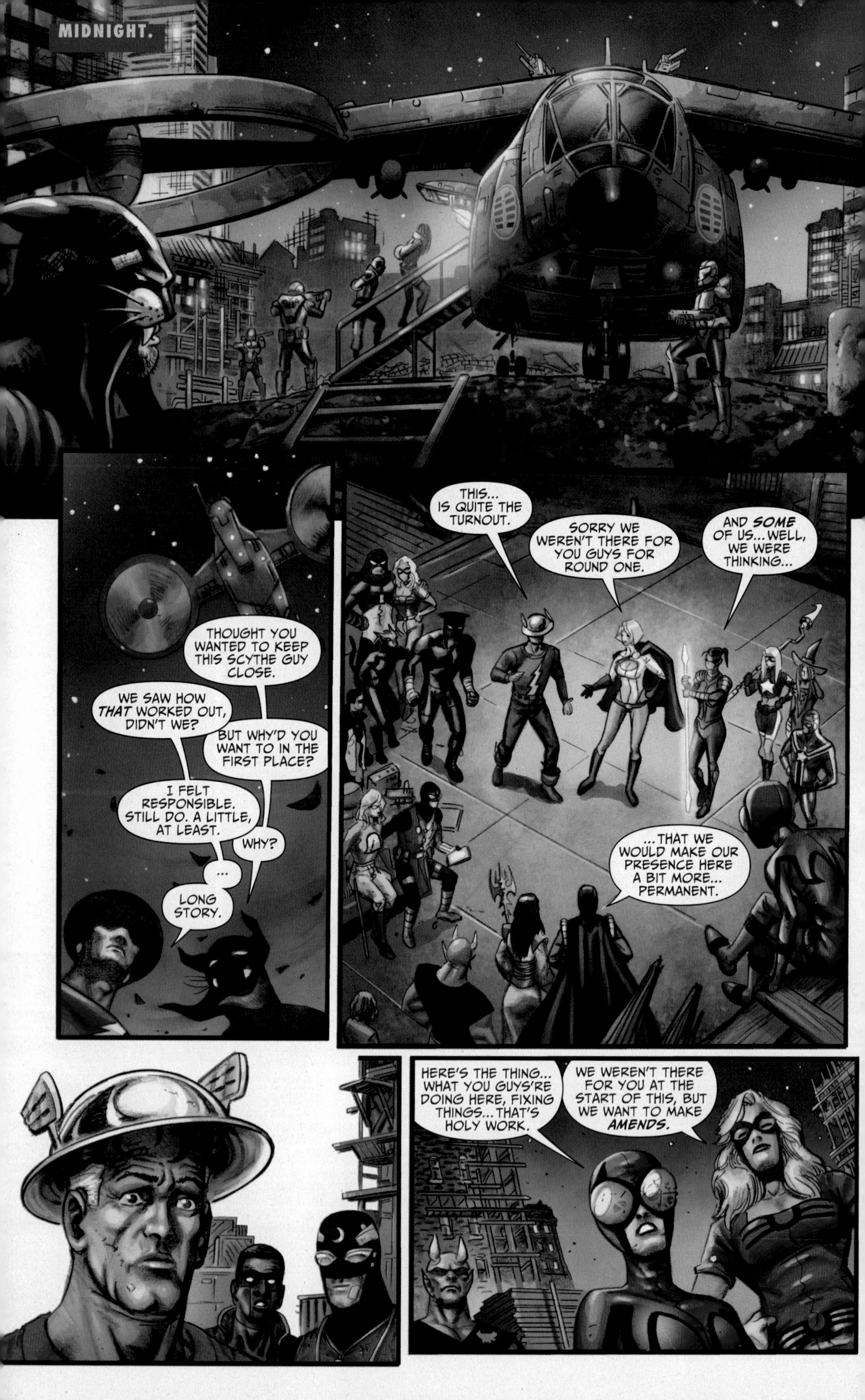
MIDNIGHT.
THOUGHT YOU WANTED TO KEEP THIS SCYTHE GUY CLOSE.
WE SAW HOW THAT WORKED OUT, DIDN'T WE?
BUT WHY'D YOU WANT TO IN THE FIRST PLACE?
I FELT RESPONSIBLE. STILL DO. A LITTLE, AT LEAST.
WHY?
...
LONG STORY.
THIS... IS QUITE THE TURNOUT.
SORRY WE WEREN'T THERE FOR YOU GUYS FOR ROUND ONE.
AND SOME OF US... WELL, WE WERE THINKING...
...THAT WE WOULD MAKE OUR PRESENCE HERE A BIT MORE... PERMANENT.
HERE'S THE THING... WHAT YOU GUYS'RE DOING HERE, FIXING THINGS... THAT'S HOLY WORK.
WE WEREN'T THERE FOR YOU AT THE START OF THIS, BUT WE WANT TO MAKE AMENDS.

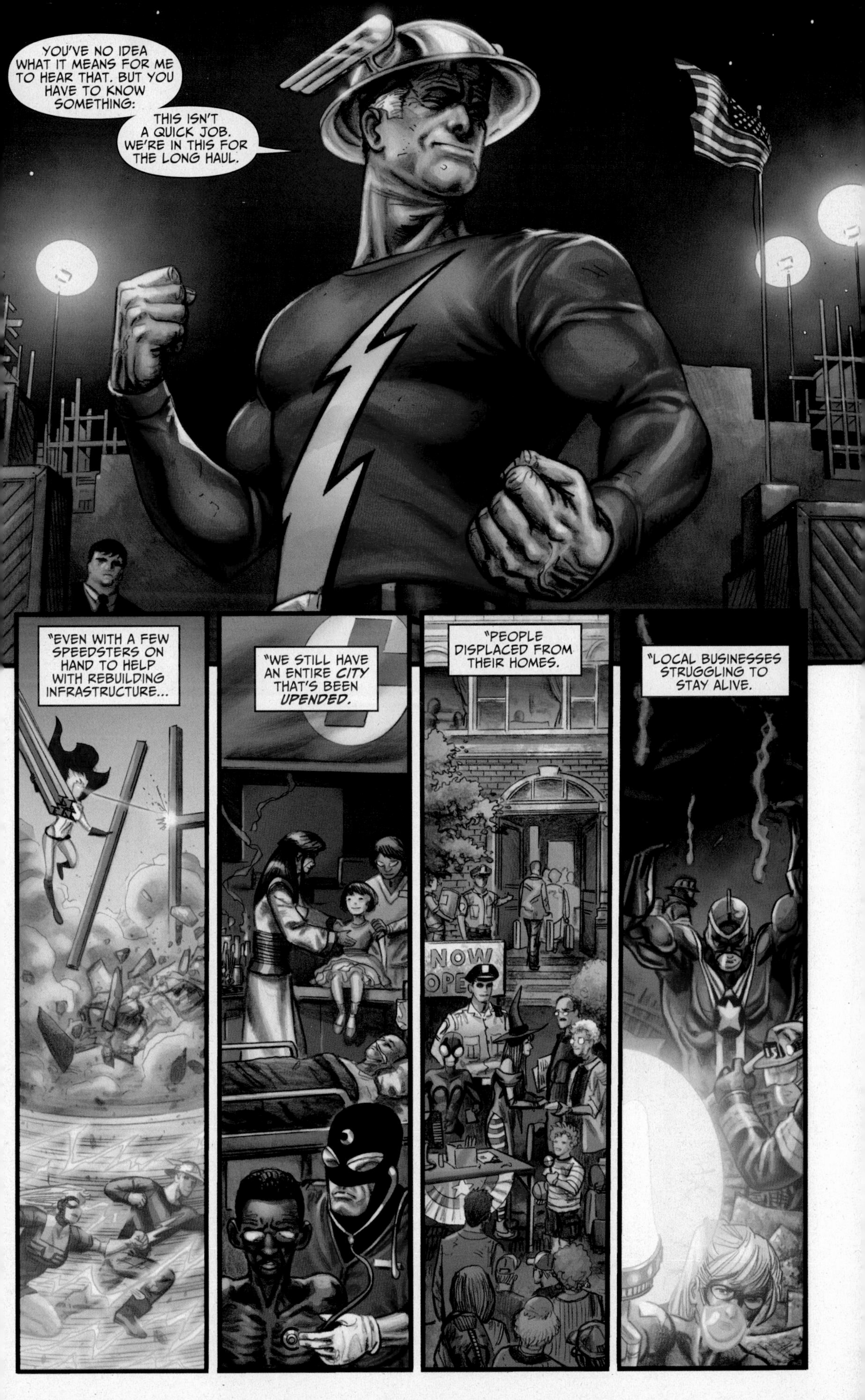

YOU'VE NO IDEA WHAT IT MEANS FOR ME TO HEAR THAT. BUT YOU HAVE TO KNOW SOMETHING:
THIS ISN'T A QUICK JOB. WE'RE IN THIS FOR THE LONG HAUL.
"EVEN WITH A FEW SPEEDSTERS ON HAND TO HELP WITH REBUILDING INFRASTRUCTURE...
"WE STILL HAVE AN ENTIRE *CITY* THAT'S BEEN *UPENDED*.
"PEOPLE DISPLACED FROM THEIR HOMES.
"LOCAL BUSINESSES STRUGGLING TO STAY ALIVE.

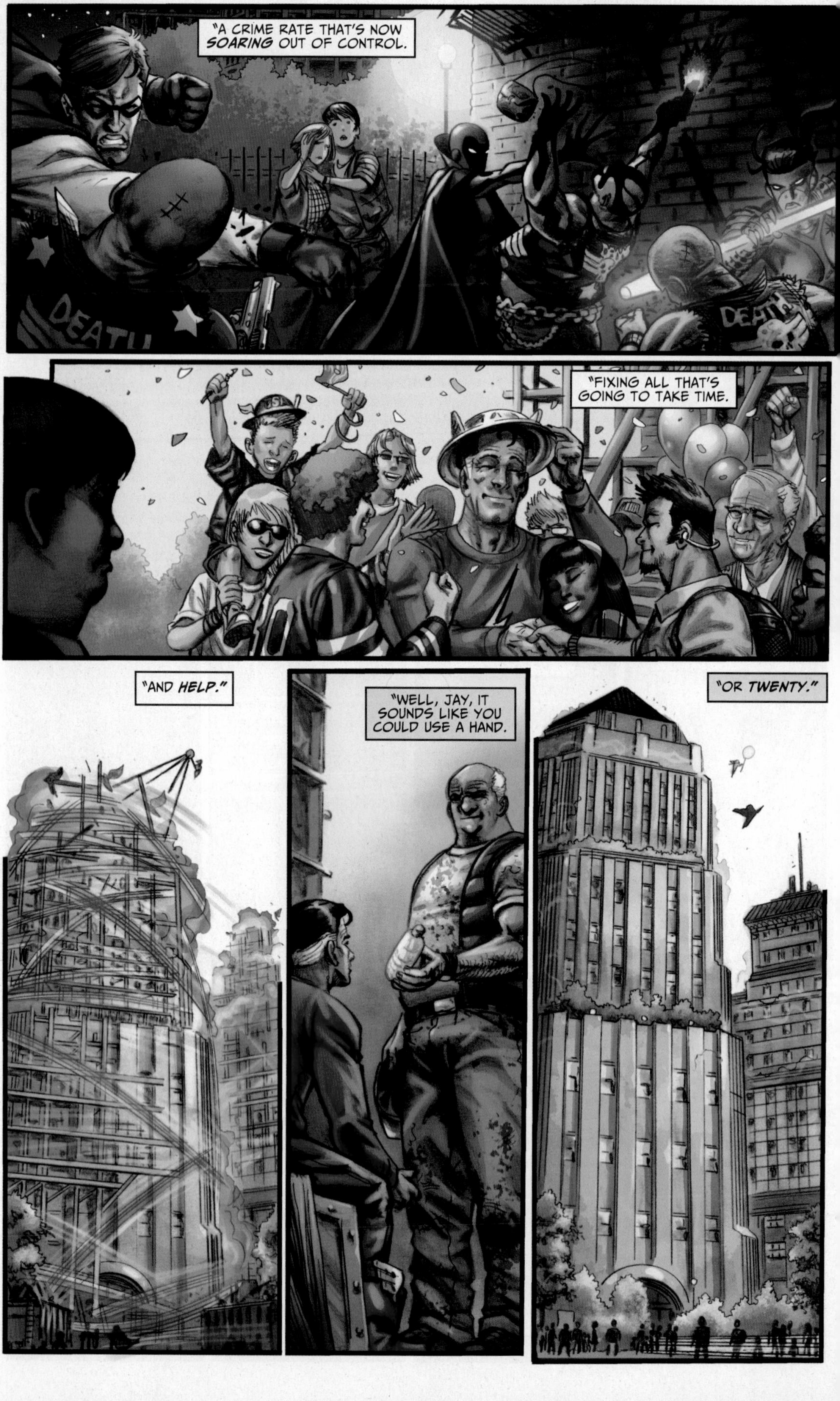
"A CRIME RATE THAT'S NOW *SOARING* OUT OF CONTROL.
DEATH
DEATH
"FIXING ALL THAT'S GOING TO TAKE TIME.
"AND *HELP*."
"WELL, JAY, IT SOUNDS LIKE YOU COULD USE A HAND.
"OR *TWENTY*."

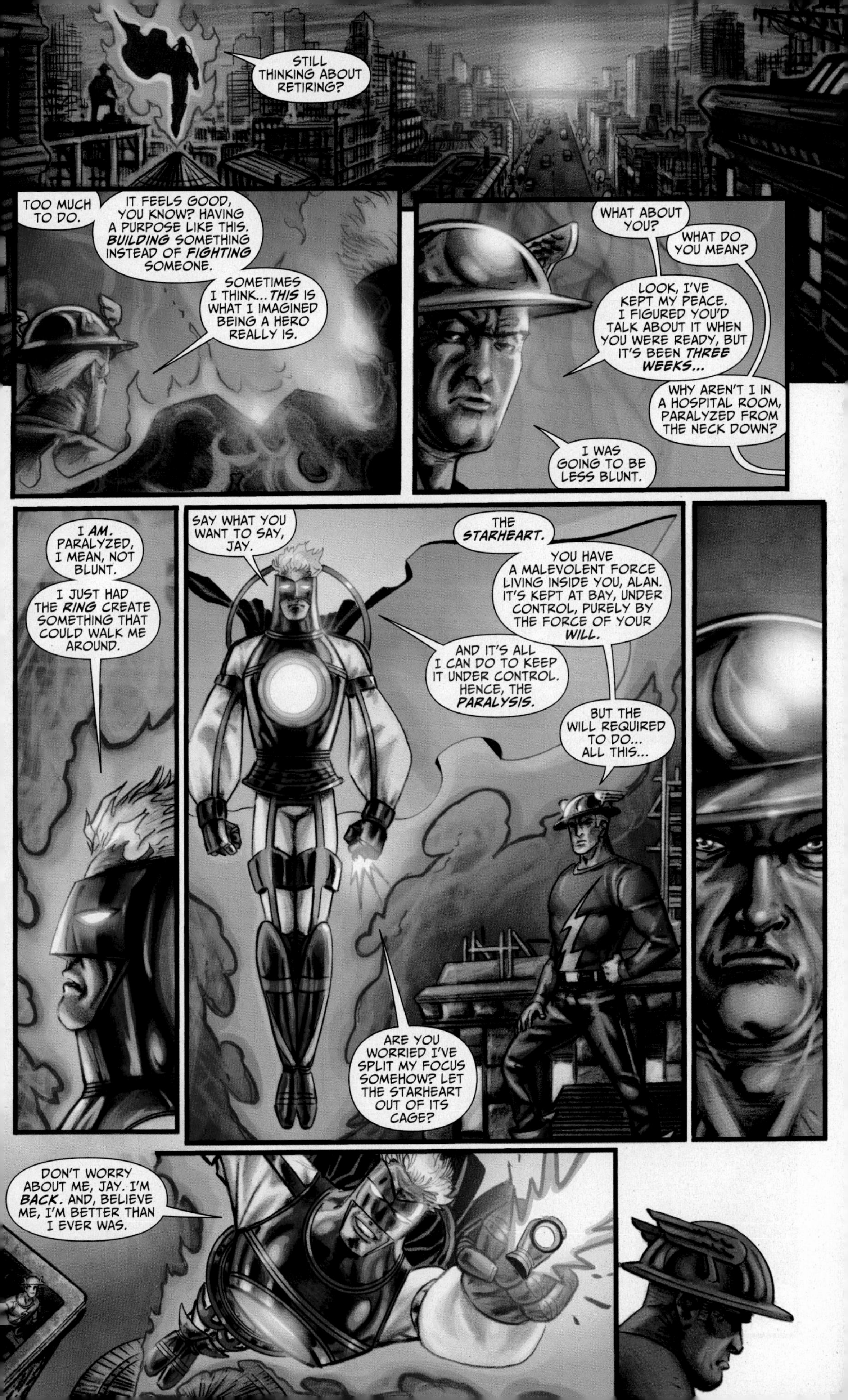

STILL THINKING ABOUT RETIRING?
TOO MUCH TO DO.
IT FEELS GOOD, YOU KNOW? HAVING A PURPOSE LIKE THIS. BUILDING SOMETHING INSTEAD OF FIGHTING SOMEONE.
SOMETIMES I THINK... THIS IS WHAT I IMAGINED BEING A HERO REALLY IS.
WHAT ABOUT YOU?
WHAT DO YOU MEAN?
LOOK, I'VE KEPT MY PEACE. I FIGURED YOU'D TALK ABOUT IT WHEN YOU WERE READY, BUT IT'S BEEN THREE WEEKS...
WHY AREN'T I IN A HOSPITAL ROOM, PARALYZED FROM THE NECK DOWN?
I WAS GOING TO BE LESS BLUNT.
I AM. PARALYZED, I MEAN, NOT BLUNT.
I JUST HAD THE RING CREATE SOMETHING THAT COULD WALK ME AROUND.
SAY WHAT YOU WANT TO SAY, JAY.
THE STARHEART.
YOU HAVE A MALEVOLENT FORCE LIVING INSIDE YOU, ALAN. IT'S KEPT AT BAY, UNDER CONTROL, PURELY BY THE FORCE OF YOUR WILL.
AND IT'S ALL I CAN DO TO KEEP IT UNDER CONTROL. HENCE, THE PARALYSIS.
BUT THE WILL REQUIRED TO DO... ALL THIS...
ARE YOU WORRIED I'VE SPLIT MY FOCUS SOMEHOW? LET THE STARHEART OUT OF ITS CAGE?
DON'T WORRY ABOUT ME, JAY. I'M BACK. AND, BELIEVE ME, I'M BETTER THAN I EVER WAS.

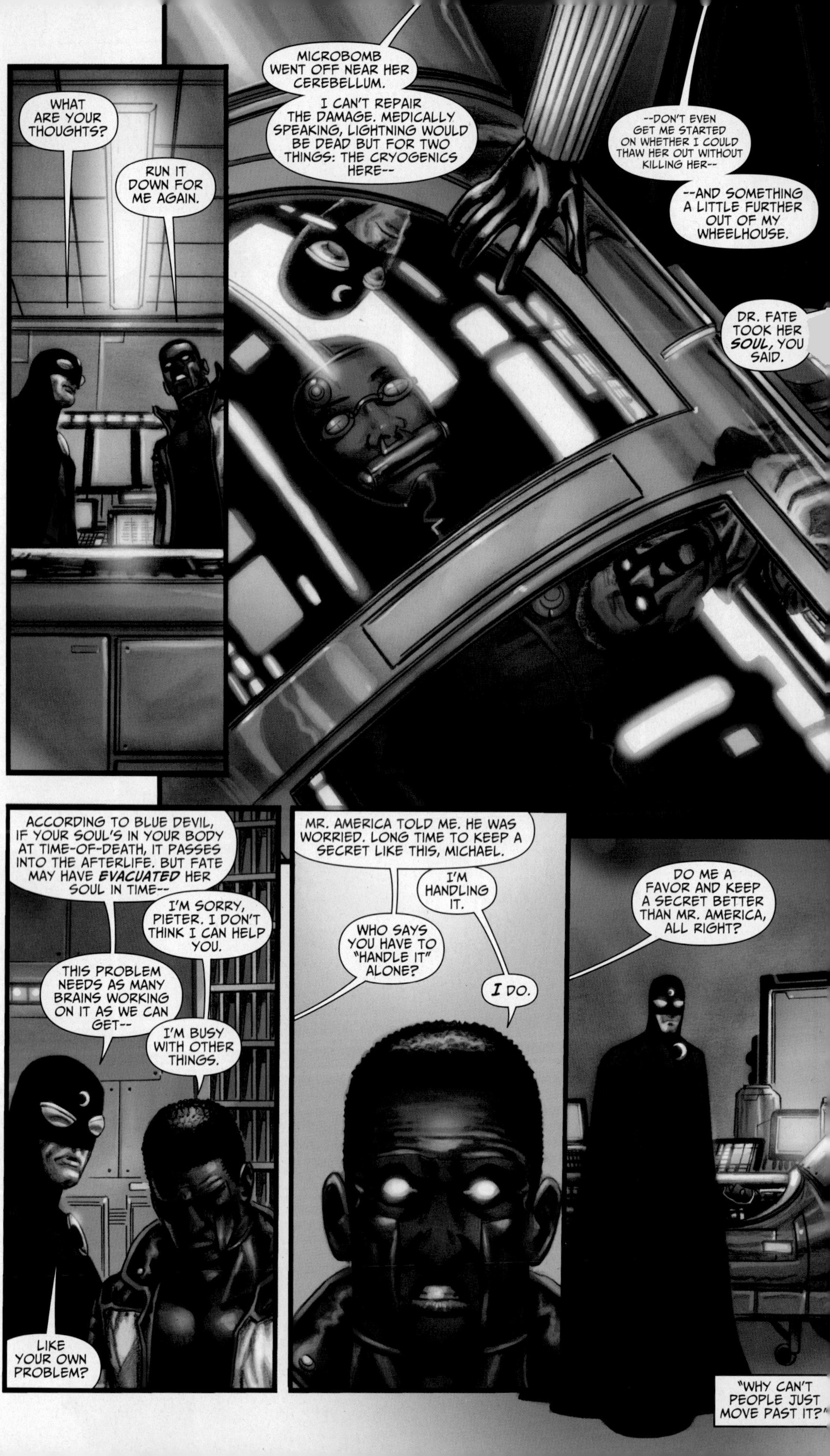

WHAT ARE YOUR THOUGHTS?
RUN IT DOWN FOR ME AGAIN.
MICROBOMB WENT OFF NEAR HER CEREBELLUM.
I CAN'T REPAIR THE DAMAGE. MEDICALLY SPEAKING, LIGHTNING WOULD BE DEAD BUT FOR TWO THINGS: THE CRYOGENICS HERE--
--DON'T EVEN GET ME STARTED ON WHETHER I COULD THAW HER OUT WITHOUT KILLING HER--
--AND SOMETHING A LITTLE FURTHER OUT OF MY WHEELHOUSE.
DR. FATE TOOK HER SOUL, YOU SAID.
ACCORDING TO BLUE DEVIL, IF YOUR SOUL'S IN YOUR BODY AT TIME-OF-DEATH, IT PASSES INTO THE AFTERLIFE. BUT FATE MAY HAVE EVACUATED HER SOUL IN TIME--
I'M SORRY, PIETER. I DON'T THINK I CAN HELP YOU.
THIS PROBLEM NEEDS AS MANY BRAINS WORKING ON IT AS WE CAN GET--
I'M BUSY WITH OTHER THINGS.
LIKE YOUR OWN PROBLEM?
MR. AMERICA TOLD ME. HE WAS WORRIED. LONG TIME TO KEEP A SECRET LIKE THIS, MICHAEL.
I'M HANDLING IT.
WHO SAYS YOU HAVE TO "HANDLE IT" ALONE?
I DO.
DO ME A FAVOR AND KEEP A SECRET BETTER THAN MR. AMERICA, ALL RIGHT?
"WHY CAN'T PEOPLE JUST MOVE PAST IT?"

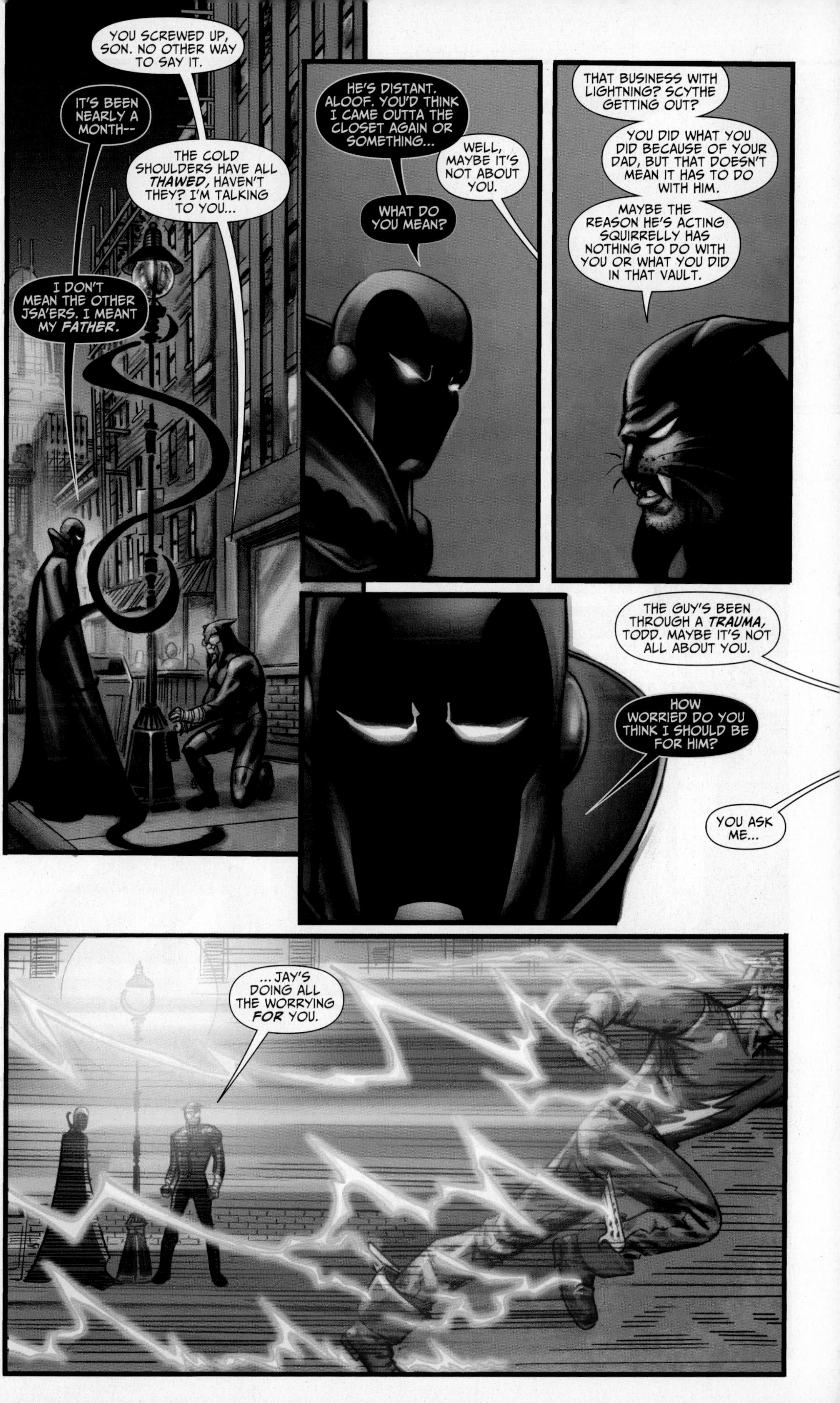
YOU SCREWED UP, SON. NO OTHER WAY TO SAY IT.
IT'S BEEN NEARLY A MONTH--
THE COLD SHOULDERS HAVE ALL *THAWED,* HAVEN'T THEY? I'M TALKING TO YOU...
I DON'T MEAN THE OTHER JSA'ERS. I MEANT MY *FATHER.*
HE'S DISTANT. ALOOF. YOU'D THINK I CAME OUTTA THE CLOSET AGAIN OR SOMETHING...
WELL, MAYBE IT'S NOT ABOUT YOU.
WHAT DO YOU MEAN?
THAT BUSINESS WITH LIGHTNING? SCYTHE GETTING OUT?
YOU DID WHAT YOU DID BECAUSE OF YOUR DAD, BUT THAT DOESN'T MEAN IT HAS TO DO WITH HIM.
MAYBE THE REASON HE'S ACTING SQUIRRELLY HAS NOTHING TO DO WITH YOU OR WHAT YOU DID IN THAT VAULT.
THE GUY'S BEEN THROUGH A *TRAUMA,* TODD. MAYBE IT'S NOT ALL ABOUT YOU.
HOW WORRIED DO YOU THINK I SHOULD BE FOR HIM?
YOU ASK ME...
...JAY'S DOING ALL THE WORRYING *FOR* YOU.

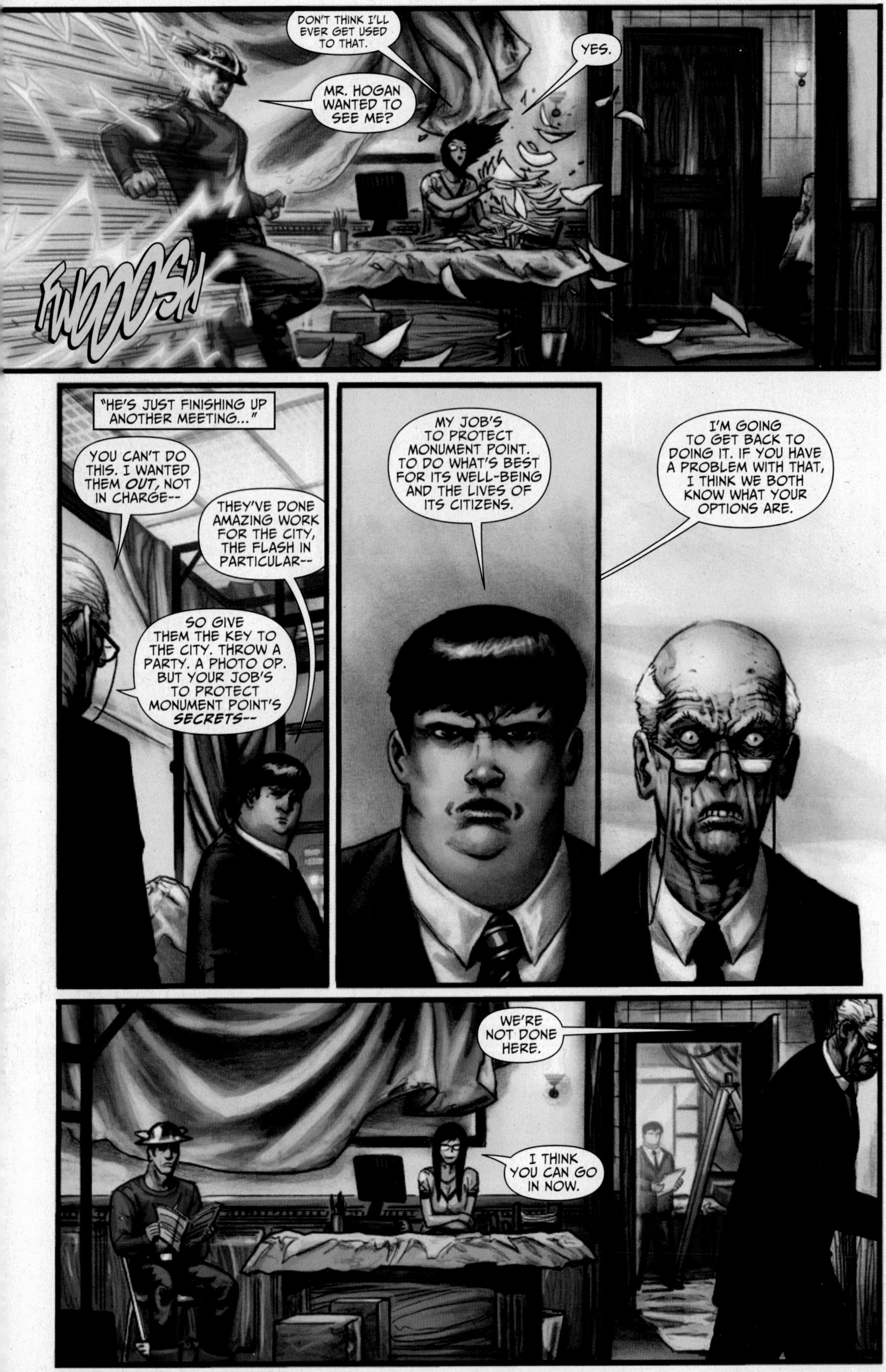

FWOOOSH
DON'T THINK I'LL EVER GET USED TO THAT.
MR. HOGAN WANTED TO SEE ME?
YES.
"HE'S JUST FINISHING UP ANOTHER MEETING..."
YOU CAN'T DO THIS. I WANTED THEM *OUT*, NOT IN CHARGE--
THEY'VE DONE AMAZING WORK FOR THE CITY, THE FLASH IN PARTICULAR--
SO GIVE THEM THE KEY TO THE CITY. THROW A PARTY. A PHOTO OP. BUT YOUR JOB'S TO PROTECT MONUMENT POINT'S ***SECRETS***--
MY JOB'S TO PROTECT MONUMENT POINT. TO DO WHAT'S BEST FOR ITS WELL-BEING AND THE LIVES OF ITS CITIZENS.
I'M GOING TO GET BACK TO DOING IT. IF YOU HAVE A PROBLEM WITH THAT, I THINK WE BOTH KNOW WHAT YOUR OPTIONS ARE.
WE'RE NOT DONE HERE.
I THINK YOU CAN GO IN NOW.

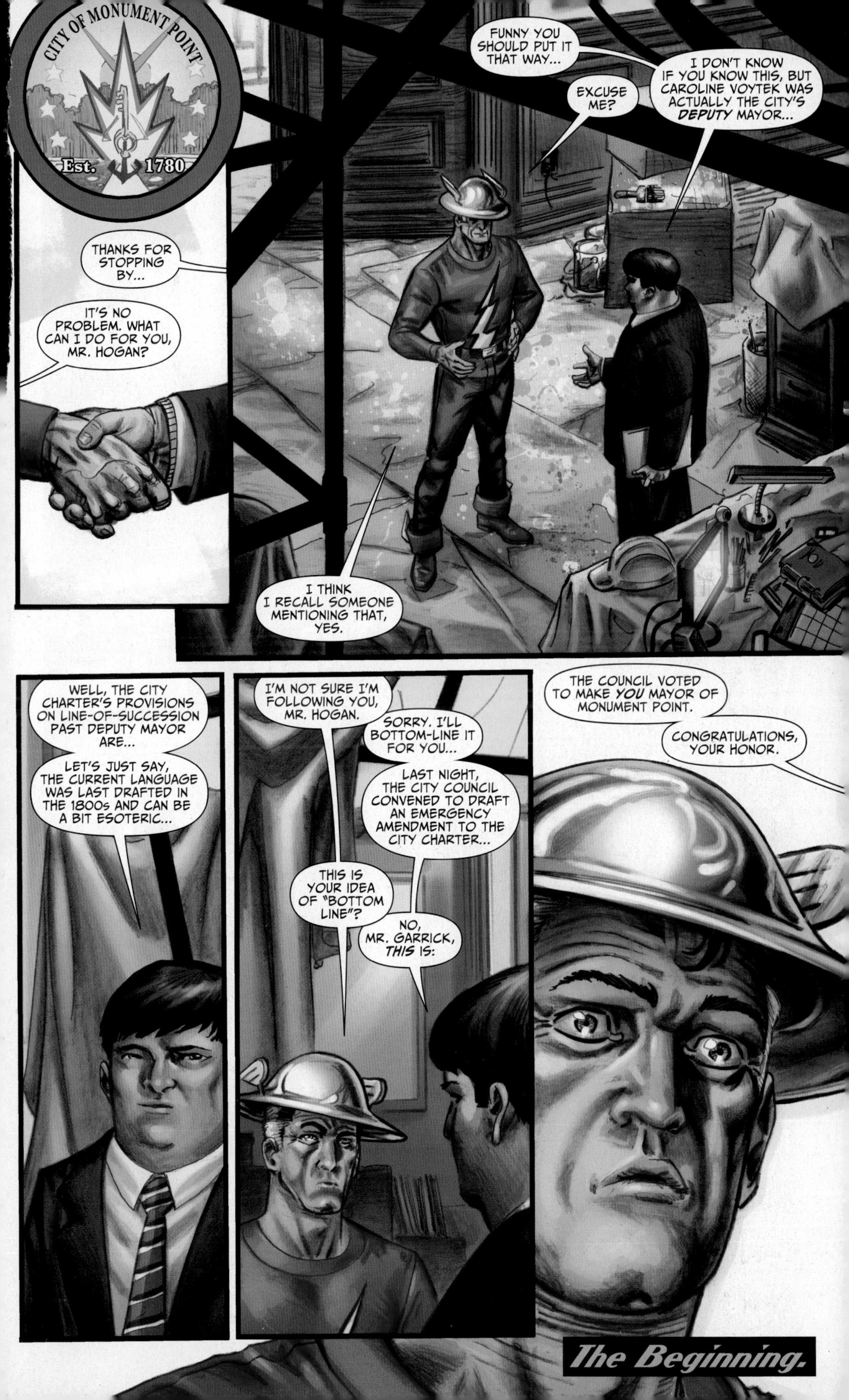
CITY OF MONUMENT POINT
Est. 1780
THANKS FOR STOPPING BY...
IT'S NO PROBLEM. WHAT CAN I DO FOR YOU, MR. HOGAN?
FUNNY YOU SHOULD PUT IT THAT WAY...
I DON'T KNOW IF YOU KNOW THIS, BUT CAROLINE VOYTEK WAS ACTUALLY THE CITY'S *DEPUTY* MAYOR...
EXCUSE ME?
I THINK I RECALL SOMEONE MENTIONING THAT, YES.
WELL, THE CITY CHARTER'S PROVISIONS ON LINE-OF-SUCCESSION PAST DEPUTY MAYOR ARE...
LET'S JUST SAY, THE CURRENT LANGUAGE WAS LAST DRAFTED IN THE 1800s AND CAN BE A BIT ESOTERIC...
I'M NOT SURE I'M FOLLOWING YOU, MR. HOGAN.
SORRY. I'LL BOTTOM-LINE IT FOR YOU...
LAST NIGHT, THE CITY COUNCIL CONVENED TO DRAFT AN EMERGENCY AMENDMENT TO THE CITY CHARTER...
THIS IS YOUR IDEA OF "BOTTOM LINE"?
NO, MR. GARRICK, *THIS* IS:
THE COUNCIL VOTED TO MAKE *YOU* MAYOR OF MONUMENT POINT.
CONGRATULATIONS, YOUR HONOR.
The Beginning.

FROM THE WRITER OF
GREEN LANTERN *AND* SUPERMAN

GEOFF JOHNS

with DALE EAGLESHAM

"This is a flawless book."
– PHILADELPHIA DAILY NEWS

"This is a flawless book..." – Philadelphia Daily News
JUSTICE SOCIETY of AMERICA
GEOFF JOHNS DALE EAGLESHAM ART THIBERT RUY JOSE
THE NEXT AGE

JUSTICE SOCIETY
OF AMERICA
THY KINGDOM COME PART 1

JUSTICE SOCIETY of AMERICA
GEOFF JOHNS ALEX ROSS DALE EAGLESHAM FERNANDO PASARIN
THY KINGDOM COME

with
DALE EAGLESHAM
& ALEX ROSS

JUSTICE SOCIETY
OF AMERICA
THY KINGDOM COME PART 2

JUSTICE SOCIETY of AMERICA
GEOFF JOHNS ALEX ROSS DALE EAGLESHAM FERNANDO PASARIN
THY KINGDOM COME

with
DALE EAGLESHAM
& ALEX ROSS

JUSTICE SOCIETY
OF AMERICA
THY KINGDOM COME PART 3

JUSTICE SOCIETY of AMERICA
GEOFF JOHNS ALEX ROSS DALE EAGLESHAM FERNANDO PASARIN
THY KINGDOM COME

with
DALE EAGLESHAM
& ALEX ROSS

SEARCH THE GRAPHIC NOVELS SECTION OF
DCCOMICS.COM
FOR ART AND INFORMATION ON ALL OF OUR BOOKS!

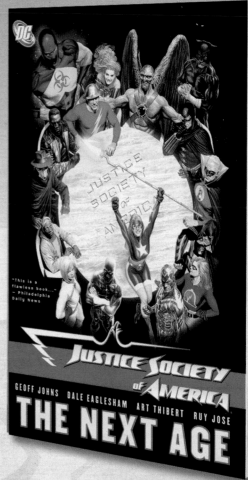

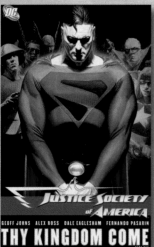

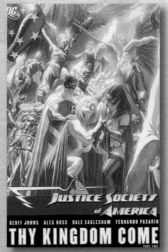

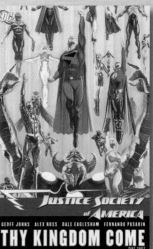